With Vine Leaves in His Hair: The Role of the Artist in Ibsen's Plays

Some other books from Norvik Press

Turning the Century: Centennial Essays on Ibsen (ed. Michael Robinson)
Robin Young: *Time's Disinherited Children. Childhood, Regression and Sacrifice in the Plays of Henrik Ibsen*

Michael Robinson: *Strindberg and Autobiography*
Michael Robinson: *Strindberg and Genre*
Michael Robinson: *Studies in Strindberg*
Freddie Rokem: *Strindberg's Secret Codes*
Eszter Szalczer: *Writing Daughters: August Strindberg's Other Voices* (2007)

Nordic Letters 1870-1910 (ed. Michael Robinson and Janet Garton)
Northern Constellations. New Studies in Nordic Cinema (ed. C. Claire Thomson)
Centring on the Peripheries. Studies in Scandinavian, Scottish, Gaelic and Greenlandic Literature (ed. Bjarne Thorup Thomsen)
Gender – Power – Text. Nordic Culture in the Twentieth Century (ed. Helena Forsås-Scott)
European and Nordic Modernisms (ed. Mats Jansson *et al*)
English and Nordic Modernisms (ed. Bjørn Tysdahl *et al*)
Anglo-Scandinavian Cross-Currents (ed. Inga-Stina Ewbank *et al*)
On the Threshold. New Studies in Nordic Literature (ed. Janet Garton and Michael Robinson)
Aspects of Modern Swedish Literature (revised edition, ed. Irene Scobbie)
A Century of Swedish Narrative (ed. Sarah Death and Helena Forsås-Scott)

Amalie and Erik Skram: *Caught in the Enchanter's Net. Selected Letters* (ed. and trans. by Janet Garton.)
Edith Södergran: *The Poet who Created Herself. Selected Letters* (ed. and trans. by Silvester Mazzarella)
Knut Hamsun: *Selected Letters*, Vols I and II (ed. and trans. by Harald Næss and James MacFarlane)

Victoria Benedictsson: *Money* (translated by Sarah Death)
Fredrika Bremer: *The Colonel's Family* (translated by Sarah Death)
Camilla Collett: *The District Governor's Daughters* (translated by Kirsten Seaver)
Jørgen-Frantz Jacobsen: *Barbara* (translated by George Johnston)
Amalie Skram: *Lucie* (translated by Katherine Hanson and Judith Messick)
Hjalmar Söderberg: *Martin Birck's Youth* (translated by Tom Ellett)
Hjalmar Söderberg: *Short Stories* (translated by Carl Lofmark)

With Vine-Leaves in His Hair: The Role of the Artist in Ibsen's Plays

by
Paul Binding

Norvik Press
2006

© 2006 Paul Binding

The moral right of the author has been asserted.

A catalogue record for this book is available from the British Library.

ISBN 10: 1 870041 67 4
ISBN 13: 978 1 870041 67 6

First published in 2006 by Norvik Press Ltd, University of East Anglia, Norwich, NR4 7TJ

Norvik Press was established in 1984 with financial support from the University of East Anglia, the Danish Ministry for Cultural Affairs, the Norwegian Cultural Department and the Swedish Institute.

Managing Editors: Janet Garton, Michael Robinson and C. Claire Thomson.

Layout: Neil Smith

Cover design: Richard Johnson

Printed in Great Britain by Page Bros (Norwich) Ltd, UK.

for

Hugh and Mirabel Cecil

Contents

Acknowledgements

My thanks first to Norvik Press, to Professor Janet Garton who commissioned this book and has given me much valued advice, and to Neil Smith who has worked so hard on its realisation. I am most grateful too to the Society of Authors who gave me a generous Michael Meyer Award to aid my work.

The Centre for Ibsen Studies at Oslo University is obviously pivotal to anyone writing on Ibsen and I have been very happy in my associations with it. I would like to express my particular appreciation of stimulus and help from its Head, Professor Frode Helland, from Assistant Professor Astrid Sæther and from Librarian Randi Meyer. Astrid was the planner of the enheartening Ibsen 2006 conference in Oslo marking his centenary and asked me to deliver a paper on *Når vi døde vågner* (*When We Dead Awaken*) relating to the ideas in this book. Earlier, in winter 2002, my friends Professors Otto Hageberg and Tore Rem of Oslo University had invited me to lecture on an aspect of *Gengangere* (*Ghosts*); this too contained material I have used here, shaped to some extent by interesting discussions following my lecture.

The Norwegian Embassy in London has given me both practical, financial and spiritual assistance as it has many another writer. I give whole-hearted thanks to the present ambassador to Britain, H. E. Bjarne Lindstrøm and to his predecessor H. E. Tarald Brautaset, to the Cultural Attaché (Minister Counsellor) John Petter Opdahl, and to Anne Ulset of the Press, Information and Culture section.

In Britain I have felt the encouragement and support of literary editors in the press who have asked me to write on Ibsen and on Nordic literary and cultural matters generally – in particular Suzi Feay, Literary Editor of *The Independent on Sunday*, Boyd Tonkin, Literary Editor of *The Independent*, and at *The Times Literary Supplement* Peter Stothard, Alan Jenkins, Lindsay Duguid and Will Eaves.

It is a pleasure to mention the friendship and hospitality in Norway of Tore Rem and his wife Norunn, whom indeed I first got to know in Britain, and of Merete Morken Andersen, Lars Saabye Christensen, Steinar Opstad, Per Petterson and Linn Ullmann and Niels Fredrik Dahl.

I have received many kindnesses during the course of my work, but I will single out here those of my friend and agent, Christopher Sinclair-Stevenson, and my friend and Shropshire neighbour Carol Wright who has read through and corrected the English text in several different versions.

Paul Binding
October 2006

Introduction

At the centre of Ibsen's last play, *Når vi døde vågner* (*When We Dead Awaken*, 1899) stands an artist, a world-famous sculptor, Arnold Rubek. His name has the same initials as that of the most famous sculptor of the day, Auguste Rodin, who, like Ibsen himself, had aroused both heated controversy and ardent admiration. Ibsen sub-titled this play, by far his shortest and most concentrated, a 'dramatic epilogue'. But epilogue to what? To the sequence of prose-dramas he'd begun with *Et dukkehjem* (*A Doll's House*, 1879) was Ibsen's first answer, later amending it, in correspondence with his French translator, Moritz Prozor,[1] to the group of plays of which *Bygmester Solness* (*The Master Builder*, 1892) had been the first. He intended now, he said, to go on to something quite new, adding that if he ever could know which work would be his last, he would write it in verse, the medium of his two watershed successes, *Brand* (1866) and *Peer Gynt* (1867). But later, when it became clear to him that his writing life had come to an end, he allowed the designation 'dramatic epilogue' to cast its backward shadow over his entire oeuvre, which had opened half a century before with *Catiline* (1850). He had, anyway, always been adamant that his plays should be read in the order in which he had written them, that its predecessor and successor were relevant to consideration of each one.

The choice of artist as the subject of the 'epilogue' in itself testifies to its importance to Ibsen. Arnold Rubek, his final protagonist, had, we cannot doubt, the capacity to create work that would rise inspiringly above the cash nexus world of the late nineteenth century. But he chose instead to follow the easier road it offered him, of fame, a title, encomia, and an upholstered life-style with an abundance of leisure. In this he reflects a dilemma characteristic of the times.

The last decades of the nineteenth century in western societies had brought unparalleled challenges to artists, so tremendous and fast-paced were the changes they witnessed. Advances in technology meant many more books and newspapers for people to read, many more concert-halls and opera-houses in which to hear complex music, many more theatres with ever-more sophisticated stages and auditoria to give an increasingly educated and affluent public works as demanding as, say, *Gengangere* (*Ghosts*, 1881), which at first greatly shocked yet excited it, or *Fruen fra havet* (*The Lady from the Sea*, 1888) which for years baffled it, though the discerning, like Norwegian writer Camilla Collett, recognized its innovative poetic penetrations from the first.

With such developments and opportunities went different expectations. It was no longer enough for artists to be inspired representatives of human passions or possessors of individualistic visions. The adoption of Darwinist evolution by the intelligentsia as the primary explanation of existence, the legacy of German Biblical scholarship that undid the concept of scripturally revealed truth, and the general loosening up and re-formation of social strata consequent on innovations in industry and commerce, all meant that there was a widely acknowledged and deeply felt need for fresh *Weltanschauungen*, in part compensatory, in part holistic, binding up the ancient, the given and the new, the future-probing.

The attainment of these *Weltanschauungen* was of course what spurred on many of the artists themselves. Their works were (and to a real extent remain) inseparable from their desire to make sense of a world whose laws no longer were coterminous with those which authority had taught them in their earlier years. Ibsen, Tolstoy, Meredith (all born 1828), Bjørnson (born 1832), Hardy and Zola (both born 1840), and such younger men as the Swedes Count Carl Snoilsky ((born 1841), Ibsen's friend and model for Rosmer, and August Strindberg (born 1849) – the art of all these writers expresses their intense struggle for a coherent philosophy applicable to men and women as they had come themselves to view them, after fighting against inherited precepts and proscriptions. The Nordic provenance of many of these artists, and of significant others not cited above, is attributable to the fact that Sweden, Norway and Denmark were fertile places for those concerned with modernity and progress.

While economically poorer than Germany, France, and Britain, they possessed people educated and secure enough not merely to receive the latest ideas from elsewhere, but to subject these to rigorous examination. And they could do so in the knowledge that their own societies, so deeply interested in what constituted true democracy, would before long be in a position to test them empirically – ideas about the relationship between the sexes, worker representation, land ownership, fiscal justice, the importance of education and the arts to communal health.

Ibsen himself, born, educated in and passionately engaged with Norway, lived in voluntary exile from it for twenty-seven years. During this period he had continuous and intimate relationships with fellow Norwegians and was fully *au courant* with what was happening in his native country, at the same time feeling free from pressures that would have hampered him had he actually remained there. He was also able to benefit, as he wished to, from the amplitude of culture on the European mainland, above all in Germany, where he resided longest. However much he relished acclamations and medals (and the evidence is that he relished them greatly) Ibsen was able, through his chosen life-style, to keep public position and even public demands from invading the private space of his mind. Though more conversant with the writings of others than he often liked to make out, he surely vindicated through his work his firm insistence on his independence. Each of his plays has an autonomy which paradoxically enables it to manifest his own deepest and hardest-won insights into self and society, and into the universe in which both perforce operate. In each one we find interplay between free beings, detached from their creator and faithful to psychological laws as he perceived them, constituting a freestanding metaphor for the essential and the good in human existence.

To examine how Ibsen saw artists of his own cultural era we have to turn to the plays of his great prose-cycle, which he began, after an uncharacteristic caesura in his literary output, in his years of exile. For it is here that he is expressly concerned with the portrayal of just such societal life as that of his readers and audiences.

I have long thought that we are justified in pushing the cycle back two years from the play cited by Ibsen himself, *A Doll's House*, to the appropriately named *Samfundets støtter* (*Pillars of Society*, 1877). Interestingly the eminent critic Toril Moi, in her ground-breaking work of revaluation, *Ibsen and the Birth of Modernism* (2006)[2] gives this play a serious attention it has too long lacked. Ibsen was forty-nine at the time of this play's publication, and behind him lay an already full life, with experiences of Norway, Italy and Germany, of obscurity and fame, of poverty and material steadiness, of marriage and fatherhood, of workaday and artistic communities, and with literary achievements of his own in many genres to his credit: historical drama, verse-drama, comedy, and narrative, occasional and lyric poetry. He thus approached his contemporary subjects with a full store of emotional, intellectual and social knowledge. For all its approximation to a 'well-made play', with its melodramatic tendency, its black-and-white moralism and its 'dea ex machina' (Lona Hessel), *Pillars of Society* represents in its width of sympathy a genuine harvesting of the riches of previous years. It was also, and seen as such, a radical literary departure for Ibsen himself, and more than that, for international drama as a whole, bringing as it does on to the stage the vernacular humdrum life of an active little sea-port, of the business-magnate's office and its dependants, and using as moral indices issues of general concern contemporaneous with the play's evolution. Moreover in Karsten Bernick, its main character, we find attributes that connect him to Ibsen's later studies in will-power. He can lead us, for instance, to those dominating figures of small-town life, the contrasting Stockmann brothers of *En folkefiende* (*An Enemy of the People*, 1882). And, prosperous, pre-eminent in his community, Bernick can stand too as prototype of the successful modern artist of whom much is asked and to whom much is given, often to the detriment of personal integrity and art alike. He is therefore of the same family as the commanding male figures of Ibsen's late plays.

Indeed Ibsen's second thoughts on the subject of *When We Dead Awaken* as 'dramatic epilogue' took him to his last three plays of the 1890s: *The Master Builder, Lille Eyolf* (*Little Eyolf*, 1894), *John Gabriel Borkman* (1896). Did they not form a unity, with *When We Dead Awaken* as an illuminating coda, a quartet in other words? Ibsen was sixty-four when the first of these appeared, and had now returned to Norway to live permanently; his exile was over. His mind was therefore inclined towards intensive review of his life and what he had accomplished in his work, and for such a review Master Builder Solness was the perfect analogue. Later in the recalcitrant person of John Gabriel Borkman he translated the artist into another kind of mage, another kind of power-wielder, the financier, and one who has knowingly gone against the moral law in pursuit of his stupendous aims. While in the play that came between these two, *Little Eyolf*, Alfred Allmers, man of letters now supposedly at work on a magnum opus, gives up writing for what one could call existential attentiveness. Does the artist, the drama asks, actually need art for his deepest ambitions, to meet the promptings of his blood and heart and mind as opposed to the societal beckonings of fame and fortune? Or can it, especially if the last are its concomitants, act as an obstruction to spiritual attainment? Cannot – or should not – some state of mind be reached, or at least striven for, which renders all artifacts redundant?

These difficult questions are asked again, posed with a greater complexity of expression, an increased intensity – and, if anything, a more palpable anguish – in *When We Dead Awaken* itself. That artefact of Rubek's which was widely acknowledged as a masterpiece, *Oppstandelsens dag*, *Resurrection Day*, betrayed, when eventually finished, the sculptor's original inspiration, even his first ecstatic attempts at its execution. Its success, which is in truth a failure, shows up painfully and sternly what Rubek has forfeited in his 'progress' from foresighted young man of modest background to world-class celebrity.

Karsten Bernick, the proto-artist, Solness the analogue for Ibsen the Norwegian artist examining his life and Arnold Rubek, the analogue for an artist of international stature, have this in common: both their success and their failure are inextricable from their relationships with women. Ibsen's examination of artists amounts also, I firmly believe, to an examination of maleness, and a valuable essay by Fredrik Engelstad[3] has already emphasized the concern with this that is the galvanic force behind the late works. Ibsen was a friend (indeed a reader) of the redoubtable feminist writer Camilla Collett (1813-1895), who in the early 1870s took him to task over his attitude towards women in both life and letters. He listened to her, and listened creatively. She was later to see herself, with some justification, as Lona Hessel in *The Pillars of Society*, whose feminine honesty brings fresh air into the fetid atmosphere of the little sea-port and with whose paean to truth and freedom the play ends. And again as Ellida Wangel in *The Lady from the Sea*, who, perhaps more than any of Ibsen's heroines, embodies 'das Ewig-Weibliche', the eternal feminine. And Ibsen did not contradict her when she made this second claim. Even while criticising Ibsen as man and writer, Collett also declared, in *Fra de stummes Lejr* (*From the Camp of the Mutes*, 1877): 'But who has also created such female characters as he? We must go back to Shakespeare to find them.'[4] And this before the great prose-cycle was underway, years before Rebekka West and Ellida Wangel and Hedda Gabler came into being!

This book is not about these great female characters but about Ibsen's masculine artists, the value of whose art is tested by their ability to see and express this truth: that every woman not only contains the universe but constitutes the universe *in herself*. Unless the male artist sees this, he is impaired, damagingly restricted by the male hegemony still in need of dismantlement, and his art will consequently be flawed. Prose-drama, as Ibsen with such sophistication refined it, was the obvious medium for explorations of this subject, presenting as it does men and women in both social and intimate contexts, face-to-face, employing everyday language, and setting the artist among his fellow-humans. The art of the future, to which Ibsen's artists aspire and to which his own art seems ever more to be pointing (and never more so than in his play of 1899) would surely, according to its own logic, constitute a fusion of male and female universes, without dissolving either, instead granting them both permanent mutual in-forming. In the wake of the successive strokes of his last years Ibsen had intimations of wonderful dramas he would never be able to write, and it is tempting to imagine that it was this fusion that characterised them.

I have written this study out of a personal debt to Henrik Ibsen who, William Wordsworth excepted, has meant more to me from adolescence on than any other writer. The first work of his I read, when I was fourteen years of age, was appropriately that first major play of contemporary life, *The Pillars of Society*. It was an overwhelming experience for me. Here, set in motion with intricate artistry, were people whose natures and interactions I could recognize and whom, because of this, I wished to understand more completely – from the haunted magnate to his rebellious, imaginative small son, from the wise, eccentric bluestocking to the sanctimonious schoolteacher presiding over the huddle of consciously virtuous wives, from the freedom-loving emigrant to the girl he loves, victim of both prurience and pity. And yet from the first I appreciated that Ibsen's accuracy in capturing lives astonishingly similar to those I could myself witness, and even the strength of his moral survey of these, were by no means the whole of his art. Like Wordsworth he was intent on what ran deeply below the surface, on what, so often unseen and unheard, unites us all, even in our painful and destructive divisions, and relates us to the natural world and to those unnameable forces that govern it. Unlike his own Hjalmar Ekdal he was not a photographer, though he revered the photographer's calling. In common with characters as diverse as Osvald Alving in *Ghosts* or Arnold Rubek in his last play he was an artist. And as I felt this to be my own avocation, however inadequate or clumsy my realisations, I soon became interested in how Ibsen depicted artists. The subject has continued to fascinate me, as I believe that we of the twenty-first century – we who have honoured the centenary of Ibsen's death all over our planet as we have honoured few other writers – stand in peculiar need of his scrutinies. Once again we are overwhelmed by technological advances which have changed the very dialogues we have with each other; once again new resources have exposed artists, for whom we acknowledge our need, to the temptations of superficial success and celebrity, at the expense of their single-minded concentration and their truth-telling.

I look at the various artists we encounter in the course of Ibsen's major prose plays, and ask what vision of art and of life radiates out from them. We will find Ibsen to be deeply versed in each of the arts he represents. This is not surprising, since it was his expressed policy never to commit himself to paper until he had observed his characters from every possible angle, investigated their pasts and listened to their conversations, snatches of which he would jot down independently of his other, more systematic notes. He also had a lively personal experience of the arts – with the exception of music which does not seem to have meant a great deal to him, even though he knew Edvard Grieg and Johan Svendsen well. He himself painted and knew painters, collected their productions, and served on a jury adjudicating them. He took a very considerable interest in sculpture, the Classical masters and Michelangelo, as well as later practitioners, including Scandinavians who were (more or less) his contemporaries and with whom he became friendly, particularly in his Rome years. With architecture he was so inward that he described it as his own trade.

Our subjects are first Osvald Alving the painter in *Ghosts*, Hans Lyngstrand the sculptor in *The Lady from the Sea*, and Ejlert Løvborg the writer in *Hedda Gabler* (1890). Of key significance to the plays in which they appear, they are nevertheless without exception subordinate in interest to another character, in all three cases a woman who has engaged Ibsen's imagination at its most searching and adventurous. In *The Master Builder* and *When We Dead Awaken*, on the other hand, the male artist-figure is not just at the very centre, he informs every cranny of the drama. Throughout our individual investigations we shall keep in sight the artist's attitude to the future, his relation to women both artistic and personal, and – a matter Ibsen learned most probably through his friend Georg Brandes – his part in that Apollo/Dionysus dialectic so influentially formulated by Friedrich Nietzsche. Dionysus and Apollo were the two gods most dear to Julian the Apostate, the subject of Ibsen's vast Goethean 'world-drama' *Kejser og Galilæer* (*Emperor and Galilean*, 1873); he honoured the pair of them in his doomed attempt to replace the official Christianity of the Empire, but distinguished between them even so. Ibsen undertook enormous researches for this two-part play, and therefore had a plenitude of ideas and feelings of his own to bring to this now classic antithesis; indeed his researches must have been contemporaneous with Nietzsche's own, since only a year separates the German philosopher's study of Greek tragedy and his own work.[5] Julian is to fail in all his endeavours, his failure tarnishing even the stature of his chosen gods. But this does not lessen the play's understanding that we humans cannot live without a 'credo' of some kind, that our very being demands some over-arching theatre of the imagination to accommodate all our activities. One of Toril Moi's achievements in her critical work already referred to is her insistence that *Emperor and Galilean*, in addition to its intrinsic merits, was a crucible through which Ibsen's art had to pass.[6]

But before proceeding further into that art, we must pay tribute to two great works of Ibsen's which in fact ante-date *Emperor and Galilean*, and from the reservoirs of which he drew constantly during all his subsequent writing life. These are, of course, *Brand* and *Peer Gynt*. Taken together they cannot but remind us of Coleridge's famous distinction in *Biographia Literaria* (1817) between the two distinct kinds of artist:

> While Shakespeare darts himself forth, and passes into all forms of character and passion, the one Proteus of the fire and flood, Milton attracts all forms and things to himself, into unity of his own ideal. All things and modes of action shape themselves in the being of Milton; while Shakespeare becomes all things, yet for ever remaining himself.[7]

Coleridge could be describing here – in reverse order – the contrasting characters of Brand and Peer Gynt, both *de facto* artists though unconcerned with the arts: Brand, the introvert, the man of conviction, certain that he knows the will of God and prepared to bend himself and all others to what he conceives as His will, apt to stay put and to dig further inwards rather than explore the wide world, a servant as he sees it of a monolithic truth; Peer, the extravert, unreliable, teller of tall stories, a vagabond, afloat on experiences too diverse to be assimilated with ease by any one person, inconstant, light of love, endearing. Brand stands for singleness of faith which never in so complex a world as ours can remain single (it is in his case *religious* faith, but might just as well be political, philosophical or artistic, as Ibsen himself admitted). Peer stands for the exact opposite: for pluralism, for the diverse life of a people who may one day come together in their differences. Both, however, learn the power of the love they tended to under-estimate before they pass from a life strewn with sadness and dangers into death, Brand through cataclysm, Peer cradled by his former sweetheart.

Throughout Ibsen's oeuvre Brand and Peer Gynt re-appear; Osvald Alving and Hans Lyngstrand, travellers both, are of Peer's tribe, Løvborg is essentially of this too, while Solness of *The Master Builder* is of Brand's party. In what I believe to be the latter play's one true peer in Ibsen's prose oeuvre, the incomparably moving *Vildanden* (*The Wild Duck*, 1884) both figures manifest themselves, for who is Gregers

Werle, so firm in his sense of his own righteousness, if not Brand, and who is Hjalmar Ekdal, with his dreams and easy slidings away from truth, if not Peer? But in *When We Dead Awaken* Rubek is a Peer Gynt (restless, inconsistent, unfaithful, but intimately human) who dies as a Brand, but a Brand who has received with understanding the earlier play's final message that 'Han [Gud] er deus caritatis', 'He [God] is the God of Love'. Well therefore did Ibsen consider that his 'epilogue' bestowed unity on the plays he gave the world over fifty years.

Ghosts
The Artist as Impressionist: Osvald Alving

1.

In the very first exchange of the play, between Snekker (Carpenter) Engstrand and his adopted daughter Regine, we learn that the so eagerly awaited Osvald, the young 'master' of Rosenvold, has now arrived home. In the second, that between Regine and Pastor Manders, we hear that he made the journey from Paris in one fell swoop:

> Han har faret i et kør lige fra Paris – ; jeg mener, han har kørt hele routen med et og samme træn. (HU IX, p. 60)

> He did the whole trip from Paris in one ... – I mean, he travelled all the way without a break. (Vol. V, p. 356)

So, before we meet him in person, we think of Osvald as the bringer of Paris and Parisian life into a remote corner of western Norway; and this is how the other characters regard him too. It is in Paris that he has been practising his chosen art of painting, it is in Paris that he has built up a burgeoning reputation that has already brought him, as Pastor Manders begrudgingly admits, favourable and frequent mentions in the papers. True, Manders speaks (to Fru Alving) about the attractions that life in 'Rome and Paris' must have had for Osvald, and Rome would indeed have been a compulsory stopping-place for any young artist of ambition like him on account of its classical monuments and art treasures. Throughout the nineteenth century Rome attracted many Scandinavian artists (writers included), especially Danes, enough to add up to a colony. And Ibsen himself lived in Rome with his wife and son from 1864 to 1868, associating closely with fellow Nordics, frequenting the

Scandinavian Club, developing friendships with sculptor Walter Runeberg, art-historian Lorenz Dietrichson, and poet Carl Snoilsky, and immersing himself in art of all periods. Twelve years later the Ibsens returned to Rome, and it was here indeed – and then in Sorrento where they went to escape the stifling city heat – that, in 1881, Ibsen worked on *Ghosts*. Something of Osvald's delight in a relaxed life-style, consequent on the very sun he pines for in Norway, surely derives from Ibsen's personal satisfaction in the rhythms of his own Italian life, with artist friends, shared meals *al fresco*, and to hand a countryside cultivated for millennia. But from the point of view of the cultural dialectic of this play Rome is not important. *Paris* is emphatically Osvald's city, his provenance, both his actual and his spiritual home, and the embodiment of his values.

He has been living and working there for some years. Two years before the action of the play, he returned, we hear, briefly to Norway, and during this visit extolled Parisian life so enthusiastically that he aroused longings in Rosenvold's housemaid, Regine. In truth he half-promised to take her there, and Regine has been learning French ever since. The opening of the play makes much of her ambition for Paris; we hear her air her pathetic little titbits of French (which her father Snekker Engstrand, such is his ignorance, believes to be English): '*Rendez-vous*', which can mean both an arranged amorous meeting and an appointment with destiny is, resonantly, the first of these. Osvald himself clearly speaks fluent French; his interview with the doctor has been in that language, and accordingly the single most tragically reverberant word of the whole drama is French; '*vermoulu*', worm-eaten, riddled with disease.

Contemporary readers and playgoers would have notions, *idées reçues*, of Paris to bring to bear on the work. Paris enjoyed a unique reputation for licence; Pastor Manders is much exercised about this, and in return Osvald inveighs against the behaviour of northern European businessmen on their trips to the city, purposefully seeking out its naughtier spots. His point (a somewhat disingenuous one) is that what they find is a comment on themselves rather than on the city; he and his friends live quite independently of commercialised vice, of such trivialised emancipation. Anyway, whatever its moral failings, however sizeable its underbelly, Paris in the second half of the nineteenth century was the acknowledged world capital of culture, of both the arts and the sciences, and proudly aware of its eminence. It generated the new. Compared to Paris all other cities, even Rome, even London, were provincial, revealing their provinciality by their entrenched resistance to the innovative and the progressive or (as in Norway's Christiania) by fostering incestuous self-protecting cliques and cabals. Interestingly we learn in *The Pillars of Society* that Karsten Bernick had as a young man visited Paris (and London too). He returned with a sophistication and a confidence which dazzled his young friend Johan Tønnesen and which he was to canalise into his career, though not without a decidedly 'Parisian' (and potentially damaging) excursion into theatre, an actress' rooms and libidinous gratification. Had Bernick been, one wonders, one of those self-indulgent Nordic visitors of Osvald's outburst?[1]

Ibsen himself was sufficiently interested in France to apply for a grant to go there in 1860, without success as it turned out. France was the home of the new drama, where the theatre was most buoyant, and by this date he had professionally directed plays by Dumas père, Sardou and, shortly afterwards, by Émile Augier (1820-1889). Augier's work with its governing theme of how moral dishonesty (as evidenced in adultery, frequentation of the *demi-monde*, financial skullduggery) undermines the claims to superiority that a complacent bourgeoisie made for itself, has distinct affinities with what Ibsen himself was to produce in *The Pillars of Society*, closer than those with Eugène Scribe, a French name so often adduced in discussion of Ibsen's literary mentors, and against whom indeed Augier reacted.

But in 1869 Ibsen really did go to France – to Paris in the first week of October, to catch a train to Marseilles from where he took a boat to Egypt for the grand opening of the Suez Canal; he was an official visitor at this. He then returned to Paris in late November, on his way back home to Dresden where he and his family were by now living. He proceeded to spend a whole fortnight in the French capital, truly not a long time but a valuable enough stretch of days for a visitor as acutely observant and as well-informed as Ibsen. Ibsen's stay in Paris is an exasperating gap for all investigators of his life, but what we do know, from his own admissions, is that he spent a great deal of his time there in the art-galleries and exhibitions that were among the city's most famous and controversial features.

The Paris Ibsen saw was a work of art in itself, and of a wholly modern kind. We must therefore super-impose on Rosenvold and the rain-beset fjord beyond Osvald's family home pictures of the city as it had evolved during the Second Empire, at the behest of Napoleon lll, with its state-of-the-art urban commodiousness, arrived at through the bold, thorough-going and taste-defining designs of the monarch's chief architect, Georges Haussmann. His work distinguished it from all other major cities, from the hugger-mugger of London with the only-too-evident dirt and squalor right in its very centre, and from Rome principally impressive for what the past, whether Roman Empire or Counter-Reformation, had left behind. In Paris, on the other hand, grand department-stores abounded, luxury-goods and luxury-enterprises were evident everywhere; this was a place of entrepreneurial opportunity, with a good deal of money around and a general will to spend freely. (The appeal of this later to the money-minded, fashion-craving Regine is obvious.) Handsome new stations unsurpassed anywhere – like the Gare St Lazare and the Gare du Nord, by the latter of which Osvald Alving would have departed for Norway – sent out arteries connecting Paris with, it would seem, just about everywhere (hence the play's insistence on the comparative straightforwardness of Osvald's journey, long and tiring though it was). Huge Universal Exhibitions were regularly staged featuring all the sciences and arts, and Paris was the indubitable world-centre for picture-dealers.

1869, the year Ibsen paid his overdue visit to Paris, was a good one for French art. It saw Monet's 'The Pheasant', Manet's 'Portrait of Berthe Morisot' (Manet's future sister-in-law, as well as an important painter herself), and his two great tributes to Spanish art: his representation of a Paris street in the mode of Velázquez, 'The Balcony', and his homage to Goya, 'Execution of the Emperor Maximilian'. It saw also Sisley's 'View of Montmartre', Cézanne's 'The Railway Cutting' and 'The Black Clock', Degas' 'Head of a Young Girl' and Renoir's 'In Summer' and 'La Grenouillère'. In the last the painter's art transmutes a bathing-place on the Seine into a true icon of happiness – that quality so intrinsic to French Impressionists at their most characteristic. Ibsen, the inveterate newspaper-reader with his self-developed antennae for what was new and significant, would, even if he were not aware of these specific works, have known what qualities they were striving to express and to promote.

In 1869 Berthe Morisot and Renoir were twenty-eight years of age, Monet twenty-nine – and Cézanne and Sisley thirty. On account of this Ibsen himself at forty-one would (after the fashion of most people past their fortieth birthday) doubtless have thought of them all as 'young' artists – Osvald is indissoluble both from his own youthfulness and from the idea of youthfulness. And truly the 1860s, the decade in which the Impressionist painters one by one emerged as major creative figures, does contain a remarkable number of durable works by painters still indisputably young. Manet (born 1832) produced in 1863 his 'Déjeuner sur l'Herbe' a totemic work for the whole movement, shocking some sections of the intelligentsia while enheartening and stimulating others – just as Ibsen's prose-plays themselves were to do (and none more so than *Ghosts*).

In addition to the achievements of these young men (and women too) – often facing contempt and rejection from academicians and conservative critics – significant work was done throughout the 1860s by an older, equally anti-Establishment group of artists. Members of the Barbizon school, who went out near Fontainebleau to paint *en plein air*, were still active; indeed the subsequently most famous of them, Jean-François Millet, did his best-known work in this decade. His first widely saluted picture, 'Man with a Hoe' appeared in 1862, and nine of his paintings were included in the Paris Great Exhibition of 1867. The Barbizon School is important to our consideration of *Ghosts* not just because it shows the strength and breadth of French painting at the time of Ibsen's Paris visit, or because it anticipates in interesting ways the Impressionists themselves (indeed Monet and Bazille, when young men, painted alongside its members), but because the socialism/egalitarianism of these artists and their emphasis on the dignity and beauty of labour seem to have become part of Osvald's own vision of things.

Though Ibsen could not have known it at the time of his visit, the Second Empire then had less than a year of life left. In July 1870 came Napoleon III's *folie de grandeur*, his declaration of war on Prussia in the hope of undermining Bismarck's plans for a united Germany. He had to resign as Emperor in September. The Prussians pushed forward, the French proving unable to stop them, and besieged Paris itself, until the surrender of the whole country in January 1871. In April 1871 began the strange two-months-long adventure of the Commune, to be put down brutally by the new French government. During the Franco-Prussian War – which distressed and stimulated French artists and writers (with Monet and Pissarro avoiding call-up by fleeing to London, where they did some of their greatest work) – the Ibsens, then living in Germany, in Saxony's Dresden, held the strongest pro-French sympathies. Young Sigurd even took the French flag to school with him, defending his cause with his fists against German schoolmates. However after 1871 France in general and Paris in particular made a speedy recovery. The capital soon got going again as Europe's (and therefore the world's) capital of the arts, and the art market flourished anew. Indeed after its defeat as an Empire the France of the Third Republic set if anything yet greater store by artistic and cultural activities, and sought to realise their commercial potential.

The 1870s were the decade in which the Impressionists truly found themselves and entered a mainstream of contemporary art. They were given major exhibitions in 1874, 1876, 1877 and 1880, the first and the last two presenting the painters under a declared 'Impressionist' banner. Parallels between the productions of Monet, Renoir and, increasingly, Cézanne, during this period and Ibsen's own work are not hard to find. Posterity has found Ibsen's work of the Seventies (until *A Doll's House*) less interesting than that of the previous decade or the subsequent one. But from the perspective of 1881 they were years of adventurous, ground-breaking, reputation-confirming work: *Emperor and Galilean* (1873) engaging with the major philosophical-cultural debates of the day while presenting as a huge 'slice of life' an important epoch which bears on the development of the western mind, and *Pillars of Society* (1877) which together with its immediate successor, *A Doll's House*, opened up new territory for readers and audiences. Yet the continuing radicalism of French painters and Norwegian dramatist was now met by a response of sufficient strength to give them status, serious critical attention and income. Their art was now widely perceived as being if not exactly a new mainstream then the most powerful of currents making for the future. Osvald in Paris feels himself part of a movement that is innovative and bold, on the one hand, and secure in its values and public role on the other.

Osvald, we're told (by Manders), is 'twenty-six or twenty-seven.' So emphatic during the writing of *Ghosts* was Ibsen that this was to be a 'domestic tragedy', a play of his own time set among the kind of people he (and his readership/audience) would know – 'the effect of the play', he told August Lindberg, 'depends greatly on the audience feeling that they are listening to something that is actually happening in real life',[2] – that we can surely assume that the play takes place (more or less) in the year of its composition, 1881. This would mean that Osvald was born 1854/1855. If, say, he went to study art in Paris when he was twenty, he would therefore have arrived there c. 1874. And if that were the year, we would have a truly happy coincidence, since on 15 April 1874 the first-ever Impressionist Exhibition opened at 35 Boulevard des Capucines in the old studio of the famous photographer Nadar – practitioner of that art to which the French laid claim as their own new art-form, and which was to feature in Ibsen's next play but one, *The Wild Duck*. The name 'Impressionist' was taken from Monet's 'Impression: Soleil Levant' (Impression: Sun Rising), which makes us in turn think of the sunrise which so terribly concludes *Ghosts*, the light brilliant on the mountain peaks and glaciers, and Osvald in his dementia crying out for it. And in 1874 French artists honoured the sun in another way: the older Manet joined Monet to paint in full daylight, by sunlight only – at Argenteuil, that *locus classicus* of the whole movement.

The kinship of Osvald's works to the Impressionists' celebrations of Argenteuil – or of social occasions at the 'Moulin de la Galette' – becomes clear when we listen to him describing his art:

> Mor, har du lagt mærke til, at alt det, jeg har malet, har drejet sig om livsglæden? Altid og bestandig om livsglæden. Der er lys og solskin og søndagsluft, – og strålende fornøjede menneskeansigter. (p. 112)

> Mother, have you noticed how everything I've ever painted has turned on this joy of life? Always and without exception, this joy of life. With light and sun and a holiday spirit – and radiantly happy faces. (p. 403)

'Lys og solskin og søndagsluft' (Light and sun and a holiday spirit) – Osvald's apologia for his own art comes close to such apologia for Impressionism in general as that of critic Edouard Drumont writing in the *Petit journal* about that first exhibition of all. The man who casually pops into it, he promises, will not '...believe himself to be entering what people solemnly call a temple of art. He will rediscover the life he has just left behind, the spectacles he catches sight of at every instant, the exact look the countryside has when he chances to observe it.'[3]

This is democratic art, unstuffy, celebratory, releasing.

The key word in Osvald's artistic credo is *livsglæden* (the joy of life); the word becomes a veritable *leitmotif*. He has learned the importance of what it means abroad; here he has entered a society which actually believes in seeking it out, in holding it up as a desideratum. The French phrases *joie de vivre* and *douceur de vivre* have become part of the currency of the entire West, which has never quite found adequate versions of them in its other languages. Northern Europe, by contrast, has never lived by a credo which gives this ideal any pre-eminence. In Norway, says Osvald, people tend to believe that existence is '*en jammerdal*' (a vale of tears) – and Fru Alving agrees with him in this assessment. She adds to her agreement with him her opinion that her own society has, for its own purpose, succeeded in making this phrase a truth. Life as a vale of tears was after all the *Weltanschauung* of Ibsen's Brand, of that Evangelicism which finds nothing in the daily stuff of life but material for sorrow, repentance, salvation or a final condemnatory judgement. For Osvald *livsglæden* is closely related to *arbeidsglæden* (love of work), indeed in France, he tells his mother, they're thought of as '*den samme ting*' (the same thing). Whereas in Norway work is conceived as harsh necessity, one more consequence of The Fall, for the society he has opted to join it is a yet further way of glorying in being alive. In his thinking here Osvald is at one with the Barbizon painters, the Impressionists' most compatible fore-runners. In life and in art they exalted physical labour – as in Millet's popular 'The Gleaners' and again in 'The Man with a Hoe'. Their own practice of working *en plein air*, antedating the Impressionists' decision to do so, constitutes a placing of the working artist beside other members of the *artisanat*. Partly made possible by the recent improvement of paint-tubes and easels for painters' convenience, it made painting no less of a manual skill than the planting, gleaning and fruit-picking they rendered on canvas. All were demanding, dignified and intensely satisfying tasks in tune with the rhythms of nature and the human body. Ibsen observed in his notes for *Ghosts*:

> The time is not long past – if indeed it is past at all – when a decent, honest manufacturer or craftsman would not feel uncomfortable at having his business compared with something like authorship; and on the other side it is quite common, especially in the newspapers, to see some mediocre work of authorship described as 'craftsmanship'. Yet the law for the craftsman and for the poet is the same.[4]

When Osvald talks of the physical exhaustion that his disease has produced in him, rendering him incapable of further work, he's surely remembering his own taking of paints, brushes and easels out of doors, his becoming a happy (and literal) labourer in the fields of art. To appreciate this is to see his situation with a new poignancy that links him to every young man incapacitated in his prime.

So Osvald comes across, though chiefly through his own remarks, as an artist consecrated to the delight of ordinary living, of men and women going about their daily business contentedly but with full sensory awareness of the world around them, *le monde visible* of Gautier's famous phrase, giving themselves equally, with no sense of psychic rift, to labour and pleasure. He is sustained in both these last by the company he has chosen to keep, men and women whose lives are governed by strong beliefs and principles but who are nevertheless free of fetters, of the prescriptions and proscriptions of the bourgeoisie, and are therefore in accord with their ideal of free love. This last contrasts with the double standards of Scandinavian businessmen, with the blinkered stuffiness of Pastor Manders who opposed Osvald's going to Paris in the first place, and above all else, it would seem, with the indulgences of his father, the Chamberlain, Kaptein Alving. Fru Alving has already given us extremely vivid cameos of her husband as a drunken lecherous sot, his mind so fuddled by drink and the brain-softening consequent on syphilis, that he has the attention-span of a baby. The long-repressed memory of him that surfaces into Osvald's mind (of his father making

him smoke his pipe) certainly confirms the truth of her portrait. But – to
an extent offsetting this – we have, in the third and last act, one of the
most powerful exchanges of the whole drama in which again the concept
of *livsglæden* is to the fore, and surprisingly:

> FRU ALVING: ... Du kom før til at tale om livsglæden; og da gik der
> ligesom et nyt lys op for mig over alle tingene i hele mit liv.
> OSVALD: (*ryster på hodet*). Dette her forstår jeg ikke noget af.
> FRU ALVING: Du skulde ha' kendt din far da han var ganske ung løjtnant.
> I *ham* var livsglæden oppe, du!
> OSVALD: Ja, det ved jeg ...
> FRU ALVING: Og så måtte sligt et livsglædens barn, – for han *var* som et
> barn, dengang, – han måtte gå herhjemme i en halvstor by, som ingen
> glæde havde at byde på, men bare fornøjelser. Måtte gå her uden at ha'
> noget livsformål; han havde bare et embede. Ikke øjne noget arbejde,
> som han kunde kaste sig over med hele sit sind; – han havde bare
> forretninger. Ikke eje en eneste kammerat, som var mægtig at føle hvad
> livsglæde er for noget; bare dagdrivere og svirebrødre –
> OSVALD: Mor – !
> FRU ALVING: Så kom det, som det måtte komme. (pp. 121-122)

> MRS ALVING: ... You were talking earlier about the joy of living. And
> suddenly I seemed to see my whole life ... everything in a new light.
> OSVALD: (*shaking his head*). I don't understand a word of what you are
> saying.
> MRS ALVING: You should have seen your father when he *was* a young
> lieutenant. He had plenty of the joy of living, I can tell you!
> OSVALD: Yes, I know ...
> MRS ALVING: Well, there was this lively, happy boy – and at the time he
> *was* like a boy – having to eat his heart out here in this little provincial
> town; pleasures of a kind it had to offer, but no real joy; no chance of
> any proper vocation – only an official position to fill; no sign of any kind
> of work he could throw himself into heart and soul – only business. He
> never had a single real friend capable of appreciating the joy of life and
> what it meant – nothing but a lot of lazy, drunken, hangers-on ...
> OSVALD: Mother – !
> MRS ALVING: So then the inevitable happened. (pp. 412-413)

Fru Alving's account of her husband when young echoes her son's
descriptions of his own Parisian life and the paintings it has enabled him

to accomplish, and not just in the concept animating it but the very vocabulary used – *søndagsvejr, et livsglædens barn*. Certainly she gives us a very significant addendum to any reading of the play which lays the blame for the terrible situation with which we are confronted too firmly on Kaptein Alving's shoulders. We have a glimpse here of a man whose capacity for happiness might, in a different freer cultural climate, and with a young wife more prepared to defy convention than Helene Alving then was, have developed into a fulfilled human being radiating his own love of life – with no need for the Johanne on whom he fathered Regine (the result of the inevitable happening of the last sentence). As it was, sex, and with it pleasure altogether, became a furtive, compulsive business, conducted and even experienced with a kind of dirtiness of spirit, again in evidence in Osvald's surfaced recollection of him as a fuddled man amusing himself by giving a little boy a pipe to smoke and making him sick. We have no need to go as far as Frode Helland and Arnfinn Åslund with their darkly ingenious interpretation of enforced fellatio,[5] but even if it were a case of this, the above still pertains; the Kaptein's vigorous and, at one time, cheerful enough sensuality, has, through the restrictions of his society, contracted to a distortion of itself, to perversion. A different Kaptein Alving would have produced a different Osvald, with no need to go away from Norway to find joy in either life or work.

Should then we see the play's central situation as amounting to a plea for Osvald's French approach to living, gloriously realised in the amplitude and colours of Impressionism and in the libertarianism of its practitioners, a plea that is also a critique of northern puritanism with all its attendant guilts, evasions and hypocrisies? We have again to consider anew 'Osvald ... maler', 'Osvald ... painter'.

2.

For Osvald the life-style of his friends is importantly the condition, the only one, in which they can produce work with the attributes he himself aspires to; it is a life-style, like the city in which it is realised, that is an art-form in itself. He is prepared to proselytise on its behalf. Hear him telling his mother his reaction to the Parisian specialist's grim diagnosis of his condition, how – denied information from her of his father's longstanding debauchery – he had to look to his own behaviour for responsibility for his illness:

> Ja, da måtte han selvfølgelig indrømme at han var på vildspor; og så fik jeg vide sandheden. Den ubegribelige sandhed! Dette jublende lyksalige ungdomsliv med kammeratene skulde jeg afholdt mig fra. Det havde været for stærkt for mine kræfter. Selvforskyldt, altså! (pp. 105-106)

> Well, then naturally he had to admit he'd been on the wrong track. Then I learned the truth. The incredible truth! This blissfully happy life I'd been living with my friends, I should never have indulged in it. It had been too much for my strength. So it was my own fault, you see. (p. 396)

'Dette jublende lyksalige ungdomsliv med kammeratene' – 'This blissfully happy life' with his artist-mates... Well, of course some of the unmarried liaisons Osvald frequented may indeed have been as full of caring and sharing as he makes out – and all readers and playgoers hope so because naturally we are all on Osvald's side, especially in opposition to the narrowly suspicious, repellent Pharisaism of Pastor Manders. Osvald presents the family life of the legally unwed (marrying would cost the couples too much!) in near-idyllic terms. But the lives of the Impressionist painters themselves – about whom Ibsen would have gathered information through gossip, newspapers and journals, and his many connections with the world of painters, cultural sponsors and critics – tell a different, rather less appealing story. Most of them cohabited with, and usually eventually married (after the 'inevitable' in the form of parenthood had 'happened') girls or women considerably lower down the social scale than themselves; *they* tended to come from the relatively prosperous new middle class. As artists working in studios in the poorer quarters of the city, they had their sexual/emotional experiences with shop-girls, barmaids, waitresses; their manner of living put young women from the bourgeoisie quite out of reach. Claude Monet, son of a prosperous Le Havre chandler, met a seamstress, Camille Doncieux, in the working-class district of Paris called Les Batignolles when he was twenty-four; they didn't marry until five years later by which time their son Jean was three. Camille Pissarro, son of a rich Jewish colonialist in the West Indies, chose as his partner Julie, an assistant to his family's cook; within ten years they had three children, but didn't marry until a fourth was on the way. Julie was later to speak harshly and regretfully of her domestic life. When Renoir – of a less well-off family; his father was a tailor – took up with the woman he was to have children by and eventually marry, he was thirty-eight to her nineteen; she was a girl from the provinces only too relieved to get a job as a seamstress. All these women – and their many sisters – bore the brunt of their male partners' initially impecunious and often precarious mode of living, and became little more than drudges, administering to their men's every need, looking after their children with hardly any assistance, and humouring, out of expediency, their every whim. Osvald might see the lives of his artist-friends in Paris as hospitable and loving – and no doubt love did flourish in these ménages, and happy hospitality at times too. For the most part, however, the women were kept busy at home while the men consorted with their mates in the celebrated cafes – or even, as Renoir so regularly did, took themselves off to their patrons' moneyed homes for sociable networking weekends. Osvald's viewpoint sounds like that of a somewhat innocent young man in love with the *Vie de Bohème* as expounded by Henri Murger in his hugely popular and influential novel of 1849. But it's unlikely that the author of *A Doll's House*, the play, after all, immediately prior (1879) to *Ghosts*, would have found much to admire in these many *de facto* imprisonments of women.

But for the true thorough-going *Vie de Bohème* beyond the pages of this novel, our minds turn to Norwegians like the writer Hans Jæger (who, born in 1854, would have been Osvald's contemporary), who dismissed Christiania as 'Siberian' and abided by Nine cock-snooking Commandments of his and his friends' devising.[6] Jæger's most famous disciple was the ten-years-younger painter Edvard Munch (1864-1944), some of whose formative creative experiences were in Paris, where he attended classes at the studio of Léon Bonnat, a favoured stopping-place for Scandinavians wanting to find themselves in Europe's most sophisticated city. But *their* bohemian manner of living, with its heavy diet of brothel-going, high alcohol consumption, drug experimentation, and calculated and toll-taking amoralism, is expressly distasteful to Osvald Alving, and, on this account as well as for chronological reasons, will be left for the chapter on *Hedda Gabler*, to which it most definitely *is* relevant.

Even so the question asks itself: how different is the attitude to women in the artistic set-ups Osvald frequents from that of his own father, even in the days of Fru Alving's warmer memories, of his pleasure-loving, attractive young manhood, let alone in his drunken, ravaged later years when his wife, we know, did all his public work for him and managed his home? Not very! Women are there to be enjoyed, to be of pleasurable service: this is the view of them behind the Kaptein's relationship with his wife, with Johanne (Regine's mother) and, one assumes, with many an unnamed other. Osvald is outwardly very much his father's son. Entering a room smoking his father's Meerschaum pipe he is mistaken by Pastor Manders for the older man. His mother too sees his father in him when she catches him making a pass at Regine, just as the Kaptein had at Johanne (two of the ghosts of the title). In truth Osvald's entire fascination with Regine, whose health and beauty he believes could assist him to recovery of that necessary *livsglæde*, seems totally of a piece with his father's attitude to the opposite sex, and with many a Parisian painter's as well.

His behaviour to her is essentially selfish. On his previous visit home, because she was attractive, and the only young person apart from himself at Rosenvold, he encouraged her to believe he would take her to Paris; she has lived on the idea of this ever since. He clearly never appreciated the effect his comparatively idle remarks, made to a considerable degree out of ennui, would have on her, and he has chosen to forget the exact words they consisted of. (Or, more likely, he *does* remember them, but prefers not to do so.) In class-terms they were very much those of the young master of the house showing off to a servant-girl. The Alvings belong, after all, to that section of land-owners who were the nearest Norway ever had to the nobility it abolished in 1814, rich, well-connected, the Kaptein's position of Chamberlain entailing regular contact with the Court. If we see Ibsen's prose-dramas as corresponding in their social scope to Balzac's *Comédie humaine* or Zola's *Rougon-Macquart* sequence, then *Ghosts* is that work of his which deals with Norway's grandest social echelon, just as *The Wild Duck* will be significant for portraying the socially humble, the economically indigent. And when on this present visit home Osvald revives the idea of Regine's accompanying him back to Paris, it is for wholly self-centred reasons; she will look after him (like all those consorts of the Impressionist painters), she will even, so he believes, administer to him the desired fatal quantity of pills when necessary. While Osvald has an insightful rider to add here when he admits: 'hun var snart bleven ked af at passe en slig syg, som jeg.' (p. 129) (she'd soon have got bored with looking after an invalid like me; p. 420), on the whole his inability to see or understand other people or himself clearly is nowhere better shown than in his dealings with Regine.

For, this last observation excepted, he doesn't get her right, doesn't see her for what she is. Even if we attribute her unsympathetic qualities to the altogether shameful, deceitful and hypocritical way that she has been treated (indeed used) – not just by her acting father, Engstrand, but by the Alvings, both Fru Alving and her husband, the real father, with their quasi-aristocratic hauteur – Regine is (the truth can't be avoided!) cold, scheming, selfish, unkind in tongue and deed, and, we appreciate at the close, amoral and greedy. Paris attracts her as a city of riches, fashion, opportunity. In Osvald himself, in the artistic pursuits of his circle, she is not the slightest bit interested. But then for Osvald she herself is primarily a body, an appealingly healthy one, just as her mother Johanne was for his father.

And so Osvald's own sexual mores can be seen as those both of a chip off the old block and a Parisian artist. When, say, Claude Monet started his relationship with his seamstress or when Renoir in his mid-twenties embarked on his with his model, Lise, it's highly improbable that these young men were virgins. Or that the women in question – come to Paris desperate for work and money – were inexperienced either. Such a milieu of wide-ranging sexual experience, little concerned with partners' backgrounds and pasts, is, of course, eminently conducive to venereal disease. Just as – readers and audience have long supposed – some woman of 'easy virtue', probably a servant, a predecessor of Johanne, (hence the 'inevitability' of his relationship with the latter) gave Kaptein Alving his syphilis, so might some of the models and female associates of Osvald's painter-mates have infected *them*. No aspect of *Ghosts* has received more, often obsessive, attention than its treatment of venereal disease – that, it used to be said, was what the play was 'about', and certainly it was this aspect that gained it its notoriety, and its acclaim. And never more so than after autumn 1883, when August Lindberg set up a travelling company to perform it with himself in the part of Osvald. To do justice to it Lindberg went to a Copenhagen hospital to watch and listen to children whose minds were affected by inherited syphilis. He was repaid; his audiences appreciated that *Ghosts* had extended the range of human experience presented on the stage, extended it further and more audaciously than any play written since the great Jacobeans. When the curtain fell on the third act on the first night in Christiania itself, there was a long and deep silence before the ecstatic applause.

Even so a major aspect of Osvald's terrible predicament has tended to go overlooked. Putting him into his Parisian artistic milieu compels us to pay close attention to some of the most interesting and ambivalent words of the play.

Telling his mother about his visit to the Parisian specialist, he (surely truthfully) declares: 'Jeg har aldrig ført noget stormende liv' (p. 104) (I've never gone in for reckless living; p. 395).

The doctor, after a most thorough examination of him, is quite sure that Osvald is suffering from syphilis and that this is an inheritance. He actually says – 'fædrenes synder hjemsøges på børnene' (p. 105) (The sins of the father are visited upon the children; p. 396) – and sticks to this diagnosis until Osvald shows him his mother's studiously false letters about the Kaptein's life and character. Even then he does not swerve from his diagnosis, and so Osvald, severely shocked, can only think that he has brought his complaint on himself. '*Det* er det forfærdelige. Uhelbredelig ødelagt for hele livet – for min egen ubesindigheds skyld' (p. 106) (*That's* the really terrible thing. A hopeless wreck for the rest of my life ... and all the result of my own thoughtlessness; p. 397).

A generation that has experienced the dreadful depredations into the community of AIDS knows that it is perfectly possible to lead a well-adjusted life, to avoid any depravity of life-style, and yet contract a fatal sexually transmitted disease. As in our time so in Osvald's. His words surely *must* amount to an admission that he has enjoyed free love himself. After all if he had not done so, he would *have* to accept the doctor's first pronouncement, whatever its clash with his picture of his father. But his filial belief in the Kaptein's rectitude proves stronger than his amazement that so comparatively orderly an existence as his own has resulted in STD of the direst variety, and so painfully he adjusts his mind accordingly.

This, I think, gives the play a particular, and profoundly resonant, irony that has long been denied it. We should hold in our minds the possibility that *what Osvald has come to believe about his dreadful condition could quite easily be the truth.* Which, one hastens to stress, is not the same as saying that it is. Our lack of ultimate certainty is surely an integral part of Ibsen's intention. Over such a matter how many of us could be 100% sure, and isn't that very position of doubt itself an integral – and metaphoric – component of existence? Thus the first and still the usual reading of the situation – that Osvald has inherited the disease from the Kaptein – is the most probable. There is no reason, in this instance, to go to the Meerschaum pipe, let alone to his father's exposed penis, to find out *how* the infection has come about, for we all should know, as Ibsen patently did, that a woman (Fru Alving) can pass syphilis on to her child without herself displaying any outward symptoms of the disease. So the verdict of his French specialist that Osvald has been – that appalling word – '*vermoulu*' from his birth is vindicated. (And we can observe here another dreadful irony in the play – that Regine, whose greatest asset is her health, an asset of which many a sailor will avail himself, to his cost, after the play's end, must also be *vermoulue*.) Nonetheless we can at the same time insist that Osvald, behaving as a younger, if more endearing, version of the Kaptein, could well have contracted the disease himself through his own amorous activities – syphilis untreated spreads through the system fast and ravagingly. Osvald's blindness to his father's *real* character and mode of life (through which, however, the light of involuntary memory breaks) may well be matched by his blindness to the precariousness of his French artist-friends' actual lives – and even of his own.

For not only is the so-called emancipation of Osvald and his friends in their attitude to women far closer to older conventions than they realise, even where this is not so, even where relationships are as sincere and open as he believes they can and should be, there's a flaw in their whole outlook, one intimately related to their artistic credo. This requires existence to be pain-free, to be unattended by gratuitous suffering – an impossibility. A humane attitude to sex which abolishes old taboos and guilts is most definitely to be welcomed, and we deeply sympathise with Osvald for this desideratum, just as we loathe Pastor Manders' canting remonstrations against it. But we must not expect it to act as some passport to permanent unadulterated bliss. We must always have our eyes open. Life can't be seen just (or even principally) in terms of delectable holiday scenes and happy shining faces, however necessary it may be at times to assert these, in the teeth of repressive, reductive creeds, as valuable (and actual) *constituents* of life.

Which brings us to Osvald's approach to art, as he has articulated it. He has absorbed *some* lessons from the leading Impressionists, their accent on the human capacity for joy, their fascination with light, but not what makes Monet, Manet, Renoir the major painters they are: their audacity in being true to ideals in themselves audacious, their probing of the relationship between the human eye and the physical world, their relentless enlargement of the painter's vocabulary. He is callow. Osvald does *not* want to keep his eyes open to life in all its complexity, and make his canvases convey that complexity. Instead, just as he prefers not to see important realities of life at Rosenvold, so he insists on the pleasant, the pleasing, even the jubilant as the fittest subjects for his brush. Youth not maturity, in Jungian terms, *puer*, not *senex*, is the spirit that guides his art.

We can see the folly of Osvald's limitation of vision in his revulsion at the familiar rain of Norway, in his recoil from the severe northern landscape that is in fact his own native one, and limitation of vision obviously means limitation of the resulting art. The play in which he appears points up these inadequacies. It is not just that in *Ghosts* West Norway's climate and landscape wonderfully context all its characters' emotional and cultural tensions, becoming the first and superb instance in the prose-cycle of Ibsen's inwardness with nature, later to inform *Rosmersholm* (1886), *The Lady from the Sea* (1888) and *Little Eyolf* (1894), but that their very inclemency – which by no means precludes the beautiful or the life-enhancing – can teach us incomparable lessons about the human condition that endless emanations of *søndagsluft* (with, one assumes, a kinder and more southern setting) simply cannot.

Besides, Osvald is Norwegian, not Parisian-French. Ibsen with his usual developed antennae had sensed the intensification of interest in their own North and in the life it supports on the part of the younger Norwegian painters.

Take Osvald's contemporaries Christian Krohg (1852-1925) and Erik Werenskiold (1855-1938) who certainly cannot be accused of ignorance of Paris or of the Impressionists; indeed Krohg positively hero-worshipped Manet. In Christiania both Krohg and Werenskiold had studios in a building on Karl Johan known, on account of its appearance, as Pultosten (Cream Cheese), which enjoyed a reputation as the centre of the Norwegian avant-garde. In the very year that *Ghosts* was written and published, Krohg proclaimed the need for Norwegian artists in the interests of their own vitality to turn to their own landscape, and to the lives of ordinary Norwegians both urban and rural. That Christmas his own picture of a representative of the proletariat, a boy-porter, 'Carry for You?' had enormous success, and further and equally well-received social studies were to follow over the years – of a middle-aged prostitute, Albertine (the subject of his scandal-provoking novel of 1886), waiting to be examined by the doctor, of the indigent on an inhospitable wintry city street queuing for bread. Krohg attacked the conservative Art Association, for having a jury for its yearly exhibition consisting exclusively of members of the higher professions, insisting that a proper practising artist should be included. Krohg, bohemian in life, radical in thought, reacted by founding the Creative Artists' Union, which by autumn the following year was able to hold an exhibition of its own. Among Krohg's most enthusiastic protégés (though their ways were to diverge) was the student Edvard Munch, who, with friends, also rented a studio in Pultosten.

And Erik Werenskiold, the artist responsible for what has proved the most widely-known and influential portrait of Ibsen (1895), was actually in this year of *Ghosts*, like Osvald, living in Paris, and shortly to write a key article on the Impressionists. Already an illustrator of the first class, especially of books with Norwegian folk themes, he created on his return to Norway a sequence of Naturalistic paintings to this day regarded as glories of the Norwegian tradition – such as 'Shepherds at Tåtøy From Telemark' (1883). Werenskiold was always eagerly involved in the artistic and political debates of Norway, whereas Osvald is impatient, even after so short a stay there as we've witnessed, to leave Rosenvold and forget its concerns. (That there's an element here of Ibsen working off his own unease about voluntary exile I have little doubt.) An Osvald delivered from his terrible affliction would, we feel, be unlikely to follow the course of either of these artists with whom he shares Norway, Paris and years.

When we consider whether the uncompromising landscapes of Western Norway do not somehow reflect the human condition more satisfactorily than those sun-blessed classical ones (among which Ibsen was, in fact, writing this play), a passage from a near-contemporaneous work, *The Return of the Native* (1878) by Thomas Hardy, springs to mind. Hardy is writing of the Dorset heathland he called Egdon:

> Fair prospects wed happily with fair times; but alas, if times be not fair! Men have oftener suffered from the mockery of a place too smiling for their reason than from the oppression of surroundings oversadly tinged. Haggard Egdon appealed to a subtler and scarcer instinct, to a more recently learnt emotion, than that which responds to the sort of beauty called charming and fair. Indeed it is a question if the exclusive reign of this orthodox beauty is not approaching its last quarter ... The time seems near, if it has not actually arrived, when the chastened sublimity of a moor, a sea, or a mountain will be all of nature that is absolutely in keeping with the moods of the more thinking among mankind.[7]

Ibsen in a scribbled note while at work on *Ghosts* seems to have concurred with this: 'The perfect man is no longer a natural product,' he thought, 'he is a cultured product as corn is, and fruit trees, and the Creole race and thoroughbred horses and pedigree dogs, and the vine etc.'[8] Is a more atavistic approach to existence called for? 'If times be not fair!' Ibsen would seem to believe they are not.

Consider the intricacies of *Ghosts*' interwoven histories. A man prevented by an ossified social position from expressing his inherent joyfulness (the Kaptein). A woman stopped from escaping an unhappy marriage and instead sacrificing her considerable capacity for love and intellectual advancement for the sake of a husband and son who never really love her (Fru Alving). A young girl, the fruit of a clandestine liaison, relegated to the role of servant in the very household of which her biological father was wealthy master, and doomed to become a seamen's tart (Regine). A once handsome and dashing man spending his last years drooling like an infant as a price for the way in which he relieved his tensions (the Kaptein again). A young man of promise and hope facing the irremediable horror of softening of the brain (Osvald himself)... Yet all these are the unavoidable consequences of the cultural conditions of the present. They follow decisions about society and self, taken long ago but as yet not fully worked out.

Paradoxically, this grim play also sounds a note of distinct meliorism, relating it to the more obviously melioristic *Doll's House* of two years before, with Nora's door-slam telling the world what women could actually *do*. In another note written on the back of a bit of old newspaper, Ibsen opines: 'The fault lies in the fact that the whole of mankind is a failure.'[9] The Kaptein, Helene Alving, Pastor Manders, Osvald, Snekker Engstrand, Regine all have this in common – that they have been incurably (Osvald literally so) infected by a cruel and dishonest culture, one that starts its poisonous work with the light in which it views the basic generative acts of humankind. There is, however, in this play the covert but surely pervasive hope that things can be otherwise than as shown, if the disease mankind has cumulatively brought upon itself is at least recognized, confronted.

Osvald's own kind of art, though, is insufficient as a harbinger of any new era; it lacks the completeness that is essential to the Apollonian vision of life. From it cannot be extrapolated conditions for any kind of Third Kingdom such as *Emperor and Galilean* tries to point towards. Yet, such is the strength of the web in which he is caught, we can't refuse Osvald our affection; he is essentially *l'homme moyen sensuel* still young and with a (limited) talent. We are in no position to think ourselves his superior.

That last note of Ibsen's contains two more very disturbing sentences: 'If a man demands to live and develop as a man should, then that is megalomania. The whole of mankind, and especially Christians, suffer from megalomania.'[10] These sentences are to be taken ironically, as protests against the repressions of the later nineteenth century, which of course include the proscriptions of Christian orthodoxy; *Ghosts* itself was to be victimised by their proponents. But in fact, such are the natural demands of body and psyche that all human beings are bound to suffer in a culture which traffics in the repressive, and none more so than professing Christians whose tenets are at variance with biology. Poor Osvald Alving is indeed to suffer doubly. An existence according to the lights of Pastor Manders and his like would be for him one of crippling limitation and denial. Yet he has perhaps been too conditioned by early influences to be adequate to the fuller way of living he has elected to embrace and to the challenges it requires.

Formally *Ghosts* constitutes a refutation of Osvald's French masters' artistic ideals. It would be hard to think of a work less Impressionist in character than this play, so tense, intense, and concentrated is it. It may indeed, as Ibsen hoped, proceed before our eyes as if we were witnesses of events at Rosenvold, but there is no question of our receiving an 'impression' of life in all its measureless amorphousness, of having its variegated components dissolved for us in the benign unity of light. It is extraordinarily tight-knit, a chamber-play (to use Strindberg's later term) in which the characters' relationships, like the strains of musical instruments, twine and intertwine, their successive remarks – and every sentence has a truth to tell – revealing more and more about their pasts, themselves, each other, with – as unavoidable destination – a coda that is at once the culmination of all these inter-relations and a retroactively resonant metaphor. *Ghosts* moves towards its appalling climax with all the inevitability, the remorseless logic of an arrow to its target – or the transmitted disease to its victim. In this it stands up as a work corresponding to the Greek ideal of tragedy (as early informed admirers appreciated, including eminently the Professor of Greek at Christiania University, P. O. Schjøtt), with its concept of Nemesis, its fusion of the Apollonian (sun-honouring) sense of order with its Dionysiac release of chaotic elements challenging it, a fusion to which Nietzsche drew attention in his provocative evaluation of the Greek art-form, *Die Geburt der Tragödie (The Birth of Tragedy)* of 1872.[11] If we take Nietzsche's view of tragedy as principally Dionysiac, then we can see the agonies the characters go through at Rosenvold as constituting a Dionysiac dance, while the sun for which Osvald cries – and which is dawning in the last moments of the play – is the emergence of the Apollonian so integral, whether he actually called it by this name or not, to Ibsen's own vision of life; it is the desired, the needed counter-force.

As important as its correspondence to classical tragedy is the play's accordance with contemporary post-Darwin readings of life. Ibsen counted among his friends in Rome J. P. Jacobsen, the translator of both *The Origin of Species* and *The Descent of Man*, and, member that he was of Georg Brandes' intellectual circle, the man probably more responsible than any other for the dissemination of Darwin in the Nordic countries. In Jacobsen's influential literary debut, *Mogens* (1872) the eponymous young man has to learn how to live in accord with nature *as completely apprehended*. He must develop alongside the changes demanded by its incontrovertible laws (the story scrupulously follows the seasons) and must accept too its capacity for eruption and destruction. When Mogens' beloved Camilla dies in a fire, he turns in his grief and rage to hostility and debauchery, but in doing this does violation to his own being. Only when he understands that the rhythms of human life and the rhythms of nature have the same source can he win through to wisdom – and indeed to happy married love. Mogens, as we first meet him, has something of the callowness of Osvald Alving, and though he seems to despise all art that lacks a chthonic origin, is in his own way a natural artist.[12]

We can register Jacobsen-like Darwinism in what Ibsen wrote on a quarto-sheet discovered with the draft manuscript of the play:

> Biologists in recent times have more and more come to recognise that the phenomena in their own particular field of inquiry can be reduced to quite a small number of natural laws; also that as this research progresses and new theories result, it appears that this number constantly diminishes, and that it is reasonable to suppose that in time we shall be faced with the realization that in reality only one such law exists.[13]

In *Ghosts* this argument is developed for us, this one law is traced, the cultural corruption revealed, with its end, its stark QED forever in sight, indeed nascent in the very opening. Yet, I believe, meliorism is present too even in the shattering ending; the immature suffering Osvald asking for the sun while his mind is in retreat, while his beloved and strong-willed mother stands by in horror as she faces up to a predicament she has never anticipated; that of having to kill the one being for whom already she has sacrificed as much as she can. It is an image both of human helplessness and of the necessity of living with greater knowledge of psychic depths and physical realities than our culture has permitted us. Meanwhile, beyond these sufferers, the sun rises for a new morning, illuminating the glaciers and peaks of the fjordland outside the windows of the imprisoning house for a new generation.

I have already used the term 'meliorism' which (from Latin *melior*, 'better') is attributed to George Eliot, and has been defined by the famous *Encyclopaedia Britannica* of 1911[14] as a belief that 'at present the sum of good exceeds the sum of evil and that, in the future, good will continually gain upon evil'. This is, of course, not to deny the strength, or even the obstinacy, of evil but to allocate an even greater strength to good and to look to its eventual dominion. 'Mor, gi' mig solen ... Solen. Solen' (Mother give me the sun! ... The sun, the sun; p. 421). The words spoken to us by Osvald in his final agonies could come to be those of a young man who takes the light of the sun, to which we all owe our life, into every part of his life to irradiate it.

No speech has become more famous in all Ibsen's oeuvre than Helene Alving's:

Gengangeragtigt. Da jeg hørte Regine og Osvald derinde, var det som jeg så gengangere for mig. Men jeg tror næsten, vi er gengangere allesammen, pastor Manders. Det er ikke bare det, vi har arvet fra for og mor, som går igen i os. Det er alleslags gamle afdøde meninger og alskens gammel afdød tro og sligt noget. Det er ikke levende i os; men det sidder i alligevel og vi kan ikke bli' det kvit. Bare jeg tar en avis og læser i, er det ligesom jeg så gengangere smyge imellem linjerne. Der må leve gengangere hele landet udover. Der må være så tykt af dem som sand, synes jeg. Og så er vi så gudsjammerlig lysrædde allesammen. (p. 92)

Ghosts. When I heard Regine and Osvald in there, it was just like seeing ghosts. But then I'm inclined to think that we are all ghosts, Pastor Manders, every one of us. It's not just what we inherit from our mothers and fathers that haunts us. It's all kinds of old defunct theories, all sorts of old defunct beliefs, and things like that. It's not that they actually *live* on in us; they are simply lodged there, and we cannot get rid of them. I've only to pick up a newspaper and I seem to see ghosts gliding between the lines. Over the whole country there must be ghosts, as numerous as the sands of the sea. And here we are, all of us, abysmally afraid of the light. (p. 384)

Fru Alving strikingly anticipates here Richard Dawkins' post-Darwinist idea of memes,[15] replicators of cultural attitudes which one mind transmits to another, or which group minds transmit to the new generations. Memes include on Dawkins' list tunes, ideas, catch-phrases but also gods, concepts, ideas. Some die, some mutate, some, alas, have all too obstinate a life. To work against the more negative memes there must be others deriving from some braver, fuller approach to existence which can adapt itself for our own unfair times. Osvald's own art will not do in this capacity, but Ibsen's play – in which it and its young creator are embodied – has already proved its forward-moving strengths.

In the overwhelming furore that the publication of *Ghosts* in December 1881 provoked, painter Christian Krohg was prominent in its defence. Arch-Bohemian Hans Jæger was another of its public apologists, as were feminist novelists Camilla Collett and Amalie Skram. To his great credit, and Ibsen's unusually fulsome gratitude, Bjørnstjerne Bjørnson came out with a fine tribute to the play. Liberals, as much as conservatives, were opposed to the play, quite failing to see even the shadow of the meliorism behind it, or the spirit of deep compassion in the portrait of misguided Fru Alving and callow Osvald. In their eyes its intent concentration on the appalling was in itself appalling. Such a heady combination of *succès d'estime* and *succès de scandale* obviously drew the vanguardist young to the work, such as the youthful painters at Pultosten. For Edvard Munch *Ghosts* always occupied a high niche in his literary pantheon. Sue Prideaux in her fine and empathic biography of Munch, *Edvard Munch; Behind 'The Scream'* describes one of the artist's first really successful paintings – 'Morning' (1884), also known more literally as 'Girl Sitting on the Edge of her Bed' – as having 'its literary roots in Ibsen'. Obviously a girl of the working-class, she confronts the new day from a rumpled bed, and we can see, even in so quiet a study, that Munch's mind has been visiting among other places the last moments of *Ghosts*. Sunrise, streaming through the window in the top left-hand corner, brings about a certain resigned sadness in the girl. The precocious beauty of the canvas didn't please Norwegian critics too taken up with finding the human subject unpalatably low-class, and their barbed words stung Munch (he was to earn many far *more* barbed; Ibsen was to tell him in person that his art was bound to bring him hostility before proper recognition, just as his own had been).

Shortly after Ibsen's death the great German director Max Reinhardt decided to honour his achievement with a new production of *Ghosts*, and commissioned Munch to paint a frieze to be displayed in one of the foyers of his new theatre. Munch accepted the commission gladly, and produced what must still rank as the most haunting and impressive visual realisations of the play. He seems to have identified himself with Osvald Alving, and yes, we say to ourselves, it was in Munch's direction that that young man, had he been less ordinary, should have gone:

'I wanted,' said Munch, tormented always by his own unhappy background, 'to stress the responsibility of the parents. But it was my life too – my "why"? I, who came into the world sick, in sick surroundings, to whom youth was a sickroom and life a shiny, sunlit window – with glorious colours and glorious joys - and out there I wanted so much to take part in the dance, the Dance of Life.'[17]

The Lady From the Sea
The Artist as Hellenist: Hans Lyngstrand

1.

Fruen fra havet (*The Lady from the Sea*, 1888) is for me Ibsen's most difficult play, *When We Dead Awaken* apart, and these two works have much in common. Both debate freedom of choice, posing the question: are those decisions we make about the direction of our lives in fact pre-determined – by innate factors, by cultural conditioning, by a potent combination of the two? Or do we have the ability to stand back from ourselves and survey our situation, to see its moral implications and its possibilities for personal fulfilment? To what extent, too, can one human being affect the course of another's life? Will an apparent surrender always be, in truth, a realisation of that individual's deepest desires?

Again both plays are profoundly concerned with the relationship of human beings to Nature. Significantly four out of the five acts of the earlier play, and all three acts of the later one are set outside, and our attention is continually alerted to natural features and phenomena, and to the effect of these on human lives – pre-eminently the sea in the first, and the high mountains in the second. Both, too, focus on mental disturbance, using its anguishes as a means of divining what is life-enhancing and what is not in the world around the afflicted person, in both instances a woman of unusual sensitivity and capacity for love. We are asked to balance confused or sick psyches against the normal – and the normative, who, of course, will have legitimate demands of their own (Dr Wangel, Fru Maja). Yet the moral proportions involved in the balancing present problems in estimation; consequently we can be uncertain what satisfaction we should take from the adjustments (or refusals of adjustment) that the characters make. This is most evident in the endings of the plays, the right resolutions, we suppose, of the struggles so intimately traced. Put simply, should we feel happy at the happy ending of *The Lady from the Sea* or should we, with our already much stimulated sense of ambivalence, qualify it? Should the deaths of Rubek and Irene which close *When We Dead Awaken* distress us, or should we do better to find beauty, even uplift, in their *terribilità* which no other fate could have bestowed?

In both plays too Ibsen gives us a sculptor. Whereas in the final play he is its major figure, a world-famous man whose predicament has the dimensions of his own Promethean work, in *The Lady from the Sea* he is a young man of no reputation at all, as callow as Osvald Alving, if not more so, while we can't be sure about his talent, only about his enthusiasm. There was, as we shall see, a personal and circumstantial reason for Ibsen's inclusion of a sculptor into the comparatively diverse cast of characters in this play, but in fact the young man's art-form is peculiarly appropriate for its discourse. *When We Dead Awaken* is a testimony to Ibsen's feeling that the sculptor's was the art most nearly approximating to his own; it raises the drama of human interaction to the height of a monument which in its turn provides metaphor, inspiration and even consolation for its onlookers. When we read the pronouncements of the greatest sculptor of the day, Auguste Rodin, on his approach to his work – whether in the form of recorded sayings, entries in note-books or paraphrases and transcriptions by Rainer Maria Rilke – we come uncannily close to Ibsen's utterances about his own creative procedures. Certainly young Lyngstrand, and nobody else, will be our conductor into the drama that stands at the very heart of *The Lady from the Sea*, and it is precisely through his project for a sculpture that we shall proceed. Nor is this the only structural contribution to the play by an artist. The very first character we meet is the painter Ballested, and he will give us a maxim, a cod-apothegm, to take through its action, and which will be pronounced at the very end also, in the words: 'Menneskene ... de kan aklam-akli-matisere sig' (HU XI, p. 157) (Men and women can acclam – acclimatise themselves; Vol. VII, p. 124). The fact that we may doubt both its value and its truth doesn't diminish its force or its dramatic effectiveness.

2.

That place is a determinant of *The Lady from the Sea* is at once apparent from Ibsen's draft and notes. Usually, he told his biographer, Henrik Jæger, he had a generalised Norwegian setting in mind for a play. Here, however, there is specificity; the town where the Wangels live derives from Molde on Romsdalsfjorden, its geographical situation in relation to fjord and open sea corresponding exactly. Molde had made a great impression on Ibsen.

In 1862, the recipient of a grant from the Akademiske Kollegium of Christiania, he made a summer journey through the Hardanger and Sognefjord districts and so north to Molde and Romsdal, 'collecting and annotating' folk-tales and folk-songs. (The first harvest of the trip, gathered in Gudbrandsdal on both his outward and his return journeys, was the material for *Peer Gynt*.) Twenty-three years later, in July 1885, he returned to Molde, in the company of his wife and son, and spent time with his friend the Swedish poet, Carl Snoilsky, the model for Rosmer in his next play, *Rosmersholm*, (1886); indeed the eponymous house was taken from Moldegård. 'One of the most beautiful places in the world for panorama' he informed his publisher, Hegel, and indeed the panorama itself features in *The Lady from the Sea*. During his stay here Ibsen liked to stand on a little jetty and stare down into the waters, and he also took several boat-trips down the fjord and out into the open sea. 'When one stands staring down into the water,' Ibsen admitted to Jaeger, speaking however about another sea-holiday, taken in Skagen, Jutland, in summer 1887, 'it is like seeing the same life that moves on the earth, only in a different form. There are connections and resemblances everywhere.'[1]

Also in his summer days in Molde Ibsen met and took a liking to a young sculptor, Jacob Fjelde (1859-1896), and sat for him.[2] The result of these sittings, a life-size bust of which there are three bronze editions, is generally agreed to be one of the best likenesses of the dramatist we have. Small wonder then that Jacob's grandson, Rolf Fjelde, famous Ibsenist, translator and critic (1926-2002) speaks of *The Lady from the Sea* as set in a 'provincial town by the Moldefjord',[3] though actually neither town nor fjord are ever named. Add to this the fact that Ibsen, earlier so professionally interested in Molde's folklore, worked two haunting local legends into the play, and I don't think we can dispute its locality, even while aware of the perils of too literal a transposition. And we will have to remember Molde in *The Master Builder* (1892) because Hilde Wangel of *The Lady from the Sea* re-appears. (The first meeting of herself and Solness ten years before that play opens, and of such seminal importance to its action, took place, we know, in the girl's home-town – presumably then Molde again.) Ibsen's Draft of 5 June 1888, five days before composition proper began, opens with a paragraph that is a landscape-painting in itself:

> The little landing place for tourist steamers. Stops are made only when there are passengers to be landed or taken on board. All around are high, steep mountains shutting out the sun. The free open sea cannot be seen. Only the bays of the fjord. Seaside hotel. Sanatorium higher up. When the play begins, the last steamer of the season is on its way north. The boats always pass at midnight. Slowly, soundlessly they glide into the bay and out again.[4]

Ibsen's first concern here is with establishing the salient features of his chosen setting: the town's popularity with and reliance on tourists, its reputation as a health resort, the presence of high mountains all round and its distance from the open sea. Also the inevitable discrepancy between its summer and winter life. He then passes on to its inhabitants, and divides them into three groups, each standing at a different angle to the place. First, its full-term residents. Ibsen's notes suggest that he saw these as prone to boredom and also to a certain eccentricity, a wilful enlargement of latent idiosyncrasies. The two are not unconnected. The community, being so isolated from the world for most of the year, is dependent for both economic and social stimulus on its summer incomers; it needs to make a memorable impression on them, and these in turn offer an expansion of a basically restricted way of life. The townsfolk relish the arrival of the steamer, and are sorry when the season for its visits ends. All this is palpable in the finished play, which is set in hot, brilliant clear weather that doesn't preclude prospects of autumn and winter. Dr Wangel is clearly a mite too fond of popping in somewhere for a drink, and has to surround himself with happy smiling faces to stave off thoughts of the more troubling aspects of life. His elder daughter Bolette pines for the amplitude of the greater world, in particular for the acquisition of more knowledge, and eventually accedes to marriage to a man she doesn't love who will take her away. Young Hilde is possessed by a constant, often sadistic, desire for things to be 'spennende', exciting, a desire that has obvious neurotic roots (and which hasn't abated when we meet her later in Ibsen's next play but one). Ibsen in this play foreshadows Chekhov, especially the frustrations and longings of *Three Sisters* (1901), and the reasons for this are not hard to find. Its setting is middle class. And, while nobody in the play is well-off (except perhaps Arnholm, and then only comparatively), and while the Wangel household, for all Bolette's capable management, often finds it difficult to make ends meet, it is a comfortable and secure enough milieu, but lacks a culture of sufficient depth or activity wholly to sustain it.

There were originally to have been other examples of trapped lives: an amorous, adulterous tailor, and an old married clerk, who years before had a play produced once, but now goes around behaving as if he's a recognised writer. This man makes no appearance in *The Lady from the Sea* as we have it, but will turn up as Vilhelm Foldal in *John Gabriel Borkman* (1896).[5] But the 'starving sign-painter with dreams of being an artist, and happy in his illusions' does survive, in the person of the painter Ballested, who constitutes in himself a telling commentary on the place and its mores. As Lyngstrand will, he matches current popular images of the artist, starting with his appearance. He sports the broad-brimmed 'wide-awake' hat, and the velvet jacket that you might expect of an erstwhile bohemian. (Robert Louis Stevenson was actually nicknamed 'Velvet Jacket' in his bohemian days, and Ibsen himself, during his first period of residence in Italy, was partial to such a hat.) Ballested still paints – though cannot find a model for the canvas on which he is at work. He came to the town with a travelling theatre company for whom he designed sets and costumes; this company went bust, and Ballested may indeed have known financial hardship, but now doesn't lead at all a bad life as a Jack-of-all-trades, while continuing to paint pictures. He does decorating and handyman jobs, runs a Dancing Academy, acts as tour-guide and is a hair-dresser as well. (Molde has clearly not gone the puritan way of Karsten Bernick's home-town during his consulate in *The Pillars of Society*.) Ibsen himself when a student in

Christiania was known as Gert Westphaler, Ludwig Holberg's Talkative Barber, so there may be an element of self-mockery here, Ballested being Ibsen's picture of how he himself might have turned out if he had not been so spectacularly gifted and iron-willed.

According to himself he has learned the secret of life, of keeping oneself reasonably happy. This is acclimatisation (though, interestingly, he finds the word difficult to articulate). While all he turns his hand to is pleasing and useful enough, to others as well as himself, he represents the artist as colourful appendage to society, something almost of a joke, a welcome decoration or diversion, posing no threat to anything or anybody, gregarious, accommodating, resilient. Though he has sympathies, only at the play's close does he appreciate the relevance of his own painting-in-progress, 'Havfruens ende', 'Death of a Mermaid' to the predicament of the Lady from the Sea herself. And then the conclusion he draws does not wholly convince. Anyway acclimatisation might easily result in existences like that of the carp, those fine fighting fish, in the Wangels' garden-pond, who perforce merely swim round and round while nearby shoals of natural-living fish move in and out of the fjord. Dr Wangel's perceptive elder daughter Bolette actually compares the life of their town to the carp-pond. And these fish when they age can be caught with tackle by the callous human, like young Hilde, abetted by Lyngstrand who is currying favour with her.

On his list of 'peculiar figures' who are 'inhabitants of the place' Ibsen put at the top a lawyer and his second wife who comes 'from out yonder by the free, open sea'. The couple, in a working week of intensest thought, matured into Dr Wangel and Ellida (who for much of the first version is called Tora; later Ibsen decided she'd been named Ellida by her father, in heathen fashion, after a *ship*).[6] Ellida's feelings of claustrophobia at living so far inland from her childhood home, the lighthouse at Sjoldviken, are reinforced by another kind of claustrophobia, the inescapability of the household of which she's become officially mistress, but of whose relationships and memories she is not an integral part. Homesickness intensifies into psychosis, exacerbated by pregnancy and compounded by the death, after a mere four or five months of life, of her baby son. She thinks the dead child's eyes had reflected all the successive moods of the sea; she pronounces the water of the fjord sick because it's brackish, lacking in the full salinity of the sea proper.

> The sea's power of attraction,' Ibsen jotted down for his own benefit. 'The longing for the sea. People akin to the sea. Bound by the sea. Dependent on the sea. Must return to it. One fish species forms a basic link in the evolutionary series. Do rudiments of it still remain in the human mind? In the mind of certain individuals?[7]

Is Ellida Wangel such an individual? Could there be in a contemporary fjord-town someone who at once points backwards to our primordial existence and forwards to a time when ordinary folk will re-experience their inherent relation to the elements? This idea, consonant with the whole post-Darwinist mind-set (see, again, Jacobsen's *Mogens* and Hardy's *The Return of the Native* with its treatment of Egdon Heath as a source of atavism) galvanised Ibsen's imagination as it set to work on this play; it is as prevalent in his first version of it as in the final one. Its importance to him is borne out by its continuation in *The Master Builder*, where Hilde Wangel has the same feeling for the air and its denizens, the birds, as her step-mother Ellida had for the ocean and its creatures, and by its furthering in *Little Eyolf* and *When We Dead Awaken*, in which Almers only truly finds himself in the desolation of the mountains and Rubek and Irene must move towards the peak to know release. That we are not with Ellida concerned simply with a case of obsessional nostalgia, with a willed regression, but with a matter of general human concern, is clear from more preparatory notes of Ibsen's:

> Has human evolution taken the wrong path? Why have we come to belong to the dry land? Why not the air? Why not the sea? The longing to have wings. Curious dreams that one can fly and that one does fly without feeling any astonishment – how to explain all this?
>
> We should take possession of the sea. Build our towns floating on the sea. Move them to the south or to the north according to the season. Learn to harness wind and weather. Something marvellous like that will come. And we – will not be there to enjoy it! Will not experience it![8]

Some of the most interesting and affecting exchanges of the play are in effect dramatisations of these speculative remarks. Take the conversation Ellida has with her old friend and former suitor, Arnholm, in which she rebuffs his somewhat platitudinous declaration that we humans belong on dry land:

> Nej. Jeg tror ikke det. Jeg tror at dersom menneskene bare fra først af havde vænnet sig til at leve sit liv på havet, – i havet kanske, – så vilde vi nu ha' været ganske anderledes fuldkomne end vi er. Både bedre og lykkeligere ... Og jeg tror at menneskene aner noget sådant selv. At de går og bærer på det, som på en lønlig anger og sorg. De kan tro mig, – deri er det, at menneskenes tungsind har sin dybeste grund. Jo, – tro De mig på det. (p. 102)

> No, I don't think so. I think if only man had learnt to live on the sea from the very first... Perhaps even in the sea... We might have developed better than we have, and differently. Better and happier... And I believe that people suspect something of this themselves. And bear with it as with some secret sorrow. Believe me, here are the deepest springs of human melancholy. Believe me. (pp. 74-75)

Arnholm protests that melancholy isn't the principal feature of human existence, that many of us pass the greater part of our lives pleasantly enough. Again Ellida cannot agree:

> Å nej, det er nok ikke så. Den glæden – den er nok ligesom vor glæde over det lange lyse sommerdøgn. Den har mindelsen om den kommende mørketid over sig. Og den mindelsen er det, som kaster sin skygge over menneskeglæden, – ligesom drivskyen kaster sin skygge over fjorden. Der lå den så blank og blå. (p. 103)

> Oh, no, it's not at all like that. The joy... is a bit like the kind of joy we take in the long sunlit summer days. It contains a threat of the long dark days to come. And this threat casts its shadow over human joy... like a passing cloud that casts its shadow over the fjord. There it lay so bright and blue. (p. 75)

What Ellida is positing here is surely but a version of the traditional Christian idea of Original Sin and Expulsion from the Garden of Eden of which we catch enough glimpses in this life to know that it is our rightful and ultimate home. Ellida seems – to judge by her later conversation – to be able to conceive of a Redeemer, and the redemption such a man will effect must take the form of our restoration to the elements. If we see this as a consequence of her material experience in

Time (an adolescence and young womanhood that ended in a father's death and a mother's breakdown) and in Space (her isolated old lighthouse-home by the shore), then this is acceptable enough; we will see it as a psycho-pathology with detectable roots in real life and therefore susceptible to rational explanation – and to cure. It would however be reductive to see it *only* as this. Ibsen in his draft wrote that her mind would be filled with: 'Images of the teeming life of the sea and of "things lost for ever",'[9] and this play's imagery is rivalled in the prose-cycle only by that of *Little Eyolf* for the beauty and majesty of what it takes from the natural world, as in her account of what she talked about with her seaman-betrothed:

> ELLIDA: Vi talte mest om havet.
> WANGEL: Ah – ! Om havet altså?
> ELLIDA: Om storm og om stille. Om mørke nætter på havet. Havet på de glittrende solskinsdage talte vi også om. Men mest talte vi om hvalerne og om springerne og om sælerne, som plejer ligge der ude på skærene i middagsvarmen. Og så talte vi om mågerne og ørnene og alle de andre sjøfuglene, som du véd. – Tænk, – er ikke det underligt, – når vi talte om sådant noget, så stod det for mig, som om både sjødyrene og sjøfuglene var i slægt med ham.
> WANGEL: Og du selv – ?
> ELLIDA: Ja, jeg syntes næsten, at jeg også kom i slægt med dem alle sammen. (pp. 88-89)

> ELLIDA: We spoke mostly about the sea.
> WANGEL: Ah! About the sea?
> ELLIDA: About the storms and calms. About dark nights at sea. And about the glitter of the sea on sunny days. But mostly we talked about whales and dolphins, and about the seals that lie out in the rocks in the warmth of the sun. And we talked about the gulls and the eagles and all the other sea-birds. And you know ... Isn't it strange? ... when we talked about such things I used to feel that he was somehow of the same kith and kin as these sea-creatures.
> WANGEL: And you ... ?
> ELLIDA: I too almost felt as though I were one of them. (p. 62)

Ellida's recollections here would, if taken as seriously as they should be, revivify her own society, provide it indeed with the art, the appeal to its deeper senses, of which it is so in need. We are surely intended to feel her superiority to Ballested's painting 'The Death of a Mermaid' or even to Lyngstrand's projected sculpture, 'The Sailor's Wife', which has something of a youth's taste for sensationalism about it. Therefore we may well ask whether 'acclimatisation', even in the terms of the play's conclusion, is really the answer for somebody of such intensity of response, though we also understand that unhappiness of such strength, such existential dereliction as hers cannot be borne, must somehow be palliated. Ellida is indeed, to repeat the phrase I have used about the eponymous Brand and Peer Gynt, a *de facto* artist who needs must reconcile her conflicting instincts – and the conflicting components of the world about her – in order to make of her life something beautiful, organic, inclusive. Small wonder then that a real artist of the stature of the novelist Camilla Collett found in Ellida a reflection of her own life, and that Ibsen replied to her declaration of this: 'Yes, there are several similarities, many, in fact, and you have seen them and felt them ... But it is many years since you, by your spiritual passage through life, in one way or another began to play a part in my writing.'[10]

In contrast Ellida's husband, Dr Wangel, is very much of the small town in which, as he tells us, he was born and bred, and some of his limitations of vision must be attributable to limitations of experience. He is one of Ibsen's subtlest and most ambiguous portraits, by no means an unaffectionate one, and this is the point at which briefly to look at him, for, a consequence of place as he significantly is, he provides one of the yardsticks against which aspirations beyond it – of the untethered imagination in general, of the artist in particular – must measure themselves.

His obstinate masculinity, reinforced by his role in the community, is as responsible for *his* difficulties as Ellida's femininity is for hers. Like so many men he requires pleasantness around him, despite (or maybe because of) his competent work as a doctor: the troubled, the disagreeable disconcert him. Though he is sincerely worried by his wife's mental health, he takes long enough to do anything about it, and for two or three years has, irresponsibly, allowed her drugs from his medical supplies to help her get through her burdensome days. In his original plans Ibsen gave him (then a lawyer) a 'reckless affair' which had cast its shadow over the rest of his life. This 'past' went, but traces of this earlier personality that it denoted remain. Something of a *bon viveur*, with a certain fondness, at the very least, for brandy – Bolette is uneasy at the thought of her father going yet again to the bar on the steamer – he doesn't hide the fact that his response to Ellida was from the very first charged with sexuality, and her later withholding herself from him in their marriage-bed spelled misery for him. His need for an attractive young wife was indeed as much libidinous as it was domestic – for in the event it is Bolette, not Ellida, who runs the home and copes with the doctor's carelessness over money. His treatment of Bolette, of whom he's fond enough, indicates that same blindness which enabled him to let his wife's situation continue. Nor is his good citizen's morality as firm as we might imagine; he's prepared to blackmail the Stranger by threatening, against Ellida's wishes, to hand him over to justice for the killing of his captain a decade before. So much for his shortcomings. These can be counterbalanced by his overall kindness, which can, at times of crisis, turn into real unselfishness, by the unstinting nature of his concern for Ellida when eventually he allows it into the forefront of his mind, by his charity to Arnholm when (wrongly) he suspects him to be the object of his wife's yearnings, by his gentleness to the seriously ill Lyngstrand, and – above all – by the profound love he feels for Ellida which survives and indeed defies all apparent reverses. Whatever Dr Wangel's deficiencies lack of heart isn't among them, and, of course, this proves to be true of Ellida too.

Dr Wangel stands for 'land', for the conservatism of the present human status quo which looks neither atavistically back nor transformingly forward, and through him we have to concede that there can be virtue, sanity and love in such a position. This makes any arguments against it the harder to pursue. But they have to be pursued even so.

The second group consists of 'summer visitors' and 'patients from the sanatorium'. We are made privy to no actual sanatorium in the play, but Ibsen makes it clear that to come to this fjord-town for health reasons is a common enough practice: Lyngstrand is both 'visitor' and 'patient', and has been staying in the town for a fortnight when we encounter him. In his draft the sculptor – probably because of Ibsen's actual experiences at Molde – has pride of place in this social group: '[The] young ailing sculptor who is trying to gather strength to withstand the coming winter. For next summer he has been awarded a scholarship and a commission and other support, and then he will be able to go to Italy. Dreads the eventuality of dying without having seen the Mediterranean countries and without having achieved anything worth while in his art. – His 'patron' is staying at the seaside hotel. Acts as guardian to the sick man. Is a man of principle. No help, no support this year. The scholarship there in black and white, "then we will see what we can manage next year". His wife is stupid, arrogant and tactless. Hurts the sick man, sometimes deliberately, sometimes unwittingly.'[11]

Lyngstrand's development in Ibsen's mind is extremely interesting. The young man's 'patron' to whom he refers gratefully is an invisible presence only, and the patron's wife has been eliminated. But, I believe, the jottings about these last two persons, so promising, were not altogether discarded but bear on the text that we have, and this I shall show. The sculptor is as closely connected to Ibsen's socio-geographical study of his fjord-town as the Wangels themselves. He is following the latest, the 'modern' method of treating tuberculosis (or 'sclerosis of the lung') then widespread and lethal: taking things easy and spending as much time as he can in the sun and fresh (sea) air. All over the coastal and mountain resorts of Europe sufferers from the disease were to be found, and, as Ibsen's notes suggest, sanatoria sprang up in suitable places to cater for their needs. With winter they went south if they could. The Scandinavian colony of Rome, of which Ibsen was such a familiar for so many years, contained numerous such, among them artists, as extant records testify. They tended to die young, and were buried in the city's Protestant Cemetery. Lyngstrand will be of their party. Like the summer birds preparing to leave at the first manifestations of autumn, like that English steamer whose last trip of the calendar year we witness, he will depart from the little town – most likely never to come back, which gives the ending of the play a particular poignancy. But this sad fact notwithstanding, he is closely linked to the third group Ibsen placed in his design for the play, which 'consists of tourists who come and go, and who figure episodically in the action'.

They don't exactly, but we are certainly aware of their presence. We have already noted how four of the five acts take place out of doors, and the exception, Act Four, is set in a garden-room with 'an open glass door leading out onto the verandah' thus giving us a view of a section of the garden. The world beyond the Wangels' house is always palpable, with both its natural and its human denizens. And in the remarkable Act Two, one of Ibsen's most virtuoso performances, movingly establishing both Lyngstrand's closeness to death and Ellida's heart-sick longing for the open sea and for the man who embodies it for her, we are actually in a public place, *Utsikten*, 'The Prospect', a celebrated view-point. Courting couples make their way to its look-out beacon, as do parties of visitors from abroad under the escort of Ballested, and all these comings-and-goings counterpoint with consummate artistry the burden of the intimate conversations among the *dramatis personae* themselves.

But this is no mere instance of imaginative theatrical effect. These young folk, these men and women have come here to admire the panorama of 'outer fjord, with its islands and headlands', and 'the mountain peaks in the distance' 'reddish gold' in the early evening, and, by doing so, they show us the universality of the need for, and the satisfaction in, nature. They also remind us of a most important truth about the times and about such places as Molde. The middle classes – like the upper classes they emulated (Molde's more illustrious visitors included Gladstone, the Prince of Wales and the young Kaiser Wilhelm) – now had disposable income enough to address, and cultivate, their instinctual delight in natural beauty. They could take pleasure-trips by steamer or railway, they could stay in comfortable hotels with other like-minded people (or if they can't afford this, at the boarding-houses and lodgings provided by local townsfolk such as the midwife, Fru Jensen, with whom Lyngstrand is staying). To travel a long way to look at a panorama such as *Utsikten* here – from Molde's equivalent look-out point, when the weather is right, you can see two hundred and twenty-two mountain peaks! – was widely judged conducive to spiritual as well as physical well-being. By the last decades of the century Molde itself was earning more from tourism than from any of the older established industries – timber and fishery. In what other play of the period is viewing a panorama the context of a whole act? What other play indeed pays homage to the tourist as this one does? In prose fiction we recall Turgenev, and Turgenev's friend, Henry James:

A Passionate Pilgrim (1875), *Roderick Hudson* (1876), *The American* (1877), *Daisy Miller* (1879), *The Portrait of a Lady* (1881), to all of which the very procedures of tourism are important. But in drama...? It was as novel, as *à la page*, as opening with a work-place was to be in his next play but one, *The Master Builder*.

And since we are dealing with Ibsen's relationship to art and the artist, we should acknowledge that the enhancement of the beauties of a place, and their organised conservation, are art-forms in themselves, and far from the least important. From the point of view of a diverse, a socially diffuse public, their creation all over the western world were phenomena of the nineteenth century. Ibsen's social antennae are noteworthy again. Take the following charming but telling exchange in Act Two:

> BOLETTE: (*til Arnholm*). Synes De ikke det er smukt heroppe?
> ARNHOLM: Her er storartet, synes jeg. Pragtfuld udsigt.
> WANGEL: Ja, De har sagtens aldrig været her oppe før?
> ARNHOLM: Nej, aldrig. I min tid tror jeg knapt her var fremkommeligt. Ikke en fodsti engang.
> WANGEL: Og ingen anlæg heller. Alt det har vi fåt i de sidste år.
> BOLETTE: Der borte på 'Lodskollen' er det endnu mere storartet at se udover ... Har De lyst at gå med os, herr Arnholm?
> ARNHOLM: Ja, meget gerne. Er der lagt vej did op også?
> BOLETTE: Å ja. Der er god bred vej.
> HILDE: Vejen er så bred at der rundelig kan gå to mennesker arm i arm. (pp. 82-83)

> BOLETTE: (*to Arnholm*) Don't you think it's lovely up here?
> ARNHOLM: I think it's magnificent. Marvellous view.
> WANGEL: I don't suppose you've been up here before?
> ARNHOLM: No, never. In those days I don't think you could get to it. There wasn't even a path.
> WANGEL: Nor any of these amenities. It's all come about in the last few years.
> BOLETTE: The view from Lodskollen over there is even better ... Do you feel like coming with us, Mr Arnholm?
> ARNHOLM: Yes, I should like to. Is there a path up there too?
> BOLETTE: Oh, yes. A good broad path.
> HILDE: Broad enough for two people to walk it arm-in-arm quite comfortably. (p. 56)

'Life,' Ibsen continued to himself, 'is apparently a happy, easy, and lively thing up there in the shadow of the mountains and in the monotony of this seclusion. Then the suggestion is thrown up that this kind of life is a life of shadows. No initiative; no fight for liberty. Only longings and desires. This is how life is lived in the brief light summer. And afterwards – into the darkness. Then longings are roused for the life of the great world outside. But what would be gained from that? ... Everywhere limitation. From this comes melancholy like a subdued song of mourning over the whole of human existence and all the activities of men. One bright summer day with a great darkness thereafter – that is all – '[12]

The man in the finished play who shows us the truth of these observations of his creator is the one incomer with whom we are engaged – and the principal representative of the artist: Hans Lyngstrand. His arrival at the Wangels' garden-gate occasions its first real dialogue – and, by no accident, its subject is art and artists. Just as the man he talks to, the painter Ballested, presents us with one conventional image of the artist, so does he. Hans is thin and pale, in obvious poor health, and his clothes suggest both refined taste and indigence. And with his very appearance at Dr Wangel's house comes the later nineteenth century's intimate and pervasive association of the artist with illness. One can give this, to begin with, a commonsensical explanation. If young men with serious ailments agreed to the programmes proposed to them by health authorities, they'd have enough time on their hands to develop all kinds of hitherto only latent interests – and how many young men in all ages have had secret aspirations to be poets, painters, sculptors? But that isn't quite enough to explain the appeal of the figure to the age.

It can surely be argued that in a society as relentlessly concerned with the cash-nexus and expansion as Western Europe was becoming in the second half of the nineteenth century the sick-bed provided one of the few impregnable retreats for the sensitive. To be 'ordered south', as so many sufferers were, was to be offered a welcome escape-route that could (if not permanently) restore mental as well as physical energies, and accordingly healthy society imaginatively pined for their paradoxical peace and freedom. One thinks of Robert Louis Stevenson for whom illness constituted the most complete antithesis to the demands of professional class Edinburgh as represented by his successful engineer father, and who embodied, if not celebrated, this antithesis in widely read stories, poems and essays. Looked at in this way the pains and anxieties caused by a disease, and even its likely termination by early death, are translated into a kind of payment for the release granted. The invalid becomes an involuntary but nevertheless self-aware martyr worthy of honour, a secular saint, who, like the non-secular kind, can be vouchsafed visions of ineffable glory. It may seem that we have met this conjunction of art and sickness already in Ibsen, in *Ghosts*, but spiritually we couldn't be further distant from that play. Osvald's paintings with their 'joy in life' are associated with health of mind and health of body like the stories of his older contemporary and fellow-syphilitic, Guy de Maupassant. Like that great writer he grieves at his loss of these, for him his disease is his tragedy. For Lyngstrand, and for some of those who meet him (though not the sensation-seeking Hilde) his disease is virtually a badge of merit, token of his creativity. For full recognition of this cultural pathology, and autopsy on its victims, society had to wait for the twentieth century to bring it Thomas Mann's *Tonio Kröger* (1903), *Der Tod in Venedig* (*Death in Venice*, 1911) and *Der Zauberberg* (*The Magic Mountain*, 1924). Lyngstrand presages Mann's representative figures[13] but Ibsen's treatment of Lyngstrand amounts to an insightful anticipation. In that opening conversation Lyngstrand tells Ballested first that he's going to be a sculptor, second that his name is Hans Lyngstrand, and third that he's *ill* (though he adds the erroneous rider that his chest-complaint is nothing so very serious). It's no coincidence that it is he, the sick artist, who will penetrate to the trauma, the personal wound behind Ellida's condition.

The history of his life that Lyngstrand gives his new friends is indeed the very pattern of that with which the career and writings of Robert Louis Stevenson had, as adumbrated above, made an English-language readership familiar (Stevenson, already one of the most celebrated artists of the day, set out for the South Seas the very year this play was published): reaction against an unsympathetic father who stands, fairly consciously, for puritanism, for a life-denying hardness connected to a rigid definition of malehood and the maintenance of a firm social position with *money*; ensuing knock-about adventurous travel which brought on illness and consequent creativity, and the prospect of more journeys ahead (including, sadly, the ultimate one at a comparatively young age). Lyngstrand relates how, after his mother's death, his father turned him out of the house and packed him off to sea. He crossed the Atlantic, went to Halifax, Nova Scotia, and then –

LYNGSTRAND: Så forliste vi i engelske kanalen på hjemrejsen. Og det var jo godt for mig.

ARNHOLM: Hvorledes det, mener De?

LYNGSTRAND: Jo, for ved det forliset var det at jeg fik mit knæk. Dette her for brystet. Jeg lå så længe i det iskolde vandet, før de kom og berged mig. Og så måtte jeg jo begi' sjøen. – Ja, det var rigtignok en stor lykke.

ARNHOLM: Så? Synes De det?

LYNGSTRAND: Ja. For knækket er jo ikke videre farligt. Og nu kan jeg jo få bli' billedhugger, som jeg så inderlig gerne vilde. Tænk – at få modellere i det dejlige léret, som føjer sig så fint mellem fingrene! (p. 71)

LYNGSTRAND: ... Then on our way home we were wrecked in the English Channel. And that was very fortunate for me.

ARNHOLM: How do you mean?

LYNGSTRAND: Well, it was that shipwreck that gave me this little weakness ... in the chest. I was such a long time in the freezing cold water before they came and rescued me. So then of course I had to give up the sea ... Yes, that really was a great piece of luck.

ARNHOLM: Oh? You think so?

LYNGSTRAND: Yes. Because this little weakness isn't really dangerous. And now I can become a sculptor, which I desperately want to be. Think of all the lovely clay I'll be able to model ... So beautifully yielding to the fingers! (p. 46)

He may be as self-deceived about his ability to sculpt as he, affectingly, is about his health. (Dr Wangel tells Bolette that in his medical opinion Lyngstrand hasn't long to live.) Even so this is a description of a true awakening. Whether good, bad or indifferent, his art is empathic enough to act as our depth-charge into the disturbed submerged inner world of Ellida, and for it to be, if at one remove, an agent in her recovery.

3.

Jacob Fjelde was only twenty-six when Ibsen met him in Molde.[14] He was a precocious young man, son of a well-known wood-carver, and had already studied in Italy. The impression he made on Ibsen must have been an unusually favourable one, since not only did the famous man sit for the unknown sculptor, but he did so with recorded patience. Two years later Fjelde was to emigrate to America where he made a fine reputation for himself. His most famous creation is the one he completed before his tragic premature death from an ear infection at the age of thirty-seven: the monument at Gettysburg to the 1st Minnesota infantry, a regiment made up mostly of emigrant Norwegian farm-boys, kin to the people he'd left behind in his home-country. (Jacob's son, Paul Fjelde father of Rolf) was also a sculptor.) The bust that he made of Ibsen from the life – now visible in bronze castings in St Paul, Minnesota, as well as in Wisconsin and North Dakota – gives him an appropriately thoughtful, serious face, behind which one can imagine imaginative and intellectual activity. Wasn't Fjelde doing here what the dramatist himself does, bringing to life people's exteriors, and suggesting the interior worlds they carry? Correspondences such as these must surely have been in Ibsen's mind as he sat for the young artist in the town he'd chosen to call 'The Rome of the North'.

But twenty years before this sitting Ibsen had known a good many sculptors, most of them young and Nordic, in the 'Rome of the South', the real city, to which they'd been drawn by its unsurpassable wealth of classical work.

At first Ibsen was to write, to Bjørnson on 16 September 1864:

Here, in Rome especially, much has been revealed to me; though I can't yet get to terms with classical art, I don't really understand its relevance to our time, I lack the illusion and, above all, the sense of personal and individual expression in the subject as in the artist, and I cannot help often seeing (as yet, anyway) mere conventions where others postulate laws. It seems to me that the classical plastic works of art are, like our heroic ballads, the products of their age rather than of this or that master; which may perhaps be a reason why so many of our modern sculptors fail when they persist, today, in trying to create heroic ballads in clay and marble. Michelangelo, Bernini and his school I understand better; those fellows had the courage to commit a madness now and then.[15]

Neither Michelangelo nor Bernini, great names though they surely were, enjoyed the blessing of fashion then, so Ibsen is demonstrating once again his independence of mind. A mind moreover unafraid of development, since by 28 January 1865 he was telling Bjørnson that, just as he had predicted, the classical was growing on him:

> Do you remember the 'Tragic Muse' which stands outside the hall in the Rotunda in the Vatican? No sculpture here has yet been such a revelation to me. I may even say that it is through this that I have understood what Greek tragedy was. The indescribably calm, noble and exalted joy in the expression of the face, the richly laurelled head containing within it something supernaturally luxuriant and bacchantic, the eyes that look both inwards and at the same time through and far beyond the object of their gaze – such was Greek tragedy. The statue of Demosthenes in the Lateran, the Faun in the Villa Borghese, and the Faun (of Praxiteles) in the Vatican (*bracchio nuovo*), have also opened great windows for me into Greek life and the Greek character, and have enabled me to understand what imperishability in beauty really is. Pray heaven I may be able to use this understanding for my own work.[16]

While *Ghosts* is the most patent and complete expression of Ibsen's 'understanding' of Greek tragedy, this is pervasive also in other works, not least *The Lady from the Sea*. The calm, the joy, the eyes looking inwards and outwards from a head crowned in a wreath can be found in poor young possibly untalented Lyngstrand as in the more talented (and never-crowned) figure of Løvborg in *Hedda Gabler*, when sober and actually writing, and in the heroic figures of Solness and Rubek. Similarly – though she is to be rewarded with devotion, and, one supposes, happiness – Ellida recalls the sorrowing women of Greek drama, Hecuba, Medea. And this Greek emotion is intimately bound up with the art of sculpture.

By the time Ibsen came to Rome, the great Danish sculptor, Bertel Thorvaldsen (1770-1844) had been dead twenty years. But he, more than anybody else, was responsible for the tradition Ibsen encountered of Nordic artists spending time in Rome, often years indeed, studying and copying the monuments of antiquity; the high regard in which these were generally held was largely his legacy too. Thorvaldsen himself (whose father, an Icelander, was a woodcarver like Fjelde's) had arrived in the city from Copenhagen on 8 March 1797, and he celebrated that day throughout his life as his 'Roman birthday', saluting it as the watershed date it had been in what turned out a triumphant career. He remained in Rome, increasingly at the very centre of its artistic life, until 1838, returning there for a further year, 1841-1842. His first widely praised work, 'Jason' (1802-03) – and Canova himself, also resident in Rome, was among the praise-givers – indicates the direction he intended his art to take. Guided by the writings of Johann Joachim Winckelmann (1717-1768) he studied Greek artefacts (both Classical and Hellenist – that is, from between 323 to 27 BCE) of which Rome contained so many examples, such as the then universally admired (and Hellenist) Apollo of the Belvedere. He learned – with special intensity between the years 1810 and 1820 – not just from the astonishing technical mastery of their makers, but from the civilisation responsible for them, imbibing its values: Apollonian indeed, honouring proportion, harmony, clarity and light, and expressing in Winckelmann's famous words *edle Einfalt und stille Grösse* (noble simplicity and calm grandeur). With Canova Thorvaldsen spear-headed the whole Neo-Classical movement which sought through promulgation – and creative emulation – of these models from antiquity to foster a new and progressive attitude to life that could and would, it was believed, unite all Europe. By 1820 Thorvaldsen was receiving so many commissions that he had to employ forty assistants to carry them out, while from 1824 to 1831 he worked on a commission that was truly a tribute to his stature: the tomb of Pope Pius VII for the Vatican, which had never turned to a Protestant artist before.

Though he himself had two children by an Italian woman, many of Thorvalden's most famous works have a strong pederastic quality, this being consonant with both Classical and Hellenistic cultures, and which, to a very real degree, accounted for Winckelmann's identification with them. 'Ganymede', 'Mercury', 'Eros', 'The Shepherd Boy with Dogs' – the titles speak for themselves. It is possible that Ibsen's initial lack of enthusiasm for the Greek sculptures he encountered, the kind that had inspired these pieces by Thorvaldsen, relates to this quality, for their homo-eroticism is shown not just in matter but in manner, and it is extremely unlikely that this had any personal appeal for him.

Thorvaldsen's reputation was still strong in the Rome of Ibsen's stay there, and the artists' hang-out he'd frequented, Café Greco in the Via Condotti, still a favoured meeting-place. His successor as the most eminent Danish sculptor of his generation was Jens Adolph Jerichau (1816-1883) who was in Rome when Ibsen was and whom he got to know. These were unusually sociable years for Ibsen; the Scandinavian colony, which we noted in the previous chapter, included many lively and interesting people who shared his own sense of liberation from the conventions and restrictions of the North. Among the up-and-coming sculptors belonging to it, were fellow-Norwegians Brynjolf Bergslien (1830-1898) whose style was to fuse Realism with National Romanticism and whose sculpture of Karl Johan on horseback can be seen outside the Royal Palace in Oslo today, and Ole Henriksen Fladager (1832-1871) whose *putto* for the baptismal font in the Christiankirke in Ibsen's own birth-place, Skien, was rescued from the great fire that devastated church and town, and so survives to the present; the Dane Frederik Stamboe (1833-1908) who, in 1861, made a famous relief of Hans Christian Andersen, and perhaps closest of all to Henrik and Suzannah Ibsen, Walter Runeberg (1838-1920), son of Finland's national (but Swedish-language) poet, J. L. Runeberg, and the creator of works now recognised as part of Finnish cultural inheritance, such as the memorials to his own father and to Tsar Alexander II. An attractive, handsome amorist, Walter was the inspiration for Ejnar in *Brand*.

Sculptures fill space just as human bodies do, yet these bodies attain stasis, defy time, as ours cannot. Yet do not actors who, night after night, go through the same motions, the same confrontations, who ritualise our despairs and joys, come near to realising what the sculptor is striving after, and for that reason may the dramatist not feel a special kinship with the sculptor? And paradoxically certain statues, and among them the very greatest, suggest not stasis, but energy, force, movement, the power of the will or of the surge of released emotion to lift the human being beyond the conditioning laws of his own being.

Ibsen himself had felt inspired by Michelangelo to begin what turned out to be his first truly great work, *Brand*. Why then would he not grant a sculptor the key insights in *The Lady from the Sea*?

4.

Ellida asks Lyngstrand what work he intends to embark on:

ELLIDA: Og hvad vil De så modellere? Skal det være havmænd og havfruer? Eller skal det være gamle vikinger – ?

LYNGSTRAND: Nej, det blir nok ikke sligt noget. Så snart jeg kan komme til, vil jeg prøve på at gøre et stort værk. Sådan en gruppe, som de kalder det.

ELLIDA: Nå ja, – men hvad skal da den gruppen forestille?

LYNGSTRAND: Å, det skulde nu være noget, som jeg selv har oplevet.

ARNHOLM: Ja, ja – hold Dem helst til det.

ELLIDA: Men hvad skal det være for noget?

LYNGSTRAND: Jo, jeg havde tænkt, det skulde være en ung sjømandskone, som ligger og sover så underlig uroligt. Og drømme gør hun også. Jeg tror nok, jeg skal få det til slig at de kan se på hende at hun drømmer.

ARNHOLM: Skal der da ikke være noget mere?

LYNGSTRAND: Jo, der skal være én figur til. Sådan en gestalt at kalde for. Det skal være hendes mand, som hun har været troløs imod, mens han var borte. Og han er druknet i havet.

ARNHOLM: Hvorledes, siger De – ?

ELLIDA: Er han druknet?

LYNGSTRAND: Ja. Han er druknet på sjøreis. Men så er der det underlige at han er kommet hjem alligevel. Det er ved nattens tider. Og nu står han der for sengen og ser på hende. Han skal stå så drivendes våd, som de dra'r en op af sjøen. (p. 72)

ELLIDA: And what are you going to model? Mermen and mermaids? Or ancient Vikings ...?

LYNGSTRAND: No, nothing like that. As soon as I can, I'm going to start on a big work. A sort of group, you might say.

ELLIDA: Ah, yes. But what will this group represent?

LYNGSTRAND: It's to be something I have experienced myself.

ARNHOLM: Yes, best to stick to that.

ELLIDA: But what's it to be?

LYNGSTRAND: Well, I've been thinking it might show a young woman, a sailor's wife, lying asleep. But she's strangely restless. And she's dreaming. I think I'll be able to make her look as though she's dreaming.

ARNHOLM: But won't there be more to it than that?

LYNGSTRAND: Yes, there'll be another figure. What you might almost call a vision. It's her husband, to whom she has been unfaithful while he was away. And he has been drowned at sea.

ARNHOLM: What did you say ...?

ELLIDA: He was drowned?

LYNGSTRAND: Yes, drowned at sea. But the strange thing is that he's returned home all the same. In the night. And now he stands by the bed looking at her. He's to stand there wet and sodden, like a body dredged up from the sea. (pp. 46-47)

With the unconscious insight of the true artist Lyngstrand has related to Ellida her own story – for though only partial, on a profound level it supplies all the truths relevant to her present condition. And Lyngstrand's involvement with his story is in itself an indication of a percipience that feeds an active imagination, and the relationship to an art-form that knows how to draw on them. Arnholm, who, for all his merits, never quite forfeits the role of schoolmaster, taxes Lyngstrand with the claim he's just made that the proposed work sprang from something he'd experienced himself. The young man explains his personal connection with the history of the betrayed sailor, and in doing so proffers an insufficiently acknowledged truth: that creative artists only rarely put experiences of their own in the forefront of their work. Their imagination is stimulated by what they've heard or seen in *other* people's lives, and then gets to work on this material, infusing it with their own personality, their own obsessions. Every major play of Ibsen's can be broken down in this way, and we only have to examine the notebooks of his admirer, Henry James, to find numerous examples of this process. (Read his account of how *The Spoils of Poynton* grew from an anecdote his neighbour told him at a dinner-party.) It is a mark of the truly creative mind, of course, that it knows what is best for it to receive; Ibsen's antennae grew the more able through practice. Lyngstrand, though the story he relates is remarkable enough in all truth, shows that he is of the company of these minds: he knew at once that what he had witnessed and heard *belonged* to him.

On his last voyage the Norwegian boat on which he was serving hired a boatswain at Halifax, Nova Scotia as a replacement for one of their crew. Though presenting himself as an American, 'Johnson' by name, he was able to read and even speak Norwegian:

LYNGSTRAND: Så var det en kveld i et overhændigt vejr. Alle mand var på dæk. Undtagen bådsmanden og jeg da. For han havde forstuvet ene foden sin, så han ikke kunde træ' på den. Og jeg var også klejn af mig og lå til køjs. Nå, så sad han da der i lugaren og læste i et af de gamle bladene igen –

ELLIDA: Ja vel! Ja vel!

LYNGSTRAND: Men bedst som han sidder, så hører jeg at han gir ligesom et brøl ifra sig. Og da jeg så ser på ham, så ser jeg at han er kridenes hvid i ansigtet. Og så gir han sig til at knase og mase bladet sammen og plukke det i tusend små stykker. Men det gjorde han så ganske stille, stille.

ELLIDA: Sa' han da slet ingen ting? Talte han ikke?

LYNGSTRAND: Ikke straks. Men lidt efter sa' han ligesom til sig selv: Giftet sig. Med en anden mand. Mens jeg var borte.

ELLIDA: (*lukker øjnene, og siger halv sagte*). Sa' han det?

LYNGSTRAND: Ja. Og tænk, – det sa' han på rigtig godt norsk. Han må ha' havt svært let for at lære fremmede sprog, den manden.

ELLIDA: Og hvad så siden? Hvad skede så mere?

LYNGSTRAND: Ja, så kommer dette her underlige, som jeg aldrig i verden skal glemme. For han la' til, – ganske stille det også: Men min er hun og min skal hun bli'. Og mig skal hun følge, om jeg så skal komme hjem og hente hende som en dr" knet mand fra svarte sjøen. (pp. 73-74)

LYNGSTRAND: Well, one evening the weather was pretty rough. All hands were on deck, except the boatswain and me. He'd wrenched his foot and couldn't walk. And I was feeling rather rotten and was lying in my bunk. So there he sat in the cabin reading one of the old newspapers again ...

ELLIDA: Well?

LYNGSTRAND: There he is quietly sitting, when I hear him give a kind of moan. And when I look at him, I see his face has turned as white as chalk. Then he starts crumpling the paper together and tearing it into tiny pieces. But he did it all so quietly. Quietly.

ELLIDA: Didn't he say anything at all? Didn't he speak?

LYNGSTRAND: Not immediately. But after a while he said to himself: 'Married. To another man. While I was away.'

ELLIDA: (*shuts her eyes, and says in a low voice*) He said that?

LYNGSTRAND: Yes. And do you know ... He said it in really good Norwegian! He must have had a flair for languages, that man.

ELLIDA: And what then? What else happened?

LYNGSTRAND: Then an extraordinary thing happened ... Something I'll never forget. He then said ... In that same quiet voice: 'But mine she is and mine she shall remain and she shall follow me, though I return home as a drowned man from the dark sea to claim her.' (p. 48)

Lyngstrand is not master of the whole history behind this – well, how could he be? – just as (again no fault of his!) he is ignorant of the all-important fact that his old ship-mate didn't drown but is alive (and has indeed just arrived in this very town with the English steamer). We can feel Ellida's horror as Lyngstrand, speaking of the seaman's death, says:

Men netop derfor har jeg fåt slig svær lyst til at gøre et kunstværk af det. Den troløse sjømandskonen ser jeg så lebendig for mig. Og så hævneren, som er druknet og som alligevel kommer hjem fra sjøen. Jeg kan se dem begge to så tydeligt. (p. 74)

But that's just why I'm so keen to make a sculpture of it. I can see her so vividly, the unfaithful wife. And the avenger who, though drowned, returns home from the sea. I can see them both so clearly. (p. 49)

The young sculptor has not only come to false conclusions, in doing so he is misrepresenting the Lady from the Sea herself, whose virtue, whose honourable dealings with other people are never in question.

The audience all but cringes here, and thinks how Ellida is being traduced. But Lyngstrand's errors have, we must recognise, their own truth, one which points to what makes *The Lady from the Sea*, so unquestionably a great work, also so teasingly difficult. Lyngstrand's story about the boatswain and his woman on the land, the story that he wants to transpose into clay, is in essentials what happened ten years before the play opens. It is a story shot through with moral ambiguities, and to come to terms with this, in relation to the whole, we must turn back again to Ibsen's draft.

'The sea,' he writes, 'possesses a power to affect one's moods which operates like the power of the will. The sea can hypnotize. Nature at large can do this. The great secret is the dependence of the human will on "the will-less".'[17]

Having made these observations Ibsen applies himself to finding the story that can really bear them out. Obviously it will focus on that woman, that prominent townsman's second wife, who 'grew up out there – by the free open sea'. She was perhaps secretly engaged in her youth to a sailor, 'an unsuccessful Naval cadet', then forced by her clergyman-father to break off the engagement, but has gone on regretting him and the life he stood for, even when married to a decent man with two almost grown-up daughters. Maybe she could meet a 'strange passenger', who'd come to the town on the steamer, who'd earlier loved her at a distance, and can now remind her of her old, unforgotten passion. No, that wasn't quite right. Ibsen now decided to turn to two Molde legends that had interested him in his earlier travels to help him fathom her plight. The first told of a sea-man of Finnish provenance – this will be the Stranger's – who, bearing out the Finns' age-old reputation for magic, can use the power of his eyes to fascinate and abduct other men's wives. The second – it surely must be told in every port the globe over – concerned a sailor who has been away at sea so long that he is presumed dead, but comes back (like Odysseus, his great literary prototype) to find his wife married to another. The stories fuse, but it will surely be at once apparent that their fusion is itself a problematic business: in the former the man is amoral, and by ordinary standards guilty in his conduct, in the latter he is innocent, wronged by Fate and possibly (at least in her heart) by the wife herself.

So Ibsen has now brought the personal into the biological/geographical situation he wants to explore. The concept of the young woman in the fjord-town longing for the open seascapes of her girlhood accords well with that of a wife missing an earlier, freer, if irresponsible love while penned in by marriage and an unfamiliar household. These, while morally sound and outwardly pleasant, demand active words and deeds, and operations on a conscious level. The sea and the first lover, on the contrary, ask only to be yielded to. This surely is the meaning of Ibsen's cryptic remark about the 'dependence of the human will on the 'will-less'' which informs the following exchange between Wangel and Ellida on the subject of that early engagement:

> WANGEL: Ja, ja. – Og så var det altså at du forloved dig med ham?
> ELLIDA: Ja. Han sa' at jeg skulde gøre det.
> WANGEL: Skulde? Havde du da ingen vilje selv?
> ELLIDA: Ikke når han var i nærheden. (p. 89)

WANGEL: Ah! So then you got engaged to him?
ELLIDA: Yes. He said I should.
WANGEL: Should? Had you no will of your own?
ELLIDA: Not when he was near. (p. 62)

The following question arises: If Ellida is a living manifestation of a potent and innate human feeling of severance from the unbounded, the elemental, and if she is also always to envisage this lost inheritance in the form of the first man who aroused her sexually – sex being as boundless as the ocean itself – how can she ever adapt herself to our restricted societised world without fatally impairing her identity? This question is, of course, fully confronted in the play, but is it susceptible to any kind of answer in the form of resolution that is imaginatively convincing? Ibsen's draft, his adumbrations of the different acts, his jotted fragments of dialogue for future use, show us that he has not only fused in the person of Ellida's lover those two very different archetypal figures (the sexually magnetic seaman and the sexually betrayed seaman) but has united also two different conflicts. There is the conflict within cultural *milieux*, reflecting a possibly unbreachable split in our civilisation, and in the psyche of humankind as it has evolved, through the millennia, and there is the conflict between specific individuals, all with temperaments, wills, backgrounds, and a complexity of feelings and needs. We can put it like this: unless she is to remain intolerably riven and therefore incapacitated for daily life, Ellida is forced not merely to hurt but to betray *either* her sincere and ardent sailor-lover *or* the kindly Dr Wangel (who for that matter is also sincere and ardent, and for whom she at her own admission feels real love). Her problematic situation does indeed relate to the ocean and to her present-day separation from it, but it's forced on her by very definite human agencies who, once established for us, cannot be turned back into mere metaphorical representatives.

There is a literal sense in which the married Ellida has actually *become* the faithless wife of Lyngstrand's tale and projected sculpture. Because she was young and vulnerable her faithlessness can perhaps be forgiven her (by us readers and playgoers, if not by the sailor himself). But even this would be to vitiate the goodness of heart which is essential to Ibsen's purpose as it has developed. A woman cannot stand appealingly for humanity's severance from the boundless while showing herself callous or self-seeking in any way. Her quest must take us beyond conventional definitions of selfhood and morality, but not flout them.

In order to cope with this Ibsen has to ensure that the sailor is a truly frightening figure, matching his designation on the list of *dramatis personae* – 'en fremmed mann', 'a Stranger'. Ibsen was so anxious that his identity be concealed that he protested in the strongest terms against German attempts to reveal it on play-bills. 'Nobody is to know *who* he is or what he is actually called. Precisely this uncertainty is the main thing in the method I have chosen for this occasion.'[18] Before we actually encounter him then, we have had impressed on us his involvement in a fearsome tale of a murder necessitating flight and name-change; we know of his insisting on a strange pagan ceremony before his flight, in which Ellida and himself are wed not to each other but to the sea, and we hear of a subsequent existence that recalls the Flying Dutchman. Wagner's opera of 1843, *Der Fliegender Holländer*, may well indeed have suggested this, especially when we recollect that the guilty voyager's good friend, the father of the heroine, was a *Norwegian* sea-captain. (Nor will this be the only instance of Wagner entering an Ibsen text dealing with the artist.) Over all over the globe he sails, in the eyes of the law a criminal, to places as far apart from each other as Archangel, California, China and Australia. Therefore by the time that we see and hear him, dedicated to abduction of Ellida from the thrall of bourgeois life, we have a difficulty seeing beyond his ritual-like stance, from which he speaks like one going through an archaic litany. To appreciate the Stranger's meaning to the divided Ellida, so inclined to leave town, home and husband to go with him, we have, I believe, to return to sculptor Lyngstrand's story, to hear again that dramatic *cri de coeur* from a bunk on a storm-tossed ship: 'But mine she is and mine she shall remain and she shall follow me, though I return home as a drowned man from the dark sea to claim her.' And at once this outcast becomes a real human being, grieving, injured, empowered by his sense of loss to behaviour beyond any rational control.

Thus the vital humanising link between the Stranger as a mysterious encumbrance from the past and the Stranger as a disturbing threat to the present is forged through Lyngstrand the artist and his creation (sculpture)-to-be.

This link having been established and accepted we are now enabled to receive the play's most imaginatively demanding passages with greater understanding. Ellida, haunted in pregnancy by the notion that she is carrying her old lover's child, and, later, that the child possesses his sea-reflecting eyes, is indeed suffering a psychosis but one to a large measure induced by association with somebody who most genuinely (cf Lyngstrand's narrative) entertained passion towards her. But a possessive passion indissoluble from power, and the psychic and physical need to exercise it over the love-object! We can see in the final ritual which the Stranger makes Ellida go through a demonstration of *one* kind of love, urgent, all-consuming, Dionysian, against another, no less strong kind, which can move beyond self to see the beloved as a person in her own right – a love that in its ultimate loftiness of vision can be termed Apollonian.

In Ibsen's first version of the play the ritual is more nearly a parody of orthodox religious ceremony, even to its being punctuated by a bell (a ship's bell in this case!). It very nearly succeeds in taking Ellida away; with each bell she is more confirmed in her feeling that she is following her *innate* self, that which belongs to the sea, to the primordial that humankind has tried so hard to forget. What she has momentarily forgotten is the individuality of each of the men competing for her. The Stranger cannot transcend himself, Dr Wangel, foolish and limited though he is, can. The Stranger's love seems inextricable from need, Dr Wangel, while also needy, loves Ellida – *because she is Ellida.* We have little doubt that Dr Wangel will remember all the stresses his marriage has been through (in fact we know him to have an excellent and accurate memory even of things that make him uneasy) but these will be subsumed in the daily love he experiences for his younger wife. In *Henrik Ibsen and the Birth of Modernism* Toril Moi writes movingly and convincingly about Wangel's bringing to Ellida an appreciation of wholeness, of humanity, that by a logical paradox, allows for frailty and inconsistency as the Stranger's single romantic-headed vision of existence could never do:

They are together. They acknowledge each other's freedom. They understand each other. They are close. But they are not one. There is still plenty of space in which to disagree, to quarrel, and to make up. This, Ibsen tells us, is what it takes to have a marriage.[19]

Viewing the whole scene of the Stranger's enticement of Ellida and Wangel's reclamation of her through the prism of Lyngstrand, we see that the Stranger really does partake of the Avenger of the young man's brooded-over history and proposed sculpture. An avenger of his very nature puts his own injured pride, and the inner turbulence it has set up, before the complexities of the lives of other people. Revenge, like the ecstasies of passion that have begotten it, is Dionysian; it cannot 'acclimatise' itself. Lyngstrand saw all this when 'Johnson' and he were together on board ship, and when his great sculpture began to take shape in his mind, and he saw a truth (without wholly appreciating its implications). That is what an artist does – see truth.

5.

From Act Three onwards Lyngstrand, the pathos of his mortal illness apart, declines as a sympathetic character. His re-sighting of the sailor and his certainty that he will surprise his unfaithful wife that very night display an immaturity as unappealing as that of Hilde, who, needless to say, finds the very notion of it 'spennende', 'exciting'. In Act Four he treats Bolette, whom he has half in mind for the position, to an exposition of what his future wife should be like, a dedicated helpmeet for the glorious career he sees ahead of him. He believes that a woman should, by degrees, become more and more like her husband. Bolette cannot forebear asking him whether it hadn't ever occurred to him that a man could become more and more like his wife. No, he says, it had not, and to defend himself from any charges of failure, takes refuge in a debased romantic view of the sexes, of the creative male whose art is made possible by feminine devotion. In Act Five he reveals himself as perfectly willing to install Hilde rather than the older (and perhaps too obviously and disconcertingly superior) Bolette in the role of his woman-in-waiting, his Solveig, the wife who'll be ready to receive him when he comes back from the Italian sojourn that will have brought him so much fame and money. Even the tragic irony of this little speech, that most probably he won't come back from Italy at all, that early death will claim him and soon, can't soften its repulsiveness. I can't but think there must be some explanation for the young sculptor's conduct here, not seen by the participants in the scenes.

Behind the mordant humour here, it should be said, surely stands Ibsen's desire to vindicate his wife Suzannah from any charge that she played such a subservient wifely role in his life – and, probably more important still, to vindicate himself from accusations that he had taken over Suzannah's life, as Lyngstrand, like too many nineteenth-century male artists, thought so right and proper. We need only think back to the so-called emancipated French artists of the last chapter, to Renoir or Pissarro. Suzannah, after all, had stood in relation to her stepmother, Magdalene Thoresen, to whom Ibsen himself was close, as Bolette to her Ellida.

But there is more about Lyngstrand to consider. Why does Ibsen make someone to whom he has accorded percipience and imagination, who indeed has vindicated himself as artist through his relationship to Ellida and his insight into her plight, then behave with such distasteful callowness, and this to the only eligible young women of the drama? We can summon to our minds here the fact that, at his own admission, he's never learned how to dance (even before his illness), and more, that he has never had a girl-friend. He knows so little about young women that he imagines them shocked when he mentions the word 'midwife', when really, as Hilde herself mockingly realises, the embarrassment is all his own. Are there not contradictions here? To get further into the mystery of Lyngstrand's behaviour we look again at Ibsen's draft. The young man has a patron, we're told, staying at a hotel in town, who is a kind of guardian to him (him evidently being estranged from his own father after his mother's death). This man will pay for Lyngstrand's studies in Italy next year, but seems to expect him to win a bursary and stand on his own feet in this one. He himself has a wife who, notes Ibsen, is not only tactless in her dealings with his protégé, but cruel, sometimes 'deliberately'. Why should this be? Ibsen hasn't scribbled down an explanation, but isn't the likely one that she is jealous of the friendship between the two of them, that she resents it? Her husband, we are told, is a 'man of principle', so there doesn't seem to be any 'improper' behaviour on his part. But on Lyngstrand's part? Could it be that what the wife (who disappears from the final play) dislikes in him is his youthful appeal, his need to win and bask in affection. And in the play as we know it Lyngstrand does indeed warmly praise his patron's goodness. The scorn that the wife was to show perhaps recurs in the attitudes towards him of both Bolette and Hilde? They deal with him, speak to him (and also about him), as if he is less than a normal grown man, and it seems to me possible that, unconsciously, they see the sickness from which he's all too visibly suffering as a symptom of this deficiency in masculinity – rather than the other way round.

This interpretation of his situation is re-enforced by the fact that there's another important if coded reference to homosexuality in the play, one present, and identically worded, in the earlier version. This concerns the crime, the killing of the Captain, committed by the seaman. Here (in Act Two) is Ellida's account of what happened:

> ELLIDA: ... så fortalte han mig da at han havde stukket kaptejnen om natten.
> WANGEL: Det sa' han altså selv! Sa' det lige ud!
> ELLIDA: Ja. Men han havde bare gjort, hvad som ret og rigtigt var, sa' han.
> WANGEL: Ret og rigtigt? Hvorfor stak han ham da?
> ELLIDA: Det vilde han ikke ud med. Han sa' at det var ikke noget for mig at høre på. (pp. 89-90)

> ELLIDA: ... then he told me that he had stabbed the Captain during the night.
> WANGEL: So he admitted it! Just like that!
> ELLIDA: Yes. But he'd only done what was right and proper, he said.
> WANGEL: Right and proper? Why did he kill him then?
> ELLIDA: He wouldn't tell me. He said it wasn't anything for my ears. (p. 63)

In this tough, rough sea-faring community – where it appears not to be too difficult for a man to confess to his beloved that he's killed somebody, where girls waiting in every port and recreation houses (such as that Snekker Engstrand will establish at end of *Ghosts*) were what were expected of sailors – what would be judged not fit for a *woman's* ears? What would be thought outside her experience? Sodomy is the most likely possibility, and contemporary audiences, so used to circumlocution and euphemism about this subject, would surely have let their minds travel in this direction as, at any rate, a viable interpretation of the line. It makes sense too. The strong sexual aura of Ellida's sailor, representing as he does the freedom and the might of the sea, must have aroused the Captain and led him into behaviour the mate simply wouldn't brook. But an erotic power – it is latent in the very narrative of the voyage back from Halifax – adheres to him wherever he goes, which explains why Lyngstrand picks up his distress so quickly – and with such lasting imaginative results. Lyngstrand, so virginal where women are concerned, is quick to respond to the emotions of a sexually charged male, so much so that he is possessed of an urge to translate them into a permanent work of art; in fact this becomes the governing ambition of his life. It is interesting that this particular sexual charge was apparent also to novelist Christopher Isherwood who in his diaries posthumously published as *Lost Years: A Memoir, 1945-1951* (2000) observed of a male lover of his: 'He was like The Stranger in [Ibsen's] *The Lady from the Sea*.'[20]

Lyngstrand's longings – made clear in Ibsen's draft – to go to Italy to see the great classical sculptures and his fear that he will die before being able to do so relate to his reaction to The Stranger. Behind the longings is the hope that proper confrontation of these statues will amount to a fulfilment for him, and why not a *personal* as well as an artistic fulfilment? Indeed how can one separate the two? Ibsen teaches us nothing if not the ultimate unity of our deeper yearnings.

Once in Rome, treading the paths of Winckelmann and Thorvaldsen – or the tubercular proselytising English Hellenist, John Addington Symonds (1840-1893)[21] – once surrounded by so many tributes in durable art, century after century, to the strength and the reality of homosexual emotions, from Praxiteles to Thorvaldsen's 'Ganymede', Lyngstrand will know a self-realisation he has previously only glimpsed with his patron, with the companionship of 'Johnson' on the ship, in his Mediterranean dreams. Apollo is the god of dreams (in distinction to the more violent Dionysiac bursts of release), sculpture is the art dearest to him, uniting as it does delight in the body (particularly the male physique) and the all-embracing calm of wisdom – and he is the god of homosexual relations. (It is Apollo who loves Ganymede). In Rome Lyngstrand may, before his premature death, be able satisfactorily to 'acc-acclimatise' himself, and so, in his own fashion, follow Dr Wangel in the direction of reciprocal love.

Ibsen's plays have a Shakespearean breadth of franchise. We know how he disliked the bourgeois male hegemony, how he looked to women and the workers to break it, for the enrichment of society, for the enrichment indeed of the life-experience of all. I see no reason, whatever his professed views on the matter – e.g. his understandable exasperation with the Danish critic embroiled in a homosexual scandal, Clemens Petersen, whose reviews had been a source of annoyance to him[22] – to believe that he didn't have deep-down a similar attitude to gays, and it seems appropriate that he should give us a (latent) representative in a play with freedom of choice as its governing theme and in which the Apollonian art-form is honoured. And we can also look ahead to *Little Eyolf* where Allmers' youthful insistence that Asta, his half-sister (as he believes her to be) should be dressed as a boy named Eyolf, and his later revelation to his wife, Rita, during their love-making, of this acted-out fantasy surely point to a strong homosexual constituent in his nature.

But, obviously, we can entertain no certainties about Lyngstrand's future, let alone about his future *happiness*. And when we take into further consideration the Stranger's dark disappointment which he will carry with him after disappearance, Hilde's hysterical make-up, partly a consequence of her home-life that can never be satisfactorily undone (we will witness its alarming manifestations in *The Master Builder*, in which she speaks of her 'parents' with scant devotion), the probable, if not perhaps unduly grave, mismatch of Bolette and Arnholm, and (even while agreeing with Moi) the strains that inevitably must attend any marriage with so fraught a past as the Wangels' own, we have to admit that ambivalence is indeed of the essence of this extraordinary, challenging play's conclusion.

Hedda Gabler
The Artist as Bohemian:
Ejlert Løvborg

1.

Osvald Alving belonged, as he hoped, to the artistic vanguard – in France; Hans Lyngstrand believed that through immersion in classical art he could rise above the limitations of the present and participate in spiritual renewal – in Italy. Ejlert Løvborg, the only living person for whom Hedda Gabler has any real feelings, is a Scandinavian writer living and working in his own country whose prime subject is the future. It is immanent in the book he has just successfully published when the play opens, and will be the main theme of his next one, the importance of which, if not the merits, we cannot doubt. *Hedda Gabler* itself is more overtly about the future even than *Rosmersholm*. Or rather *approaches* to the future. Which attitude to what lies ahead of us is the most conducive to individual and social health? How can we recognize the more destructive memes that will impair our reception of it, and even vitiate the culture-to-come?

Hedda's supreme tragedy is that she can find no future for herself, not even in pregnancy, when the future should be at its most appealing; isn't she now responsible for a new life and isn't she playing her part in the continuation of the human race? Indeed her very inability to envisage the future is in good measure the cause of her bitter resentment at being pregnant. Nor can she can find a future for Løvborg. Quite the contrary: she is intent on his denying himself one. She engineers him into a position of appalling self-humiliation, and then encourages him to extricate himself by subscription to a bleak anti-life code of honour from the Ancient World – Roman, Viking, Japanese samurai – and kill himself. She also commits to the flames that very study of the future which would have been Løvborg's own passport to it, an act consciously mimetic of child-murder. The book was the baby of Løvborg and Thea, the pregnancy that brought it into being their intent and creative collaboration.

But Løvborg's own urge to self-destruction was an important feature of Ibsen's original conception. It's hard to see him accepting for the rest of his life Thea's neutering regimen, and therefore hard to see him, for all his recent success and apparent renewed belief in himself, as other than somehow collusive with Hedda's dark design for him. Significantly, though, he does not *literally* carry this out, and the actual circumstances of his death have an untidiness that will prevent its being released into future years as an appropriate completion of a valuable life. As for Løvborg's opposite, his three-fold rival (academically, and over both Hedda and Thea) Jørgen Tesman, *his* future, both intellectually and emotionally, would appear a vicarious one: the long laborious task of re-activating the dead man's achievement, side by side with a former admirer of both whose feelings are now all with the deceased. We have the decided feeling that if the two survivors ever did form a partnership of the flesh as well as of the study, the presences of Hedda and Løvborg will be strong to the point of stranglehold.

Over the sitting-room that is part of the play's set hangs a portrait of General Gabler, whose surname Ibsen imposed on the work's title (initially it was just called *Hedda*), in order, as he said, to show that his eponymous central character is still more daughter than wife – or, more specifically, late military man's daughter rather than up-and-coming academic's wife. This portrait in itself therefore constitutes a denial of the future. Old even when he begot Hedda, General Gabler is of the irreclaimable past, and in fact proved in his last years utterly unable to adjust himself to the future, to life in a new forward-looking society. In the drafts he is said to have died 'in disgrace', after 'dismissal' from the army, and we certainly know that by the end his financial affairs were in a bad way (a 'disgrace' indeed for one of his social standing). He left Hedda no money, hence her desperate wish to be married, to be financially secure, and mistress of a house worthy of her rank, and all as speedily as possible – in conventional terms to procure herself a safe future, even though the constituents of it are not to her taste. She has, of course, deceived herself that this is what she really wants, and already by the time we encounter her, she is only too aware of this. This safe future – however can she bear it?

What the General *has* left Hedda, apart from his pistols, is his set of Spartan or Roman Republican values which obviously haven't served him so very well, and are certainly obsolete in this contemporary world of jobs, salaries and competition by qualifications and publications which the play inhabits. These values are 'bad' memes, and correspond to Hedda's temperamental inheritance from him: a certain audacity (by no means coterminous with true courage), a need for excitement and physical stimulus that turns in on itself when thwarted. This also ties in with Ibsen's related, equally post-Darwinist preoccupation that persons can come into the world, corresponding to psychological or physical types for which the future can have no use, and therefore no place. Indeed we might be tempted to put, for different reasons, both Hans Lyngstrand and Bolette Wangel from the previous play into this sad category.

Not that the room which the General's portrait dominates speaks of the future either. Hedda says that the whole house has an old-maids' aroma of lavender and pot-pourri, which she attributes to Tesman's Auntie Julle. Her old friend Brack laughingly says that this scent is a relic of its previous owner-occupant, Lady Falk, the widow of a cabinet-minister now consigned to history. The house lacks the electric light that you would expect in a Christiania house of its standing, as William Archer pointed out in his preface to the play; likewise there is no telephone, in the 1890s such a telling emblem of civilization's future. (The first Norwegian telephone directory dates from the previous decade.) Indeed the whole household, with old Berthe looking after things, is something of a time-warp, and this is accentuated by old-fashioned Auntie Julle with her constant clucking concern, and her clothes and the hat that rouses Hedda's sadistic mockery, and her cherished sister, Auntie Rina, so long an invalid, first sinking, and then dying off-stage.

Ejlert Løvborg is the one antidote to General Gabler's code, to the fussy tunnel-visioned preoccupation with the past that is Tesman's – and in a different sense his two aunts' also – and to such a mean-minded self-serving representative of a complacent and dishonest present as Brack.

83

Isn't he a writer, an artist, an historian of our future? He is one of Ibsen's most disturbing creations since, no matter how keen we are to rank him above the others, we never succeed long in doing so. Those vine-leaves never arrive in his hair.

2.

Ejlert Løvborg's latest book (it is implied that he has had previous work published) has, when the play begins, been out in the world only a fortnight, but already it has made him something of a celebrity, and has even brought him money. But it no longer interests him; he has, he says, moved on.

> LØVBORG: Det var netop det, jeg vilde. Og så skrev jeg bogen så at alle kunde være med på den ... (*smiler, sætter hatten fra sig og trækker en pakke i papiromslag op af frakkelommen*). Men når dette her kommer, – Jørgen Tesman – så skal du læse det. For det er først det rigtige. Det, som jeg selv er i ... Og dette her handler om fremtiden.
> TESMAN: Om fremtiden! Men, herre gud, den véd vi jo slet ingen ting om!
> LØVBORG: Nej. Men der er et og andet at sige om den alligevel ... Det er delt i to afsnit. Det første er om fremtidens kulturmagter. Og dette her andet ... det er om fremtidens kulturgang.
> TESMAN: Mærkværdigt! Sligt noget kunde det aldrig falde mig ind at skrive om.
> HEDDA: ... Hm – . Nej-nej. (HU XI, p. 341)

> LØVBORG: That was just what I wanted. So I wrote a book that nobody could disagree with ... (*smiles, puts down his hat and pulls a packet wrapped in paper from his coat pocket*) But when this one comes out ... Jørgen Tesman ... then you're to read it. Because this is the real thing. I put some of myself into this one ... And this one deals with the future.
> TESMAN: With the future! But ye gods, we don't know anything about that!
> LØVBORG: No. But there are one or two things to be said about it, all the same ... It's in two sections. The first is about the social forces involved, and this other bit ... That's about the future course of civilisation.
> TESMAN: Amazing! It just wouldn't enter my head to write about anything like that.
> HEDDA: ... Hm ... No-no. (Vol. VII, pp. 215-216)

This sets up the really significant contrast between these two men of the same age (thirty-three) and the same academic background, a contrast that Hedda immediately notes and judges in her old admirer's favour. This does *not* lie simply in the fact that one, Tesman, is occupied with the distant and localised past – with the crafts of medieval Brabant, with which his wife is so heartily bored – while the other is looking ahead. It consists in the differences of a cast of mind expressed in approaches and methodology. Earlier, before Løvborg succumbed to debauchery, when he was still a member of the academic world, their work was clearly much of a kind. Otherwise how could he be the one long-standing serious rival to Tesman of Aunt Julle's statement? Doubtless in his period of dissipation the standard of Løvborg's work fell, but now his writing not only is a testimony of his recovery but surpasses anything he's done before. Tesman, after he has had a peek at this recent production, is amazed at how well-written it is, with a sobriety of style he hadn't expected. It's apparent that even this book he is now intellectually disowning is a more arresting, a more 'modern' work than what Tesman is engaged on. He does not eschew fact-finding and seeing to accuracy of detail (by implication Tesman concedes that these are present in it, as in the earlier years of their rivalry, and we hear from himself that he enjoys thorough research) but what has occupied him most is trying to trace the currents in society, trying to determine which are strong and which less so, and in which direction the stronger are flowing. It should go without saying that Ibsen's declared aims over the years have not been dissimilar. Instead of trying to win the approval of academic committees with some potential reference-book, a quarry for later students, he has been bold enough to stand above what he has gathered together, to survey it, think hard, and come to provocative and original conclusions: he has given not just industrious students but serious-minded men and women a compass-bearing for the difficult terrain of contemporary living. Such a task (which obviously involves the imagination as well as the intellect) is foreign to Tesman's concept of what a historian should do. *He* could never have said of a book that it contained part of *himself*! But – and this is one of Tesman's more attractive traits – he can recognise the merits of work of Løvborg's kind, and will hail them when eventually he has perceived them. (It is, however, noteworthy that he, a professional historian, knows nothing of the éclat occasioned by his old friend's book.) And he atones for lack of his immediate interest by genuine enthusiasm for the new project:

> Nej, Hedda, du kan aldrig tro, hvad det blir for et værk! Det er visst næsten noget af det mærkeligste, som er skrevet. (p. 361)

> Oh, Hedda, you've no idea, it's going to be ever so good! One of the most remarkable books ever written, I'd almost say. (p. 236)

Even if he doesn't grasp all the complexities of Løvborg's thought, he does unequivocally recognise its originality and importance.

And it's worth pointing out here that Løvborg's modernity of style provides an explanation for an aspect of the play that has often aroused adverse criticism: the easy portability of so ambitious a work, the availability (and again the portability) of a working draft of it which, though admittedly only with great labour, can be the means of its restoration. Like Nietzsche Løvborg will have written sequences of connected apothegms, some expanded into discursive paragraphs, others retaining their epigrammatic nature. It might resemble the following from *Die fröhliche Wissenschaft* (*The Gay Science*, 1882) under the heading 'Our eruptions':

> Countless things that humanity acquired in earlier stages, but so feebly and embryonically that nobody could perceive this acquisition, suddenly emerge into the light much later – perhaps after centuries; meanwhile they have become strong and ripe. Some ages seem to lack altogether some talent or some virtue, as certain individuals do, too. But just wait for their children and grandchildren, if you have time to wait that long: they bring to light what was hidden in their grandfathers and what their grandfathers themselves did not suspect. Often the son already betrays his father – and the father understands himself better after he has had a son.
>
> All of us harbour concealed gardens and plantings; and, to use another metaphor, we are, all of us, growing volcanoes that approach the hour of their eruption; but how near or distant that is, nobody knows – not even God.[1]

Differences between Tesman's and Løvborg's work would inevitably have arisen for all their common base. Tesman is the academic as researcher and as professional man linked to a post in an institution, closely bound up with matters such as salary and career-structure, Løvborg is the academic as independent thinker, sage, artist. Anyway their very clothes should have told us all this before any dialogue between them occurred: Tesman wears 'comfortable, slightly slovenly, indoor clothes', Løvborg 'an elegant, black, and quite new suit. Dark gloves and a top hat...' This suggests a further contrast still, one rich in cultural implications for the times: the academic as dutiful civil servant (Tesman's bursary is from the State), as diligent boffin, and the academic as man-of-the-world, as, in terms of today, the man-of-the-media (he has attracted a lot of attention to himself in the press), Society figure, dandy.

At this point it must be insisted that Tesman's work, however tedious or risible to Hedda and Brack (though not to Løvborg, who respects him) is of itself not just competent but of proper interest and value. Brabant is fascinating territory for the cultural or social historian.[2] From the early fifteenth century onwards, artefacts made in the villages of Brabant, including such luxury items as its unique and sought-after tapestries, were an essential component of trade in the greatest Brabantine city, Antwerp. When Antwerp became *the* entrepot for two-way commerce between Europe and the Spanish colonies of the Americas, and therefore for at least half a century the richest city in the world, the crafts of its hinterland not only swelled its exchequer but made an important cultural contribution to the ever-more internationally minded societies which the port reached. There is therefore nothing in the least narrow or peripheral about Tesman's choice of subject, which anyway, as Hedda involuntarily admits in the course of her exasperations to Brack, he sees as part of a whole:

> Ja, De skulde bare prøve det, De! At høre tale om kulturhistorie både sent og tidlig – ... Og så dette her om husfliden i middelalderen – ! Det er nu det aller græsseligste! (p. 331)

> Well, you ought to have a try at it! Hearing about the history of civilization day in and day out ... And then this stuff about medieval domestic crafts ... ! That's the most sickening of the lot! (p. 206)

Ibsen's notes and drafts reveal not so much ambivalence about Tesman as his intentness on finding a man one can sympathise with and even, qualifiedly, praise, but who is wholly deficient in attributes that arouse admiration – or passion. The result of this quest will be one of Ibsen's subtlest, most memorable portraits, a part almost as wonderful a gift to an actor as that of Hedda herself. Initially he writes for his own benefit that Tesman is 'undistinguished as a person, but an honourable, talented and liberal-minded scholar'.[3] Not long afterwards he notes that Hedda 'can respect his learning, she can recognize his nobility of character, but she is embarrassed by his insignificant and ridiculous bearing, makes mock of his behaviour and utterances' (*ibid.*, p. 481). But this is more to do with outward personality rather than with inner qualities, and the fruit of these last awaits assessment. '...Tesman isn't really a scholar,' Ibsen then notes, 'but a specialist,' adding cryptically 'The Middle Ages are dead – ' (*ibid.*, p. 487). No question then of Tesman being able to extrapolate from them notions of the future stretching beyond the close of the nineteenth century!

By the time Ibsen is writing more detailed synopses of the three acts, he has come to the conclusion that Tesman is 'good-natured, hard-working, of good average intelligence, formerly his school's "shining light" but lacking independence, vacillating, has never learned to help himself' (*ibid.*, p. 492).

The word 'average' is a key one here. Paradoxically, in view of the enormous attention and popularity *Hedda Gabler* has received as a study in morbid psychology, neither Tesman nor his beautiful bored wife is so very out-of-the-ordinary. The opposite is true; they can't transcend the conventions they have grown up with, and don't really want to, they are unable to think, let alone behave creatively. And here Tesman's attitude to history mirrors only too completely his personal and societal life; he has been accustomed to following examples, and is truly thrown when confronted with the innovative, the purposefully forward-looking. His book on the important subject of Brabantine crafts, postponed indefinitely by the play's end, would surely have been a worthy labour much like any other hard-working scholar's, but very probably weighed down by a surfeit of footnotes, cross-references, citations from other authorities etc. in which he patently delights and which keep him away from independent and therefore disconcerting thoughts. Is he not 'Tesemann', thesis-man? His position is identical to his wife Hedda's in that the great challenge to him comes from his contemporary Løvborg. He is nervous of one so recklessly defiant of social mores, and, besides, Løvborg's writing makes him bewilderedly aware of his own limitations, some of which he hadn't suspected.

'Tesman is positively losing his head,' Ibsen observed in the course of composition, 'All his material meaningless. New visions! A new world!' (*ibid.*, p. 484).

But he differs from Hedda in being able to see some distance beyond himself, if not so very far then enough to recognise quality he could never himself attain. And in the end he will discover – if for ultimately self-serving reasons – the ability to dedicate himself to the editing of Løvborg's revolutionising work, though Ibsen's comment to himself is surely apt: 'How grotesquely comical that those respectable people Tesman and Mrs E. should try to piece the scraps together as a memorial to E. L. He who so thoroughly despises the whole thing – ' (*ibid.*, p. 486). By which Ibsen means not the lost work, of course, but the whole paraphernalia of academe, and even beyond it: the wearying labyrinth of publishers, critics, reputations, social positions, the cash nexus itself.

And so we arrive at Løvborg the man, catalyst to Tesman's career as historian and his life as proud husband and happy father-to-be, and the focus of what capacities Hedda Gabler has for love or admiration. How are we to view him as a person and a writer/artist? We shall, I think, find that of all Ibsen's many jottings about him the most pertinent is 'Løvborg leans over towards "Bohemianism"' (*ibid.*, p. 482).

3.

Any attempt to place Løvborg culturally has to have recourse to two exemplarily closely-argued essays in historical research: 'Ibsen and the Immoralists' by Evert Sprinchorn (1972)[4] and 'How Ibsen found his Hedda Gabler' by Håvard Nilsen (2003)[5] – and to consider these alongside Ibsen's disclosure to his son Sigurd about the models for Tesman and Løvborg. All these examinations, however, lead us to Georg Brandes (1842-1927).

Sprinchorn sees the origin of *Hedda Gabler* in the heated public intellectual duel of 1889-1890 between Brandes and the then widely respected Professor Harald Høffding. Brandes was a passionate advocate of the ideas of Nietzsche, whom he, more than any other man, had championed, indeed promoted, beyond Germany and who had caused him to revise many of his own earlier tenets, those he'd formed under the influence of John Stuart Mill. In the spring of 1888 Brandes had given a series of controversial and, before long, cult-forming lectures eagerly reported in the Copenhagen newspaper *Politiken*, and so creating an atmosphere that made them seem like a continuation of that 'morality debate' which had swept Scandinavia in the middle of the decade, its subject the relationship between the free love ideal and the full emancipation of women. Brandes' opponent Høffding had since 1883 held a chair in philosophy at Copenhagen University, the very institution that had found even the *younger* Brandes too heterodox in his thinking and so driven him to Germany to flee Danish philistia. In the nine-month-long debate with which Sprinchorn is concerned, Høffding stood for the *via media*, and among the accusations he levelled against Brandes was that of reneging in his new enthusiasms on the very ideals for which he had previously proselytised. Brandes, increasingly sharing Nietzsche's desideratum of a powerful elite that could through its defiance of a tired ethical system invigorate a society grown timid and smug, espoused an 'aristocratic radicalism' (the title of his 1889 essay), to which Høffding retaliated with his 'democratic radicalism', which could, and did, align itself with the Social Democratic movement. In particular Høffding objected to Nietzsche's 'unshakeable faith that to a being such as "we are" other beings must be subordinate by nature and have to sacrifice themselves'. To quote Sprinchorn: 'Brandes retorted that the German philosopher passed Høffding's understanding because Nietzsche was unique and mysterious; a demon whose thoughts moved in great leaps but that he, Brandes, could understand, for Høffding was a *citoyen* and he was a Bohemian' (that all-important term again!)[6]

Sprinchorn's contention is that Ibsen transposed these two Danish adversaries into the two rivals of *Hedda Gabler*. Høffding with his safe chair and public virtue and unexceptionable standpoint became Tesman,

Brandes with his daring, advanced views and general panache Løvborg, exuberant, iconoclastic, sexy.

This last adjective is important in its literal as well as its general contemporary sense. Sprinchorn has important ballast to his argument. Brandes, a relentless, indeed a ruthless amorist, much given to vaunting his sexual prowess, had one affair which ended with the tragic suicide of the woman, Victoria Benedictsson (1850-1888), a Swedish writer of some renown who had attended his epoch-making lectures on Nietzsche. Publicity, both in the press and in gossip, linked Brandes' name with her peculiarly appalling death. We can compound the above link with other features of Victoria's life: a domineering father who brought her up as a boy; her own expressed feeling that she was a man in a woman's body (she used for her writing the masculine pseudonym Ernst Ahlgren); her marriage to an older man whom she did not love but by whom she had two children; her lack of maternal feeling for these (though she was a good stepmother).

Knowledge of the affair had a deleterious effect on Brandes' reputation, not least on his ability to acquit himself of charges of immorality/amorality during the public wrangling with Høffding. Nor can the news of 1889 that Nietzsche had gone incurably insane have aided his cause, the philosopher writing to his greatest advocate letters of wildest paranoia with such signatures as 'Nietzsche Caesar'.

Håvard Nilsen's brilliant essay also takes us to Brandes as Nietzsche's apologist, and like Sprinchorn's posits the great Danish literary critic as the original of Løvborg. But one of his principal reasons for doing so is his very different candidature for the model for Hedda, Lou Andreas-Salomé (1861-1937). Brandes first met Lou Salomé, as she then was, in 1883; for two years she had been the object of Nietzsche's intense love (he actually asked her to marry him) and had made contributions to *Also Sprach Zarathustra* (*Thus Spoke Zarathustra*, 1883-1892). A great admirer of Ibsen, she had already begun a study of his women which was finished and published in 1892 (to contain an, at first sight, unexpectedly hostile account of Hedda), and Nilsen's point that Brandes must surely have mentioned to Ibsen himself this beautiful, talented and fascinating woman so intimately connected to radical intellectual-artistic circles, seems unanswerable. Lou, born in St Petersburg into the Russian aristocracy, was, like Hedda, the daughter of a General; like Hedda, she was fascinating, even *séduisante* in manner, expressed liberated views, but held herself from sexual demonstrativeness to the point of coldness. Having been a member of one *ménage à trois*, with Friedrich Nietzsche and the philosopher Paul Rée, she married passionlessly a leading sinologist Friedrich Carl Andreas (hence the full name by which she is best-known), but Nilsen seems to think that Brandes, always anything but passionless, made up yet another triangle with her at the apex. Brandes, who propagated in reviews in both Denmark and Britain a connection between Løvborg and his friend Hoffory (just as later he gave the world the letters between Ibsen and Emilie Bardach so crucial to *The Master Builder*), did so, thinks Nilsen, as a smoke-screen. Nilsen also reminds readers that an earlier reference in Ibsen's oeuvre to the vine-leaves in the hair that is Hedda's wish for her old admirer concerns Julian the Apostate in *Emperor and Galilean*, whom Brandes always believed to be based on himself.

This last is not at all impossible. Although Ibsen had been drawn to the subject and had actually begun work on the play before the two men actually met, on 14 July 1871, they had been in lively and enthusiastic correspondence (including the dispatching of poems). Ibsen and Brandes certainly prove the truth of William Hazlitt's dictum that 'the youth of friendship' is its best part. In its earlier phase these two mighty intellects admired and responded to each other with a kind of deep gratitude for one another's existence. When Ibsen had read the first volume of Brandes' *Hovedstrømninger i det 19de Aarhundredes Litteratur* (*Main Currents in Nineteenth-Century Literature*, 1872), the text of lectures given in the November of the previous year, he wrote to its author a letter vital to any study of Ibsen's attitude to the future. He praises to Brandes precisely those qualities in his work which had offended, no, outraged so many, including members of Copenhagen's philosophy faculty:

> A more dangerous book could never fall into the hands of a pregnant writer. It is one of those books which set a yawning gulf between yesterday and today. When I was in Italy I could not understand how I managed to exist before I went there. In twenty years people will not understand how anyone managed to live spiritually in Scandinavia before these lectures.[7]

But over the years this pitch of mutual admiration was not maintained, and while it would be over-simplifying the case to say that Brandes' embrace of Nietzsche's ideas, themselves in the process of defiant and usually eccentric development, was the cause of a widening gulf between these two great Scandinavians, it would not be altogether untrue either. Perhaps the real difference between them was that Ibsen being an imaginative writer, concerned with the creation of flesh-and-blood human beings, could not opt for seeing life in black-and-white terms, but had to remain open to all human possibilities, all shades of attitude and inconsistencies of conduct. The man responsible for Dr Stockmann was also, after all, the author of *The Wild Duck*. After the furore caused by Bjørnstjerne Bjørnson's *En handske* (*A Glove/ Gauntlet*, 1883), one of the first salvoes in the Nordic 'morality' wars, Brandes was apt to feel that Ibsen had not rallied, as he should have done, to his – and indeed Nietzsche's – side. In this play Bjørnson, with a lusty enough life of his own behind him, argued that an answer to the problem of a double moral standard was for men and women to demand purity from each other. This met with nothing but derision from Brandes, who, like Hans Jæger, believed the exact opposite, that the sexes should enjoy the same freedom, the same opportunities for satisfaction and resourcefulness. Brandes was unimpressed by Ibsen's apartist stance, which he thought tended to conservatism. He thought that, in making Rosmer such a 'eunuch-like' character, he had already half-joined the wrong party.

The complexity of Ibsen and Brandes' relationship is in itself a fact which should discourage us from making any kind of equations. Nilsen and Sprinchorn have directed us most admirably to the appropriate terrain for Ibsen's play. But nobody was more aware than Ibsen of the variety of factors that go to the making of any one individual – ancestry, parentage, cultural context, early experience, education. While he almost certainly borrowed traits, maybe, as he saw them, *principal* traits from individuals, he was very unlikely to put them whole into a work of art, to write the dramatic equivalent of a *roman à clef* – let alone if they were as well-known, complicated and gifted as Brandes, whom Ibsen continued to see as a pioneer for human freedom, and Benedictsson and Salomé with whose accomplishment he was familiar.

Alongside our knowledge (and his) of these individuals we must put Ibsen's statement about Hedda herself: 'Hedda is fundamentally conventional'.[8] The play surely goes on devastatingly to vindicate this. And whatever they were, however self-obsessed we may deem them, Brandes' friends Victoria Benedictsson and Lou Andreas-Salomé were in *no* sense conventional; they raged against conventionality and defied it. They both had fine intellects and creative gifts which have indeed amply survived them. Brandes' failure to respond to Benedictsson's feminist novel, *Fru Marianne* (1887) hurt her irreparably, but it and its predecessor, *Pengar* (*Money*, 1885) are living works of literature to this day, radical and sensitive. Hedda Gabler is as far distant from their creator as she was from a woman who conversed as an equal with Rilke and Freud..

For Hedda, as we shall see, is conventional only *partly* because her insecurity of social position after her father's death forces her to take note of the proprieties. The conventional is embedded in her very nature, her awareness of the past constitutes an inherited meme. She is dependant on what the herd thinks, if only to find out how best she can startle or offend it. And while this same adjective cannot quite be applied to Løvborg, I see no good reason for considering him some sort of genius, a Georg Brandes, a man with qualities that can survive him. Hedda's admirer is a clever and thoughtful man who has scored one success, and who might, had he been a wiser, more adjusted person, well have achieved another, greater still. William Archer, in his 1907 preface to the play, asks the reader what evidence there is for finding Løvborg so remarkably gifted, for surely we can't take Tesman's hyperbolic praise as a time-transcending critical judgement. All this brings us to the only original model that Ibsen himself acknowledged for this character, and whom Archer – who was in a position to know about the people in Ibsen's drama – writes about in so lively a way that he deserves quotation in full. The story indeed derives from Brandes himself, who had given it out to the world, using somewhat coyly the name of Holm for the late academic it features. Anyone familiar with that world would have identified him at once as Julius Hoffory. Hoffory, though a Dane, was one of Ibsen's principal translators into German, to whom he made many confidences about his plays:

A young Danish man of letters ... was an enthusiastic admirer of Ibsen, and came to be on very friendly terms with him. One day Ibsen was astonished to receive, in Munich, a parcel addressed from Berlin by this young man, containing without a word of explanation, a packet of his (Ibsen's) letters, and a photo which he had presented to Holm. Ibsen brooded and brooded over the incident, and at last came to the conclusion that the young man had intended to return her letters and photo to a young lady with whom he was known to be attached, and had, in a fit of aberration, mixed up the two objects of his worship. Some time after Holm appeared in Ibsen's rooms. He talked quite rationally, but professed to have no knowledge whatever of the letter-incident, though he admitted the truth of Ibsen's conjecture that the 'belle-dame-sans merci' had demanded the return of her letters and portrait. Ibsen was determined to get to the root of the mystery, and a little inquiry into his young friend's habits revealed the fact that he broke his fast on a bottle of port wine, consumed a bottle of Rhine wine at lunch, of Burgundy at dinner, and finished off the evening with one or two more bottles of port. Then, he heard, too, how in the course of a night's carouse, Holm had lost the manuscript of a book; and in these traits he saw the outline of the figure of Ejlert Løvborg. Some time elapsed and again Ibsen received a postal packet from Holm. This one contained his will, in which Ibsen figured as his residuary legatee. But many other legatees were mentioned in the instrument – all of them ladies ... so generous that their sum considerably exceeded the amount of the testator's property. Ibsen gently but firmly declined the proffered inheritance; but Holm's will no doubt suggested to him the figure of that red-haired 'Mademoiselle Diana' who is heard of but not seen in Hedda Gabler and enabled him to add some further traits to the portraiture of Løvborg. When the play appeared, Holm recognised himself with glee in the character of the bibulous man of letters, and thereafter adopted Ejlert Løvborg as his pseudonym.[9]

We can perceive at once what went from this sad history into the play: the alcohol addiction, the irresponsibility that enables a man not to know where he has put (or misplaced) a document of value to himself and others (for it represents hard work and emotional investment on Thea Elvsted's part, never mind the public for whom it is intended) and the frequenting of prostitutes for, of course, Archer's hearty circumlocutions cannot altogether disguise the fact that the 'carouse' was a visit to a brothel or that red-haired Diana was, if not a mere tart, a 'madame'. It is perfectly possible that Ibsen did indeed think about the Høffding/ Brandes debate, that aspects of his friend and (for the most part) intellectual ally were present when he breathed life into Løvborg – didn't he himself famously say that he never wrote a line without wondering what Georg Brandes would think about it? – and that behind Hedda he saw Victoria, brought up like a boy, a suicide because she didn't enjoy reciprocal love with anybody, and Lou at the apex of at least two emotional triangles. This last fact is surely important. Hedda herself stands in no fewer than *three* triangles in each of which she appears at first to be the commanding figure but in which, in truth, she is the weakest member: Tesman, Løvborg, Hedda – Tesman, Thea, Hedda – Løvborg, Thea, Hedda. Further this situation greatly appeals to Judge Brack who has long practised and favoured the triangular. So that behind the three triangles just referred to stands another, far less appealing one: Tesman, Brack, Hedda – one that, maybe mercifully for the woman's pride and dignity, will never come about.

So in pointing our minds in such directions the researches of Sprinchorn and Nilsen have enriched our reading. But Hoffory's story should not be relegated to second place, first, because the adventures of the manuscript and the misadventures of its author provide the dynamics of the plot and, in tandem with Hedda's pregnancy, the prime symbol of the work, but also for another reason. Hoffory's status is more akin to Løvborg's, and by extension this enables us to see Tesman and Hedda more clearly.

Ibsen's interest is in what effect the ideas of such as Brandes, and behind him Nietzsche, are having on contemporary society in a period of flux, on otherwise ordinary men and women who are intelligent and educated and high enough on the social ladder to influence others. (We shall see that this is exactly the section of Norwegian society which was drawn to 'Kristiania-Bohêmen'.) Once again Ibsen stands as diagnostician of his times, applying himself to the creation of autonomous-seeming but representative individuals. Løvborg and Hedda are there to tell us, not about Georg Brandes and a Swedish novelist or a Russian-born intellectual femme fatale, but about their contemporaries – and ourselves.

So we should ask ourselves instead: are the personalities of Hedda and Løvborg helped or hindered by the value-systems on offer in the world about them? And if hindered, why? Is it not true that every one of Hedda's disabling attributes we could find without difficulty in family or neighbourhood: insecurity resulting from change in financial position; inability to respond sexually as desired to a partner for whom one does not feel enough; difficulty in satisfactorily filling leisure; apprehension, more, resentment at, pregnancy; ambivalence about the gender-role expected. All these problems are constituents of the human condition as we know it, even if they can be seen as products of a civilised society rather than a more atavistic one. Placing Hedda too close to Victoria Benedictsson and Lou Andreas-Salomé or Løvborg to Brandes tends to diminish the character's representative nature so essential for the discussion of conventional marriage which *Hedda Gabler* powerfully conducts.

For the Tesmans' is a marriage contracted within an educated and reasonably enlightened section of society but as lacking in love and as informed by material consideration as any arranged bourgeois union of an earlier era. Tesman has got to the age when he needs a wife to make his social standing complete, he needs her every bit as much as Hedda needs a husband, and for similar reasons. He does not love her – not in any empathising or altruistic way, not as Dr Wangel loves Ellida – as Ibsen makes plain in his notes; she is a feather in his cap, a piece of property on a par with the acquisition of house and furnishings on terms he can't properly afford and which puts him heavily (and, for one of his temperament, uncharacteristically) into debt. Trite but persistent and strongly expressed social judgements that there's something amiss with a good-looking woman who by twenty-nine hasn't got a husband have similarly guided Hedda into wedding Tesman, on top of her financial need to find a well-off man to support her. No society that condones, and even applauds, such a marriage is a healthy one, and consequently it is only to be expected that her situation can *produce* unhealthiness, those pathologies in Hedda – her obsession with the pistols which had started before her marriage, her increasing fascination with some coronation ceremony that will ecstatically unite sexuality, honour and death. But that most emphatically does not mean that she started life as a 'monster' or even as an exceptional person. There's nothing to suggest that she's particularly intelligent; her complete lack of interests which leads to her confessed devouring boredom, her failure to demonstrate intellectual curiosity at any point, her blindness to what is of value in the work of either Tesman or Løvborg, all indeed point to modest brains. What could have redeemed her is a *Weltanschauung* comprehensive enough to suit her make-up, her forceful impetuousness, while giving her a breadth and adequacy of context. Ejlert Løvborg could perhaps have supplied this: the expression, if not the propagation of *Weltanschauungen* is what writers like himself do. In fact what he does give her is entirely destructive; he abets not so much what is wildest in her as what is weakest. Ibsen himself remarked during composition: 'Hedda feels herself demonically attracted by tendencies of the age. But the courage is lacking. It all remains theoretical, and idle dreams.'[10]

4.

Løvborg himself is under the impression that he can stand as man of the future, as well as one dedicated to assessing its possible shape. In a draft Ibsen makes him say: 'How pitiful to toe the line to the morality of the day. The ideal would be if a present-day man could live the life of the future' (*ibid.*, p. 486). And what would that be like? '[His] idea is that a way must be found towards a companionship between man and woman, whereby the true spiritual individual may emerge' (*ibid.*, p. 487). He is thus linked to the Scandinavian 'morality debate', could even have taken part in it. He has had sexual relations with neither Hedda nor Thea, but has enjoyed this preferred companionship with each of them. In both cases the companionship has the strongest sexual charge, in both cases too it ends with betrayal. Discussing him in his notes, in relation to the women, Ibsen says:

> [Thea Elvsted] 'labours for his moral regeneration'. For Hedda he is the subject of fearful, alluring fantasies. In real life she hasn't the courage to take part in such things. (*ibid.*, p. 483)

And:

> Ejlert Løvborg is a double nature. It is a fiction that one only loves one
> person. He loves two – or more – (speaking frivolously) by turns. But how
> to explain his own situation? [Thea Elvsted], who forces him into
> respectability, runs away from her husband. Hedda, who eggs him on
> beyond the limits, flinches from the thought of scandal. (*ibid.*, p. 484)

Put like this Løvborg sounds sympathetic enough, as sinned against as
sinning,. And if we listen to Thea's account of the effect he's had on her,
with the dramatic and surprising result adumbrated above, we see that he
has not only charm and sexual charisma but the rarer capacity to
transform, for somebody else, the very appearance of reality. (We shall
encounter still further instances of Ibsen's interest in influence, in
powers of persuasion emanating from the unconscious, already so
important to *The Lady from the Sea*, in his next play *The Master
Builder*). That Løvborg has real feeling for Hedda is beyond doubt, and
his repetition of her name when first they are alone together is one of the
great moments of the play, abundantly justifying Ibsen's choice of title.
His ensuing *cri de coeur* both convinces and moves. 'Å Hedda, Hedda,
– hvor kunde du dog kaste dig slig væk!' (p. 345) (Oh Hedda ... darling
Hedda, how could you throw yourself away like that?; p. 220).

Nevertheless Ibsen was right to insert that parenthesis '(speaking
frivolously)' for there is something, even in such scenes, disengaged
and narcissistic in his behaviour to both women, behaviour that
parallels his academic career. Born into a comfortably off, well-
connected family (see the conversation between Tesman and Brack in
Act One), he has been the focus of its hopes, the promising young
scholar who was to confirm their fine social name, until his profligate
behaviour upset them so much that (according to Tesman) they
disowned him. Hence his need to take a tutoring job at Thea's
husband's home to support his intellectual work. In order for this to
reach completion, it was necessary for Thea to organize his days, but
despite her success – this is her greatest mistake in her dealings with
him – she can't trust him to keep a control on his taste for wild living
when he's out of her sight. If he is grateful to her for her solicitude, he
also treats her abominably not just in the scene in Act Three where he

lies to her about what has happened to 'their child', his book, but earlier, in Act Two, where he snubs her cruelly for her concern.

No, Løvborg is *not* sympathetic (though – a different matter – one can *sympathise* with him, out of knowledge of one's own or one's friends' frailties). There is not really enough evidence that he has concerns beyond those of his own ego, nor that his debauchery is not by now an ingrained habit, conveniently relieving him of all responsibility to his own talents and to the expectations of others. Debauchery was indeed an integral part of his life even when his 'companionship' with Hedda was at its firmest, in fact it had its own peculiar role to play in it; she would elicit from him accounts the details of which held her fascinated. There is no exchange more important to the play's most urgent preoccupations than that in which this becomes clear:

LØVBORG: Ja, Hedda, – og når jeg så skrifted for Dem – ! Fortalte Dem om mig selv, hvad ingen af de andre vidste dengang. Sad der og tilstod at jeg havde været ude og raset hele dage og nætter. Raset døgn efter døgn. Å, Hedda, – hvad var der dog for en magt i Dem, som tvang mig til at bekende sligt noget?

HEDDA: Tror De, det var en magt i mig?

LØVBORG: Ja, hvorledes skal jeg ellers forklare mig det? ... Spørge mig ud om – om alt sligt noget!

HEDDA: Og at De kunde svare, herr Løvborg.

LØVBORG: Ja, det er jo netop det jeg ikke begriber – nu bagefter. Men sig mig så, Hedda, – var der ikke kærlighed på bunden af forholdet? Var det ikke fra Deres side, som om De vilde ligesom tvætte mig ren, – når jeg tyed til Dem i bekendelse? Var det ikke så?

HEDDA: Nej, ikke ganske.

LØVBORG: Hvad drev Dem da?

HEDDA: Finder De det så rent uforklarligt, om en ung pige, – når det kan ské sådan – i løndom –

LØVBORG: Nå?

HEDDA: At en da gerne vil kikke lidt ind i en verden, som –

LØVBORG: Som – ?

HEDDA: – som en ikke har lov til at vide besked om?

LØVBORG: Det altså var det?

HEDDA: Det også. Det også, – tror jeg næsten.

LØVBORG: Kammeratskab i livsbegæret. Men hvorfor kunde så ikke *det* ialfald ble't ved?

HEDDA: Det er De selv skyld i.

LØVBORG: Det var Dem som brød.

HEDDA: Ja, da der var overhængende fare for at der vilde komme virkelighed ind i forholdet. Skam dem, Ejlert Løvborg, hvor kunde De ville forgribe Dem på – på deres frejdige kammerat!

LØVBORG: ... Å, hvorfor gjorde De ikke alvor af det! Hvorfor skød De mig ikke ned, som De trued med!

HEDDA: Så ræd er jeg for skandalen.

LØVBORG: Ja, Hedda, De er fejg i grunden. (pp. 347–348)

LØVBORG: Yes, Hedda ... And then when I used to confess to you...! Told you things about myself that none of the others knew at that time. Sat there and admitted that I'd been out on the razzle for whole days and nights. For days on end. Oh, Hedda ... What power was it in you that forced me to reveal all those things?

HEDDA: Do you think it was a power in me?

LØVBORG: Well, how else can I explain it? ... Cross-examine me about ... about all those things!

HEDDA: And that you could answer, Mr Løvborg.

LØVBORG: Yes, that's just what I find so incredible ... Now, afterwards. But tell me then, Hedda ... wasn't it love at the back of it all? Wasn't it on your part a desire to absolve me ... When I came to you and confessed? Wasn't that a part of it?

HEDDA: No, not exactly.

LØVBORG: Why did you do it, then?

HEDDA: Do you find it so hard to understand that a young girl ... when it can happen like that ... in secret ...

LØVBORG: Well?

HEDDA: That she should want to find out about a world that ...

LØVBORG: That ...?

HEDDA: ... that she isn't supposed to know anything about?

LØVBORG: So that was it!

HEDDA: That as well ... I rather think it was that as well.

LØVBORG: Our common lust for life. But then why couldn't that at least have gone on?

HEDDA: That was your own fault.

LØVBORG: It was you who broke it off.

HEDDA: Yes, because there was an imminent danger that the game would

> become a reality. Shame on you, Ejlert Løvborg, how could you offer such violence to ... to your confidential companion!
> LØVBORG: ... Oh, why didn't you play it out! Why didn't you shoot me down, as you threatened?
> HEDDA: I'm much too afraid of a scandal.
> LØVBORG: Yes, Hedda, at bottom you're a coward. (pp. 222-223)

The reality is, of course, that instead of firing at him, Hedda would have given herself to him! But... Note the many, carefully presented, inconsistencies here. That Løvborg speaks in terms of confession but feels no regret for his (past?) way of life. That Hedda, even though she now admits she was on the point of offering herself, still sees such action as belonging to the domain of the sinful. That there's an explicit element of 'game' about the whole thing, though what is at stake here is the relationship of man and woman, than which nothing can be more important. Løvborg and Hedda betray in this scene, I think, their privileged class-base, and not just in Hedda's fear of scandal, her inability to see far beyond the parameters of their own social milieu, but in their distance from their own hearts, in their delight in experimentation and their avoidance of ultimate seriousness.

It is at this point that we should see them in the light of the movement that held such an appeal for their like, *Kristiania-Bohêmen* and its leader Hans Jæger (1854-1910).[11] I do not mean here to suggest that Jæger is a model for Løvborg, who would however have been a mere two or three years his junior, but that this 'writer, philosopher, political activist' is a vital point of reference for the play and the society in which it is set.

Hans Jæger's early life appears to us today as a template for the defiant artist of the second half of the nineteenth century: the pietistic, respectable, educated home; the running-away to sea at sixteen; the escapade with a foreign whore (in his case, in Plymouth, England); the contraction of syphilis and the tardiness in getting it diagnosed, so that ever afterwards sexual activity was impaired; the exploration of other philosophies to find an alternative to the Christianity he detested because of the narrow-visioned churches that served it and its permeation of authority in all of its forms; the difficulty in supporting himself (but Jæger, interestingly, became a stenographer to the Storting, the Norwegian Parliament, which only confirmed his contempt for the Establishment and the *bien-pensant*); the heavy drinking and whoring; the need to propagandise on behalf of a set of revolutionary (or generally outrageous) ideas, some of them decidedly unappealing even to other anti-bourgeois – that of killing all old people, for example. (Jæger expected to be the centre of attention wherever he went, and isn't this true of Ejlert Løvborg also? Exhibitionism is one of the qualities that their world, and their position in it, have developed in both Hedda and her admirer – witness her behaviour with the pistols to Brack.) Jæger saw himself as a missionary for sexual freedom, and what he preached reflects contradictions that, through the conduct of Løvborg, are fully shown up by Ibsen in *Hedda Gabler*.

Jæger was ahead of his time in his insistence that women needed sexual fulfilment as much as men. Indeed he thought that happiness in society depended on both sexes developing their capacities for sexual pleasure, and even proposed that he should start a school where women could be educated in their sexuality! Not so endearing to our post-feminism generation is his obsession with prostitutes, which he passed on to his greatest young disciple, Edvard Munch, a willing enough convert, though we can only applaud Jæger's work on public recognition of them and of the conditions, physical, social and psychological, in which they lived. We should appreciate too what courage it took for him to insist just how integral prostitutes were to a society that officially preferred to disown them. While he involved himself with his close friend and ally Christian Krohg's novel about a mature whore, *Albertine* (1886) and with the series of paintings of her by him, it was only up to a certain point, that of the artist against sexually squeamish Philistia. For Jæger did not really care for Krohg's depiction of Albertine, he thought it 'tourism', the production of someone who had failed properly to identify with its subject. Despite this shrewd assessment, he does not seem to have differed from Krohg and Munch in failing to see a discrepancy between their brothel-going and their promotion of sexual equality, thus revealing, for all the sincerity of his Leftism, a decided class-bias. Nor when we turn to the subject of his and his friends' liaisons – the struggle for Oda Krohg, for instance – do we feel that a transposable freedom has been attained, in all this tangle of over-weening egos.

Kristiania-Bohêmen had its Nine Commandments, as previously noted, the first and last of which must certainly interest readers of *Hedda Gabler*: '1. Thou shalt write thy life.' (and intense self-preoccupation and self-presentation characterised all these Bohemians, pre-eminently Munch, who under Jæger's influence, began a scrutiny of his own unhappy young life in order to realise it on canvas), and '9. Thou *shalt* kill thyself.' (Of those in-between perhaps number 3 comes also to mind as one pretty thoroughly lived up to by the subscribers: 'There is no limit to how badly thou shalt treat thy family and all elders and betters.')

Jæger did *not* commit suicide, but a young friend of his did, and this death he turned to advantage by putting it into a sensational novel (reminding us of Ibsen's comment on Hedda that she easily envisaged herself taking part in a work of fiction: 'If an interesting female character appears in a new novel or a play, she imagines it is she who is depicted'[12]). The story of Jæger, Fleischer, and the book *Fra Kristiania-Bohêmen* (From the Kristiania Bohemians, 1885) is vividly given, in crystallised form, in Ketil Bjørnstad's fine re-creation *Historien om Edvard Munch* (*The Story of Edvard Munch*, 1993), where the author enters via letters, journals and writings into Munch's mind to the point of stream-of-consciousness and makes us see the case through the eyes of one for whom Jæger was a true mentor (though later there was a break between them):

> *From the Kristiania Bohemians* confiscated in Norway. Scandal. The novel about Johan Seckmann Fleischer, a student at the military academy, who on the Wednesday after Easter Monday 1884 the previous year had stood on Tjuvholmen, loaded a revolver, cocked it, felt the touch of cold steel against the roof of his mouth, and stood, legs apart, to support himself when he pulled the trigger. Fleischer, the suicide candidate, painfully aware of his wasted life, his miserable wasted life, the ability to live withered for want of the right conditions. The hopeless emptiness, instead of a free, open life together among free, open men and women who only recognized one rule for social life, which was love, freedom and worldly happiness. The Bohemians' last commandment: 'Thou *shalt* take thy own life'. A suicide which was virtually ordered and arranged by Jæger, so that he could later write the book about Fleischer's death. Naïve Fleischer who, after a summer in the mountains, told his mother that the farm girls had let him sleep with

them. A young man quite unable to control his own life. But Jæger took control of it and led him to disaster. At his friend's burial, he had stood there taking down the priest's funeral address in shorthand so as to be able to reproduce it in his book.[13]

Unsurprisingly Jæger had difficulty in finding a publisher for this book, and when it eventually was taken by a small socialist press, its career got off to a nervous but dramatic start both good and bad for its publicity-minded author: authority judged it obscene, and ordered copies to be confiscated from shops on publication day itself. This, in view of its lurid descriptions of sex acts and his unequivocal hostility to Christianity, to its ethics and to its upholding of chastity and marriage, Jæger must have expected, though he was patently less prepared for being prosecuted – for blasphemy, the following April – and was horrified at being sentenced to eighty days imprisonment, which he served, after an idyllic seaside summer in Munch's company, from October to December 1886, very far from forbearingly. All this had the result of making *From the Kristiania Bohemians* a cult book, and Munch was to place it alongside the Bible and Dostoyevsky as influences on him. As for Ibsen's reaction to Jæger's novel: he loathed it, and had nothing but contempt for its author for having produced it, and this despite his having been an ardent defender of *Ghosts*. Jæger thought that Ibsen, once so vanguard, had grown conservative with the years, and, where sexual matters were concerned, Brandes, as we have seen, tended to think this too.

This was not the case – at least not in terms other than those of the Kristiania-Bohemians or the Nietzschean apostles. Ibsen understood that just as religious orthodoxy refuses to allow for the variety of human emotions, so does its obverse, the almost fanatical compound of nihilism and libertarianism that the Bohemians embraced. *Hedda Gabler* is surely a demonstration of this, of the negativity of an approach to human life that derides pregnancy, scoffs at marital or indeed emotional constancy and domestic pleasures, as thorough and crippling an exclusion as that which believes that outside a home with babies there are no valid experiences. And in life, while Ibsen's marriage knew great strains, while his emotional fixations on Emilie Bardach, Helene Raff and Hildur Andersen may have caused trouble to himself and others, he did maintain a relationship, indeed a household, with Suzannah and Sigurd, and wrought no lasting havoc on anybody else. Compare this with the ghastly embroiled lives of the young Munch, the young Strindberg, of Staczu Przebyszewski, Oda Krohg and Dagny Juel and indeed Hans Jæger himself. Out of Munch and Strindberg, of course, came art of the greatest kind – the Kristiania Bohemians liked to claim Munch's 'The Sick Child' as their own – but these men had gifts quite transcending the wild living and vaunted enmity to others which their fellows practised and preached, largely to the detriment of self-realisation.

Jæger's Løvborg-like concern with the future was to persist and to lead him, an increasingly lonely man, into the world of both theoretical and political anarchism. He praised Ibsen, whatever his other reservations, for his comparative lack of nationalistic fervour, while he himself moved, following Kropotkin, towards Europeanism and internationalism with a forward vision one has to admire: *Anarkiets bibel* (Anarchy's Bible, 1906); *Socialismus ABC* (The ABC of Socialism, 1906-1910, which was however never finished).

5.

It is Ejlert Løvborg whom Hedda envisages crowned with vine-leaves, both during the course of the play, and before its action, at the time when their friendship was at its most intense; and he it is who so signally fails to wear them. This conscious symbol is therefore inextricably bound up with the artist as Ibsen wishes in this work to present him.

Lorenz Dietrichson remembered that during the period of Ibsen's first residence in Rome, the period of *Brand, Peer Gynt* and the preliminary work on *Emperor and Galilean*, members of the Scandinavian Colony with whom both he and Ibsen consorted, would wear garlands of vine-leaves at parties or celebratory dinners. They thus became associated in Ibsen's mind with his own (comparative) bohemian days, with the warmth, wine and fellowship that made them at the time so refreshing a contrast to the fraught earlier years in Bergen and Christiania. They were a means too of connecting up with the classical Rome that fascinated him, with the cult of Bacchus (the Roman name for Dionysus) whose emblem they were.

They appear fleetingly in *Peer Gynt* – and while the reference is to their absence not their presence (no more than Løvborg is Peer actually wearing them), their implication for *Hedda Gabler* is most interesting. Peer Gynt, middle-aged, in exile from Norway, is at large in North Africa, now an entrepreneur with many dubious ventures to his discredit. He comes across the tent of a Sheikh, and an ensemble of Arab dancing-girls, to one of whom he represents himself as the subject of their song, the Prophet, while she purports to believe him. Quoting Goethe – 'das Ewig-Weibliche zieht uns an' ('the eternal feminine draws us on') – he abducts her (as he thinks – Grieg's famous music here deliciously recaptures her sensual slyness) and they gallop through the desert on the white charger of romantic poetry. Somewhat affronted during their dalliance by her comments on his (Prophet's) venerable years, he assures her of his real youthfulness, and Anitra decides to play him along:

> ANITRA: Ja, du er ung. Har du flere Ringe?
> PEER GYNT: Ikke sandt? Der; grams! Som en Bukk kan jeg springe!
> Var her Vinløv i Nærheden, skulde jeg mig krandse.
> Ja minsæl er jeg ung! Hej, jeg vil danse! (HU VI, p. 166)[14]

> ANITRA: All right, you are young. Have you any more rings?
> PEER: Aren't I? There; catch! I can leap like a stag!
> If there'd been any vine-leaves here
> I'd have made a wreath to put on my head.
> By God, I'm young! I'll have a dance![15]

Peer is about to be made a total fool of. Anitra flatters him into disrobing himself, parting with his bag of money and Arab kaftan, and after surprising him by rapping him over the knuckles in what he thought was a love-game, speeds back across the desert, leaving him bereft. The vine-leaves are therefore doubly connected with deception; Peer wishes to wear them in order to deceive Anitra into believing him a lusty young man, Anitra encourages his fantasy so that she can deceive him to her advantage even more than she already has, and make off with his property. *Hedda Gabler* will subject the image to further elaboration, but we can note that, even three years before the play's action, Løvborg and

Hedda were far too old to be indulging in their wild games; coronations for gallantry, like fooling around with pistols, belong to the self-experiments of adolescence, not to a scholar of thirty and a general's daughter expected soon to get married. And during the course of the play Løvborg deceives Hedda a further two times, first, by going off to the brothel instead of returning to her probably drunk but nevertheless heroic-poetic, and second, by not killing himself in the high Roman manner. It seems improbable that Ibsen had, when writing the later play, forgotten this farcical episode in his earlier work.

But his use of a wreath of vine-leaves in *Emperor and Galilean* is far more extended and serious. In Act One of Part Two ('Kejser Julian', 'The Emperor Julian'), Julian, his emperor-cousin Constantius being dead, arrives in Constantinople to take up his throne. He wants all his subjects to be free to worship whom they wish and as they wish, but it is hard for him to jettison his decided animus against Christianity, for the official status it had held, a position encouraging professions of faith for the sake of job-security or personal advancement, and leading it to practise and promote ruthless intolerance against all and any other creeds. Julian himself remembers, with a nostalgic tenderness, the old gods whose influence on people had been, it seems to him, more accepting of humanity's vagaries, more benevolent, non-proscriptive, more in harmony with the visible workings of Nature and its seasons, instead of being authoritarian, anti-sensuous, and rigid and often blind to the natural world. At a small shrine Julian performs an ancient rite, declaring:

Så har jeg da åbenlyst og i ydmyghed udgydt olje og vin for eder, I velgørende guddomme, der så længe har måttet savne denne for eder så højst sømmelige ihukommelse. Jeg har opsendt min tak til dig, o Apollon, hvem nogle af vismændene – og især de fra østerlandene – tillægger navnet sol-kongen, fordi du bringer og fornyer det lys, hvori livet har sin grund og sit ophav. – Jeg har bragt mit offer til dig, o Dionysos, du henrykkelsens gud, der løfter menneskenes sjæle ud af lavheden og bærer dem op til et for ånden værdigt samliv med højere ånder. – Og, skønt jeg nævner dig sidst, har jeg dog ikke derfor mindst ihukommet dig, o Fortuna! Stod jeg vel her uden din bistand? Visselig ved jeg, at du ikke længere selv lader dig tilsyne, således, som tilfældet var i den gyldne tidsalder, hvorom hin uforlignelige blinde sanger har fortalt os. Men det ved jeg dog – og deri er alle andre visdomsvenner enige med mig – at det er dig, som har en væsentlig andel i valget af den ledsagende ånd, god eller fordærvelig, som skal følge ethvert menneske på hans livs-gang. (HU VII, p. 175)[16]

I have thus openly and humbly, poured out oil and wine for you, beneficent deities, who so long have been denied this most fitting act of remembrance. I have sent up my thanks to thee, Apollo, to whom some wise men ... especially those from the east ... give the name of the Sun-King, because thou bringest and renewest that light which is the source and origin of life ... I have sacrificed to thee, Dionysus, thou god of rapture, who dost lift men's souls from baseness, and bearest them up to a worthy life of communion with higher spirits ... And, last but not least, I remember thee, Fortuna! Would I stand here without thy help! I know indeed that thou dost no longer appear unto men as in the golden age of which that blind and greatest poet of all has told us. Yet I know ... and all other lovers of wisdom are at one with me ... that it is thou who dost largely determine the choice of attendant spirit, good or evil, which is to accompany every man on life's journey.[17]

Of this Trinity Julian favours at this point Dionysus, as most particularly representing all that the former state religion had been most repressive towards. And so he organises a ceremonial in which he enters the city-centre in the guise of his god, mounted on an ass, attended by men, women and young people, most of them in states of great excitement, some all-but-naked, some appearing as 'fauns and satyrs', and among others musicians, jugglers, dancers.

> ... *han er klædt som guden Dionysos, med en panterhud over skuldrene, vinløvkrans om panden, og i hånden en med grønt omvunden stav, på hvis øverste ende der er fæstet en pinje-kongle.* (p. 190)

> *He is dressed as the god Dionysus, with a panther-skin over his shoulders, a crown of vine-leaves on his brow, and in his hand a thyrsus, wreathed in green leaves and tipped with a pine cone.* (p. 339)

And stepping out of the rout, in which, to common view, these lovers of wine are all too plainly a crew of drunkards and these jubilant Maenads whores off the streets, Julian gives the bewildered but fascinated crowd an address:

... ingen gud er bleven så miskendt – ja, latterliggjort – som denne
henrykkelse bringende Dionysos, hvem Romerne også kalder Bakkus.
Mener I, han er en gud for drukkenbolte? O, I højst uvidende, jeg ynker
eder, hvis I tænker så. Hvem anden end ham er det, seerne og digterne
skylder sine vidunderlige gaver? Vel ved jeg at nogle tillægger Apollon
denne virksomhed, og det visselig ikke uden al føje; men da er
sammenhængen hel anderledes at forstå ... (p. 192)

... no god has been so misunderstood ... ridiculed even ... as Dionysus, this
god of ecstasy, whom the Romans also call Bacchus. Do you think he is the
god of drunkards? Oh, you ignorant creatures, I pity you, if that's what you
believe. Who else endows seers and poets with their miraculous gifts? I am
well aware that some ascribe this activity to Apollo, not entirely without
reason, I confess; but in a context which demands an utterly different
interpretation ... (pp. 340-41)

Dionysus was not only the god of wine and the grapes that produce it,
he was their originator. Though later the lover of innumerable women
and with a regular retinue of members of the opposite sex possessed by
their desire for him, Dionysus had as his first love Ampelos, a boy later
killed by a bull. Dionysus' grief could be only assuaged by the fruit-
bearing vine that grew from Ampelos' body; he relished the juice of its
first grapes, which for him was the dead boy's blood in drinkable joy-
eliciting form. Dionysus then took the grape all over the known world,
Europe, North Africa and Asia, and even eastwards into India. Where
grapes could be grown and wine be made, there also were Dionysian
festivals when the body was sent into wild transports, and the normal
laws of behaviour were abandoned through the sheer bliss that wine-
consumption brought on. This in itself told you something about the
truth of existence, which neither Apollo, so dedicated to reason and
proportion, nor the mentors of the Judaeo-Christian tradition knew (or if
they had known, had done their best to disguise). The panther, black and
sleek and incredibly fast, became the wine-god's animal, and the rod he
carried, the thyrsus, a plant stalk, usually decorated as in Ibsen's stage-
directions with ivy-leaves and a pine-cone at its tip, represented the
god's energetic penis, much more interested in the giving of pleasure
than in procreation. He was associated with the bull, despite – or
sometimes because of – its featuring in some legends as Ampelos' killer;

hence the tearing apart of bulls or of portions of bulls' flesh which became rituals in Dionysian orgies.

More germane to the concerns of Ibsen and other nineteenth-century visitors to Greek mythology is his connection with the goat. 'Satyrs' and 'fauns' are respectively the Greek and the Latin (Roman) terms for the same creature, half-man, half-goat, and male followers of Dionysus would accordingly wear goat-skins, as in Julian's orchestrated procession. The following story is often adduced as explanation for this. A king in Attica, Icarius, to whom Dionysus had taught viticulture, killed a goat because he had found it destructively nibbling at a vine. He then made a portion of its skin into a vessel for holding wine. What Icarius had not appreciated was that the goat, as much as the vine itself, was dear to the god. Killing the animal was therefore tantamount to murdering Dionysos himself. In some versions Icarius and his friends put on what remains of the goat's skin, and dance round the wine vessel; in other stories Icarius dies, and the dance is performed in remembrance of his terrible death-dealing blunder, a ritual combining recognition and re-enactment of this with a frenzied emanation of spirits such as ordinary life could not accommodate. This, according the Alexandrian Eratosthenes (c276-194 BCE), is the origin of 'tragedy' (Greek 'tragos', a goat), an idea to be developed by Nietzsche in his declaredly partisan Dionysian interpretation of the art-form.

In his remarkable presentation of Greek mythology, *The Marriage of Cadmus and Harmony* (1988) Robert Calasso has this to say about Dionysus:

> Dionysus, of all the gods, is the one who feels most supremely at ease with women. His enemies 'used to say that he revealed the religious mysteries and initiations so as to seduce other men's women.' ... Dionysus doesn't descend on women like a predator, clutch them to his chest, then suddenly let go and disappear. He is constantly in the process of seducing them, because their life forces come together in him. The juice of the vine is his, and likewise the many juices of life. 'Sovereign of all that is moist,' Dionysus himself is liquid, a stream that surrounds us. 'Mad for the women,' Nonnus, the last poet to celebrate the god, frequently calls him, 'mad for the girls'. And with Christian malice Clement of Alexandria speaks of Dionysus as *choiropsales*, 'the one who

touches the vulva': the one whose fingers could make it vibrate like the strings of a lyre. The Sicyonians worshipped him as 'lord of the female sex'. Dionysus is the only god who doesn't need to demonstrate his virility, not even in war.[18]

Yet Dionysus, who can at times be represented as decidedly effeminate, was also the winner of many campaigns and contests. His strength derives from his confidence in his own specifically male equipment. To look forward to *Hedda Gabler*, can't we see Ejlert Løvborg easily enough in terms of the above? The overpowering sway he holds over Hedda and Thea; and always Mademoiselle Diana – or her like – to take into consideration!

Julian's procession into Constantinople as Dionysus fails for predictable reasons that he himself was unable to predict. Though it arouses a sensation, it is, for one thing, too *voulu*; it lacks that spontaneity that guarantees genuine response, however limited, to a movement, a 'happening'. Too much of the present and the past have to be brushed aside to make room for Julian's new broom. We can understand the reasons for his choice of the pagan gods over the imposed Christian pantheon, but the fact remains that the former have had their day, one which came to an end. And while the latter need not command unthinking devotion, it demands to be taken on board and dealt with on its own terms. It seems to have been Ibsen's own hope – the Third Kingdom – that only after working *through* the Christian legacy can something without the contradictions and rigidities of early Christian orthodoxy be reached. Two points, even in the tableau referred to above, can at once be noted. First, Julian's riding into the city on an ass, however dissimilar his attire and attendants, inevitably brings to mind the Christ he is trying to supplant, to the point of appearing parodic of him. Second, Julian's enthusiasm for his cause – too much bound up with his own ego and its requirements – is in itself blinding him to possibilities only too painfully obvious to the more objective: that the witnessing crowd will be more curious than impressed, that the kind of retinue he himself will attract is made up of self-indulgent riff-raff who will not do any movement any good. Shortly afterwards a graver deficiency in vision becomes apparent. Julian's very unease at the way his attempts at restoration of the old religion have been received makes him first more wary, then more belligerent in his attitude. There is, if at a deeper level, that same deceit we encountered in Peer when wishing for vine-leaves. Julian gives an audience still appareled in the fashion of his god, saying:

> ... og hvis du i dette øjeblik finder mig træt og en smule afkræftet, så er det fordi jeg nylig har fejret en højtid til ære for den guddommelige Dionysos ... Se her, – endnu sidder kransen i mit hår. (p. 196)

> ... if you find me, at the moment, tired and a little worn, it is because I have just been holding a festival in honour of the divine Dionysus ... Look ... the wreath is still in my hair. (p. 344)

But his determination to bring about a revival starts up a ceaseless paranoia in him; he sees Christian hostility everywhere, including in his former friends and good counsellors, and bit by bit he adopts a near-fanatical beleaguered position which will be his ultimate downfall. This crown of vine-leaves is a hollow crown indeed.

In the same way, we feel, Brandes and his followers like the Kristiania Bohemians may have preached pluralism but were as often as not exceedingly intolerant where Christianity was concerned. Many seized on, say, the new scholarship of the Bible or the discoveries of Darwin determined to throw every item of the Christian faith to the wolves, and this being a complex affair, and not, as they jeered, a simple one, a great deal that was life-enhancing got jettisoned. It is interesting that perhaps the most spectacularly creative spirits of the movements we've been visiting in this chapter – Strindberg and Munch – liberated themselves from this all-or-nothing anti-Christianity. It was a liberation because the faults of their fellows were exactly what they themselves were condemning in Christians: a rigid negative judgement of what had sustained millions of human beings and was a part of the very civilisation of which they were beneficiaries. Strindberg's *Påsk* (*Easter*, 1903) must be one of the most beautiful tributes to the gentler, forgiving side of Christianity ever penned.

Dionysus offered himself as an alternative to Christ through attributes they shared as well as through those which, in the minds of such as Emperor Julian, distinguished them: the association with the vine, the drinking of its juice as 'blood', the attendants drawn from all walks of life including some of the shadier ones, but always served with dithyrambic joy, not with programmes of self-denial. He offered expansion not service: 'Have I been understood? *Dionysus against the Crucified?*'[19] ends a book Ibsen could not have read, though its writing predates *Hedda Gabler* by a couple of years: Nietzsche's *Ecce Homo* (not published until 1908). Nietzsche had already in the same year, 1888, in *Der Antichrist* (*The Antichrist*), discriminated between Christianity's *Sklavenmoral* ('slave morality') and his own *Herrenmoral*, ('nobleman's morality'), but in this strange disjointed but impassioned autobiography he inveighs still more savagely against what was for him not just the western hegemony but the blight of its civilisation. Only the authenticity of Nietzsche's unique tormented genius makes tolerable its diatribes, and perhaps not even then, and in the hands of some disciple, a Bohemian of only good-to-average abilities, a Løvborg for example, it would be, more than anything else, a recipe for self-destruction:

> *Now my hammer rages fiercely against its prison* ... the italicised line provides the occasion. Among the decisive preconditions for a *Dionysian* task is the hardness of the hammer, *joy even in destruction*. The imperative 'become hard', the deepest certainty *that all creators are hard*, is the actual mark of the Dionysian nature ... (*ibid.*, p. 111)

> What defines me, what sets me apart from all the rest of mankind, is that I have *unmasked* Christian morality ... Blindness in the face of Christianity is the *crime par excellence* – the crime *against life* ... The millennia, the peoples, the first and the last, the philosophers and the old women – except for five or six moments of history, me as the seventh – on this point they are all worthy of one another. The Christian has hitherto been the 'moral being' ... more absurd, mendacious, vain, frivolous, *harmful to himself* than even the greatest despiser of mankind could have allowed himself to dream. Christian morality – the most malicious form of the will to the lie, the actual Circe of mankind: that which has *ruined* it. (*ibid.*, p. 131)

Well, it is not hard to find examples, even from lives led in Ibsen's plays (the marriage between Rosmer and Beate comes to mind), where Christian value-systems as conveniently promulgated by state and its instruments, have done dreadful psychic damage. But morality *tout court*, that's a different matter. If we look at our play's central quintet of

Tesman, Hedda, Brack, Løvborg and Thea, we can see behind them a society where the traditional Christian values, faith, hope and charity, have grown weaker and other less positive values have replaced them. Tesman and Thea are indeed kind people, capable of self-sacrifice, but they also lack depth and amplitude of vision, and something in the world around them has eroded their capacity to be as impressive as, by rights, they should be (even remembering Thea's temporarily successful reclamation of Løvborg). And in the quintet's three innermost members can we not find that 'joy in destruction' of which Nietzsche speaks, and which was to be one of his most potent and dangerous legacies?

But in *The Birth of Tragedy*, published in 1872 when he was a prodigious and industrious professor of Classical Philosophy at Basel University (and still in his twenties), Nietzsche pits Dionysus not against Christ, but against Apollo. Dionysus can stand for not just acceptance of the destructive principle, but psychic participation in its working. The energy of Hedda herself and of the play she dominates culminates in her playing wild dance music on the piano (and music is par excellence Dionysiac) before she kills herself. Nevertheless the play *in distinction to its characters and action* seems to me an Apollonian creation; we can only bear its violence of speech and thought and deed because we view them from the perspective of wisdom, of hard-won appreciation that, all evidence to the contrary, human beings and their inter-relationships are worthy of our sympathies and understanding. It is thus profoundly *anti-Dionysian*, though at the same time it unflinchingly and with deep feeling enables us to understand why the desire for the Dionysian arises in societies ossified by conventions and exhausted ethical precepts that justify and perpetuate them.

We must now look at the specific instances in the play itself when Dionysian artist Ejlert Løvborg is decked with vine-leaves, in all except the literal sense of those words.

The first mention of the Dionysiac garland occurs in Act Two. Hedda has deliberately broken Løvborg's resolve to stay behind quietly with herself and Thea rather than go to Brack's little stag party which could well present him with temptation. She has done this in a peculiarly cruel – and successful – manner by disclosing to him the worries Thea has expressed in confidence to her, thus betraying the one, and insulting the other. Wounded, Løvborg rebels against such solicitude, and this moment constitutes the real breaking-off – as Hedda had intended – of the fruitful relationship he'd sustained with Thea for more than two years and which had just recently made her abandon her own marriage. But of course the decision to go to Brack's is the beginning of the end for Løvborg. Does Hedda know this? Certainly spoiling things between her old admirer and her old school-friend is not her only intention. Both her father's Spartan soldierly code and her own Kristiania-Bohemian one protest at the Puritanism and lily-livered approach to self and living that could make a man stay away from traditional tests of manhood by closeting him with soft drinks and two 'respectable' women. Maybe she does indeed want him to prove during the course of the evening a strength of will she is well-placed by experience to doubt; or again maybe she actually wishes him to come home drunk (the word 'het' would suggest as much); it will upset Thea, and it is how a true Dionysian bohemian should behave.

> HEDDA: Klokken ti, – da kommer han altså. Jeg ser ham for mig. Med vinløv i håret. Hed og frejdig – (p. 355)

> HEDDA: Ten o'clock ... and back he'll come. I can just see him. With vine-leaves in his hair. Flushed and confident ... (p. 230)

The last adjective is significant: the vine-leaves are a symbol of rejoicing, of letting one's own desires and not conventions be the arbiter of one's behaviour, a drinking of life-giving Ampelos' blood. They also, in classical iconography, often represent maturity, a ripe maturity with a sense that decay will follow not so long afterwards; no callowness of youth here that has to be afraid of real possibilities, or cosseted away from them. The possibility of Løvborg's triumphant return as one fully adult and fully independent, embodying masculinity as it most appeals to her – not that of a virtuous-living scholar, but of a red-blooded initiate who has just passed with flying colours a peculiarly hard test – excites Hedda and brings out in her a terrible and revealing honesty. She is jealous of Thea who at least has done something bold – leaving her Sheriff husband – as opposed to herself who has opted for a man she thinks a ninny, and with rare genuine emotion she exclaims:

HEDDA: Å, dersom du kunde forstå, hvor fattig jeg er. Og du skal ha' lov til at være så rig! (p. 355)

HEDDA: Oh, if only you knew how destitute I am. And you're allowed to be so rich! (p. 231)

Somehow this admission reinforces Hedda's psychic ability to keep Thea a prisoner to whom she will be able to exhibit Løvborg as someone who chose to follow *her* plan. Thea wants to leave, Hedda will not let her.

HEDDA. Snak! Først skal du få thevand, du lille tossehode. Og så, – klokken ti, – så kommer Ejlert Løvborg, – med vinløv i håret. (p. 356)

HEDDA. Nonsense! First you're going to have some tea, you little goose. And then ... at ten o'clock ... Then Ejlert Løvborg will come ... with vine-leaves in his hair. (p. 231)

Of course precisely where they believe themselves to be strong is where both Hedda and Løvborg, in different but related ways, prove themselves weak. Hedda exalts in her power over others, but in truth it is a power that can only be realised through bullying, privilege (she is after all in her own new home), and duplicity. 'Jeg vil for en eneste gang i mit liv ha' magt over en menneskeskæbne' (p. 355) (For once in my life I want to feel that I control a human destiny; p. 230), she declares. But does she control Løvborg's? Her taunting her old flame into leaving the house that evening would certainly appear to be what seals his destiny; but in truth, it is sealed by compulsions from deep within himself. It is possible, more, probable, that Løvborg doesn't give her a thought all the time he's away from her house.

The complexity and strength of Løvborg's feelings for Hedda and of hers for him are of course at the heart of the play, and they defy reductive judgement, tidy categorization. But we can't leave it at that. We return again to that moving exchange screened by Hedda's photograph album (and never do we like Løvborg more than during its course):

LØVBORG: (*med harmfyldt stemme*). Hedda Gabler gift? Og det med – Jørgen Tesman!
HEDDA: Ja, – så går det.

LØVBORG: Å Hedda, Hedda, – hvor kunde du dog kaste dig slig væk! (p. 345)

LØVBORG: (*with bitterness in his voice*) Hedda Gabler married. And married to ... Jørgen Tesman!
HEDDA: Yes ... That's the way of it.
LØVBORG: Oh Hedda ... Darling Hedda, how could you throw yourself away like that? (p. 220)

Moving certainly, but hasn't his regret too aesthetic a quality to come entirely from the heart? Isn't his inquiry just a touch too detached? Why and how, he protests, could a glamorous young woman with whom he had had good times go and legally chain herself to so egregiously *un*glamorous a man? Shortly afterwards he makes Hedda answer the following direct question:

Var der ikke kærlighed i forholdet til *mig* heller? Ikke et stænk, – ikke et skær af kærlighed over det heller? (p. 347)

Was there no love in your relationship to me either? Not a trace ... Not a suspicion of love in that either? (p. 222)

Hedda's answer, with which he does not disagree, is that already noted, that their relationship was essentially one of comradeship. Charged with erotic currents as it may be, this differs little from male camaraderie, particularly as found among Bohemians. Yet this very camaraderie can often involve the heart without acknowledging it, a painful and potentially dangerous state of affairs.

What happens that fateful evening at Brack's and afterwards is totally consonant with Løvborg as Hedda's bohemian boon-companion, and involves those very activities about which in the old days she had so persistently and obsessively liked to question him – such as the visit to Mademoiselle Diana of whose charms he had long been a devotee. Yet the news of his conduct – which involved humiliation by authority – comes as a shock to her. Why? The truth is that, predicated on causing offence to the bourgeois establishment, such acts as extreme drunkenness and brothel-going bring out the bourgeois as well as the voyeur in Hedda – and maybe the same is really true of Løvborg himself, for what are his antics but a deliberate inversion of generally accepted codes (just as Jæger's Nine Commandments were a conscious inversion of the biblical Ten)? And in truth there's nothing so very impressive or unusual about his dash and daring; he is merely availing himself of opportunities to licence available to every man in Christiania if he wishes to pay for them. Ironically he turns out as big a servant of the cash nexus as the fussy virtuous Tesman with his perpetual home-comforts and salary-prospects. There was perhaps naivety as well as lack of proper psychological foresight on Hedda's part, hence the acuteness of her disappointment:

> BRACK: Men det blir nok en dyr spas for Ejlert Løvborg, det gale menneske.
> HEDDA: Nå!
> BRACK: Han skal ha' gjort voldsom modstand. Skal ha' slåt en af konstablerne på øret og revet hans frakke istykker. Så måtte han da med på stationen også.
> HEDDA: Hvoraf véd De nu alt dette?
> BRACK. Fra politiet selv.
> HEDDA:(*ser hen for sig*). Således er det altså gåt for sig. Da har han ikke havt vinløv i håret. (pp. 367-368)

> BRACK: ... But I fear this will have been a costly interlude for that imbecile Løvborg.
> HEDDA: Oh!
> BRACK: Apparently he put up a spirited resistance. Struck an officer of the law over the head, and tore his tunic. So he had to go along to the police-station too.
> HEDDA: How do you know all this?
> BRACK: The police told me themselves.
> HEDDA: (*looking away*) So that was how it was. He didn't have vine leaves in his hair. (p. 242)

The sordid episode not only disabuses Hedda of her ideas about Løvborg, it disabuses her of her faith in her own somewhat factitious symbol. With her old admirer's failure to qualify for it goes her whole ideal. It isn't workable; Dionysian revelry is perhaps essentially a literary concept. We have already noted how she likes, Bovary-fashion, to imagine herself as the heroine of every book she takes a liking to. Translated into terms of real life it means just such an exhibition of bodily yearnings and satisfaction as, in the end, she has always shrunk from. She is a Bohemian in the head only; she cannot translate her pinings after a richer, less boring life into any world that includes the bodily. Hence the intensification of her death-wish that follows her learning the truth about Løvborg.

To an important extent this scene between her and Brack is a dress-rehearsal for what is to follow between them after Løvborg's death: the scales torn from her eyes about the brilliant scholar-artist, and the increase in Brack's hold over her which he will work so unscrupulously. The absence of vine leaves connotes now the abandonment of Hedda to the emptiness of her own dreams, and her vulnerability to the one man who unfeignedly represents the furtive, greedy, dishonest, capitalist attitude to sex and sexual relations that all future-minded people have very properly scorned. So when she sees Løvborg again, and he admits to her his desire to do away with himself, her urging him to carry out this terrible action is not only a longing for their one-time code to be at last vindicated but a wish to punish him for a betrayal of it which has put her at the mercy of a man she dislikes, even despises. (But – and this especially pains and humiliates her – a man to whom she feels a measure of sexual attraction.)

> HEDDA: Og hvad vej vil De så gå?
> LØVBORG: Ingen. Bare sé til at få ende på det altsammen. Jo før jo heller.
> HEDDA:(*et skridt nærmere*). Ejlert Løvborg, – hør nu her – . Kunde De ikke sé til at – at det skede i skønhed?
> LØVBORG: I skønhed? (*smiler.*) Med vinløv i håret, som De før i tiden tænkte Dem –
> HEDDA: Å nej. Vinløvet, – det tror jeg ikke længer på. Men i skønhed allikevel! For én gangs skyld! (pp. 374-375)

> HEDDA: And what are you going to do then?
> LØVBORG: Nothing. Just put an end to it all. The sooner the better.
> HEDDA: (*taking a step towards him*) Ejlert Løvborg ... Listen to me ... Couldn't you let it happen ... beautifully?
> LØVBORG: Beautifully? (*Smiles*) Crowned with vine leaves, as you used to imagine?
> HEDDA: Oh, no. I don't believe in those vine leaves any more. But beautifully all the same! Just for this once! (p. 250)

When he appears, smiling, to go along with her fantasy, just as he used to in the society games which he refers to, she tells him with dark deliberateness – but with truth – that she no longer believes in those vine-leaves, in other words that the Bohemian paganism that had sustained their relationship for some seasons, and underscored her attraction to him, has collapsed. She is too late to find any other surrogate faith; she must now face the reality she despises. She is a woman expecting a baby trapped in a loveless but highly respectable marriage to a most presentable man she can't physically stand. But there will be no other course for her than to go along with convention-blessed normative life (with the commonplace get-out of an affair). To endure this she has to see first that the representative of her former alternative value-system, the Dionysian, is got rid of, that he is ritually quasi-religiously slain – and with her ordination and her blessing. And Løvborg himself, robbed now of his self-esteem, not least by this last announcement of hers, (seemingly) submits.

Hedda and he make two contrasting farewells within a matter of seconds.

When she tells him of her loss of faith, he says, with bitter mocking irony: 'Farvel, frue. Og hils Jørgen Tesman fra mig' (p. 375) (Goodbye, Mrs Tesman. And remember me to your husband; p. 250).

But when she gives him the pistol to remember her by, and emphasizes the beauty of the deed she now expects of him, his wording undergoes a movingly significant change: 'Farvel, Hedda Gabler' (Goodbye, Hedda Gabler; *ibid.*).

By calling her this, he is cancelling out her crippling, mistaken marriage, saluting her by the name of their old friendship. But Ibsen leaves us to imagine what pain there must be in his heart – after hearing from her own lips that the woman to whom he once confided otherwise unutterable details of his intimate life wants him dead.

But of course though he keeps her pistol, he does *not* use it to kill himself, and there is not a shred of evidence that he ever intended to do so. He is dissolute, depressed, tormented, yes, but lacks, even though he may somewhat partake of, the General's daughter's consuming nihilism (a mindset Nietzsche disapproved of, perhaps aware of how closely it connected with that of so many of his followers). And Hedda reveals the extent of its consumption of her, how under its sway she has forfeited common humanity, when we hear her greeting the news of the fatal shooting (she doesn't know that Løvborg is in fact already dead nor the true circumstances). She exclaims, virtually instantly, not with shock and not at its sadness nor its wastefulness but at its beauty – a chilling aestheticism which has vanquished not only all feelings for a man once dear to her but any respect for life as such. She finds it difficult to forego the congratulations she thinks due to the suicide (as she sees him) for having the courage (as she sees it) to leave life early, courage to give his act of departure some ritual splendour that will defy the *muflisme* (to use Flaubert's term) of conventional contemporary life – even though there were, by mutual agreement, no vine-leaves. This is the consequence of the Dionysian *Weltanschauung*: when the triumphalist orgy is over, there can only be exhaustion; ecstasy, as its name proclaims, may wonderfully fill the minute but has nothing to offer any longer, more durable future.

Perhaps Hedda's true epitaph is what she says to Brack:

Å det latterlige og det lave, det lægger sig som en forbandelse over alt det, jeg bare rører ved. (p. 388)

Everything I touch seems destined to turn into something mean and farcical. (p. 263)

And when she protests this, she does not know the worst of it. That he was found dying with a pistol in his pocket in Mademoiselle Diana's boudoir, and that it is impossible as yet to say whether the red-haired whore shot him and then put the weapon back in his trousers herself, or whether Løvborg was on the point of pulling the gun out and turning it on her. Either way it presents another alternative – a terrible one for Hedda. Either she faces what she has always dreaded most, scandal (her father's fate) or she is bound further to Brack, in a middle-class adultery such as she has always looked down on. It is important that we do not know the answer to the immediate cause of Løvborg's death; he is thus denied any kind of resolution, and we are denied any stronger emotion for him than an un-Nietzschean pity. And our ignorance compounds our sense of Hedda's trappedness, that apprehended condition which will tip her into death. Besides – what difference would more precise knowledge make? Dionysus' vine has been proved sterile.

The indignant, contemptuous, withering criticisms that *Hedda Gabler* received when it came out, both in Scandinavia and in Britain, surprise us today, when the play is probably Ibsen's most popular, with more regular productions to its credit than all but the top Shakespearean handful. The condemnations that contemporary critics made, centring especially on the character of Hedda herself, we attribute to the timidity of the age, to its reluctance to confront the psychic diseases it not merely harboured but fostered. We smile a little when we read that *Morgenbladet* found Hedda 'a horrid miscarriage of the imagination', that *Samtiden* bewailed the fact that the play 'leaves us with a sense of emptiness and betrayal'.[20] Yet I wonder if today, in our relativist aversion to moral judgement on a work of art, in our liberal inclusiveness, we have not sanitised the play, or, at any rate aestheticised it, so that it commends itself to us for its (truly galvanising) theatrical effectiveness rather than distresses us as it should in its cultural diagnosis. Those early reviewers who shuddered at the picture it gave of contemporary society, in Norway and elsewhere in the West, were at least responding to and acknowledging Ibsen's unflinching awareness of moral inadequacy and self-blindness, paying tribute to the darkness which sooner or later shows itself to be the inner state of all its people. It is surely, even remembering *Rosmersholm*, Ibsen's bleakest work, the one in which the absence of virtue seems to cry out between the interchanges, where all the characters' deficiencies add up to culpabilities, and where these connect to that most essential component of existence, sexuality. 'Bad faith, bad sex!' could be its motto. From Brack's repellent predatory approach which will shun no means of obtaining power over those who attract him to Tesman's fussy need for gratification and comfort from women, from Hedda's prurient curiosity about sexual behaviour she refuses to engage in, out of fear and an obsolete code, to Løvborg's loveless self-indulgence masquerading as modern-style freedom, from Auntie Julle's spinsterish distance from the flesh to Mademoiselle Diana's commercial proximity to it, the picture appals. And no system of thought, no art proffers itself to lift these victims away from their auto-destruct into any communication of body and spirit that will prove creative, life-enhancing – no joyful Sunday scenes by Osvald Alving or Hellenic sculptures by Hans Lyngstrand. Only the art of world-weary epigrams, the pronouncements of an intelligence that shows its decadence in its convinced superiority to basic human feelings. The act of generation in *Hedda Gabler* is denied its proper end, the birth of a new life; instead there is the unkindest and most ignoble termination of all, the self-inflicted death of the woman who, through nature, would have brought it about. The male phallus, instrument of Eros, is translated into the pistol, instrument of Thanatos. Instead of a man in his prime, sexually and mentally, wearing a victor's crown made up of leaves that betoken the everlasting, he gets a bullet in the groin. And that says it all!

The Master Builder
The Artist as Challenger: Halvard Solness

Whereas in the three plays we have so far considered the artist is a component of an interactive group, in each of which another figure commands more attention – Helene Alving, Ellida Wangel, Hedda Gabler – in *The Master Builder* the artist has dominion over all others. Not since *An Enemy of the People* of ten years before (1882) had Ibsen accorded a man this central position; the problems of Solness as artist are inextricably involved with his problems as a male, and a male in a world in which – if too slowly – the female as an autonomous being is granted increasing recognition. Is Solness' art – architecture – which he has served so unsparingly too bound up with his masculinity, too little concerned with admission of The Other? Do in truth the defects of his fairly ruthless, mostly unquestioning masculinity reveal themselves in his productions which have brought him, up to the point at which we encounter him, unqualified success?

Ibsen's French translator Maurice Prozor was right,[1] as Ibsen himself conceded, to see *The Master Builder* as a vital predecessor of *When We Dead Awaken*, where also the dominance of an artist in the play provides a way of looking at the dominance of the male. As I intimated earlier, *The Wild Duck* apart, *The Master Builder* is in my opinion Ibsen's intellectually densest as well as most emotionally searing play. His relationship to it is of an extraordinarily intimate kind, as its mostly admiring critics were quick to point out. However the intimacy is not in the least that of a self-portraitist, but springs from the fact that the central situation is for Ibsen so perfect a correlative for the tensions in his life at the time of writing. Though it is the work of a man of sixty-four, it is informed by a preoccupation, at once fearful and adventurous, with the future.

1.

On 13 March 1891, Ibsen, still living in Munich, replied to a letter from the family member of whom he had always been fondest, his sister Hedvig (now Stousland). Skien, their native town, was, she had informed him, shortly to celebrate the completion of extensive rebuilding following the great fire of 1886:

> Dear Sister, I thank you warmly for the letter which I received last month and which I must no longer delay answering.
>
> I was very glad indeed to learn that Skien, too, is now to have its Public Festival Hall. It is sure to be a large and fine one, up to date in every respect and worthy of the modern town.
>
> And you go on to say that a variety of entertainments will be given to celebrate the opening of this hall.
>
> I wish very much that I could have been present at them. I suppose I would have met only a very few of my childhood acquaintances. I would have been surrounded by a new generation, all strange to me. But perhaps not altogether a stranger. For through all these long years of absence I have always had a feeling that I still belong to my native town.
>
> Had these festivities taken place some years ago and I had been told of them, I would have written a song or a poem and sent it home. I hope and trust that it would have met with a kind reception there.
>
> But I no longer write poems and songs of the kind required. So this is out of the question. And yet I wish with all my heart that I could take part in some way.
>
> And therefore I wish that you would have this letter read aloud, so that everyone present may know that I am with you in thought on this festive occasion, as I have many a time been with you before, both in your sorrows and in your hopes of brighter days to come.
>
> It was in 1850 that I was last in Skien. Not long afterwards the town began to pass through a period of spiritual storms, which spread from there over a wider area.
>
> I have always loved stormy weather. And, although I was absent, I went through this tempestuous period with you. That I did take part in it – some of my writings bear witness to that.
>
> Then great calamities befell the town, devastating it again and again. The house where I was born and where I spent my earliest years, and the church – the old church with the angel of baptism under the raftered roof

– were burned down. All the things to which my earliest recollections were attached have been burned – every one of them.

So you can understand how impossible it would be for me not to feel myself deeply and personally affected, together with you all, by the blows that struck our common home.

But I beg of you also to believe that it gave me a keen pleasure to read of the rebuilding of the town in a handsome and beautiful style, of the growth of the town, and of its progress in many directions.

It seems to me that gladness and hope must fill your hearts when you think of the future of our town.

I wish I could have said this and much more to you personally. But, in my own way, I am with you in spite of the distance that separates us.

And if I come to Norway again, as I hope I shall, then I will come and see my home again, the old and yet new home.

Dear Hedvig, this is what I particularly wanted to say to you today. I shall do my best to let you hear from me soon. Farewell! Remember me to your own family and to other relatives.

Your affectionate brother,
Henrik Ibsen.[2]

This letter adumbrates, to a quite remarkable extent, the central features of the first play Ibsen wrote after his return to Norway to live, after twenty-seven years' residence abroad.

First the fire.

His hometown of Skien had, in fact, been *twice* devastated by fire – in 1854 and again in 1886. Both this letter and *The Master Builder* ask the question: how does physical destruction of a place affect its people's relationship to their own, and each other's, past? As long as it stands, a house, to use a convenient microcosm, is informed by the experiences of its inhabitants; it offers them daily reminders of these, binding the most disparate individuals together. But when that house has gone – whether through fire or any other calamity – then that continuous linkage to the past has gone too, and accordingly the present itself is also changed. Therefore those bonds between fellow-inhabitants have loosened. The experiences of earlier years are confined now to each person's head where they have to co-exist with much else, including the traumas brought on by the disaster responsible. Here we come to one function of the artist in whatever medium: as giver-back of what has irretrievably gone, as one who can un-destroy.

In Ibsen's play fire destroys the first house of Solness and his wife Aline, inherited from Aline's mother. As a consequence of this disaster their children, twin baby boys, die, though by a terrible irony they were successfully brought through the actual fire. The Solness' loving instinctual marriage dies too, and a major reason for this is the destruction of that physical context which had nurtured it. It cannot survive the transportation. Conscious (that is to say, artificial) attempts to restore the good of the past – by rebuilding the nurseries, for example – are doomed to failure. We appreciate from the very first that the Solness' new house can never and will never be the hoped-for *home*. Aline, Fru Solness, movingly tells Hilde about what destruction of her first and only home has entailed:

> Nej, det er de små tab i livet, som skærer en så ind i hjertet. At miste alt det, som andre folk regner for næsten ingenting ... Bare småting. Der brændte nu alle de gamle portrætterne på væggene. Og alle de gamle silkedragterne brændte. De, som havde hørt familjen til i så langsommelige tider. Og alle mors og bedstemors kniplinger – de brændte også. Og tænk, – smykkerne da! ... Og så alle dukkerne ... Jeg og dukkerne blev ved at leve sammen siden også. (HU XII, p. 103)

> No, it's the small losses in life that cut deep into the heart. Losing things that other people think nothing of ... Just little things ... All the old portraits on the walls were burnt. And all the old silk dresses were burnt. Things that had been in the family for years and years. And all Mother's and Grandmother's lace – that was burnt too. And even the jewels! ... And all the dolls ... The dolls and I had gone on living together. (Vol. VII, p. 425)

This passage is often taken as an indication of Aline's severance from normal human feelings. She grieves more, it is said, for lost objects than for her own flesh and blood. For me the passage is a statement of a disturbing and rarely acknowledged truth. Nobody (and least of all her husband) denies the depth of Aline's grief for her dead babies. This is an emotion beyond adequate words, as all who have endured such a bereavement know. But to keep our bearings through life we need objects that have long had associations for us, particularly cherished ones: they are props for our identity when this is under threat. Reduce these to ashes, and we are too often bereft, helpless. Aline's emotion-choked sentences most certainly do not tell us that she rates family jewels, or even her loved nine dolls, *above* her dead children. But they *do* reveal that her precarious relationship with her husband, her co-survivor, is insufficiently strong to enable her to withstand the tragedy, to move forward from it into a living future. Had the destruction by fire been less total she herself would have been better enabled to see life as a continuity, even if one with dreadful notches on its chain. Every bombing raid the world over leaves casualties as desolate as Aline Solness.

Other forms of destruction than the literal and visible can overwhelm a household, a community, however, and in his letter to Hedvig Ibsen refers to one that distressed him enormously. In the 1850s an evangelical movement swept through Skien taking with it Ibsen's mother, younger brother and indeed Hedvig herself. Ibsen detested the narrow-minded religious fervour promoted by Gustav Adolf Lammers who, in his rigidity of faith, waged war on all ambiguities, on the myriad complexities of existence. In *The Master Builder* Ibsen is undoubtedly remembering Skien when he makes Solness defy the God of his pietistic youth and condemn as harsh and anti-human His 'all or nothing' demands, a God who will even use a life-taking fire as instrument:

Det var for at jeg ingenting andet skulde ha' at hæfte mig ved. Ikke sligt noget, som kærlighed og lykke, forstår De. Jeg skulde bare være bygmester. Ingenting andet. Og så skulde jeg hele mit liv igennem gå her og bygge for ham. (p. 117)

It was so that I should have nothing else to cling to. No love or happiness or anything like that, you see. I was to be a master-builder, and that was all. I was to spend my whole life building for Him. (p. 439)

Solness' subsequent riposte to the Almighty, made, significantly, on a church-tower, is pivotal to his whole career, and to the lives of others too, including that of the girl Hilde Wangel, who from ground level witnesses his delivery of it. Solness undoubtedly stands for his creator here who, repelled by a thunder-hurling loveless Jehovah, attacked Him and His dedicated servant in his first major work, *Brand* (1866). Doesn't his letter to Hedvig show that sympathetic feeling for those under the fervid evangelist's sway was an important constituent of his mind when writing that work? He who 'always loved stormy weather' went, he says, 'through this tempestuous period with you.' Even from the comparatively serene height of 1891, Ibsen saw his assault on narrowness of religious creed as a watershed work, for, a consequence not without irony, it brought him not only wider acclaim than any he had hitherto known but an 'official' worldly reward too, a lifetime government pension enabling him to devote himself to writing. Yet he could not have written *Brand* had he not been able to enter into that faith which his siblings had embraced, and in *The Master Builder* we can discover in Solness a curious nostalgia for church-going days, and a pining after faith, even though his awareness of its shackling of the soul and of the cruelty and falsity of its demands is as strong as ever.

In *The Master Builder* Solness, like Ibsen a creator on an ample scale, also sees his career as inseparable from defiance of the intransigent God of his boyhood. And we know that he is right to so regard it, whatever construction we place on it and however ambiguous and self-deceiving we find the renunciation. For what is indisputable is that personal achievement, reputation, success and money all came to Solness only *after* he had announced to God that he would make no more buildings honouring Him, that he would thenceforth busy himself only with houses for *people*. This last sounds a laudable and sympathetic enough ambition, especially if seen as a way of giving others what he himself has recently been denied; but its stressful genesis calls its purity into question, and how satisfactorily it has been realised is one of the hard questions the play demands that we ask.

Ibsen's fellow-feeling with his sister even when their religious positions were in opposition is borne out in the letter's references to a kind of telepathic communication between himself (wherever he might happen to be living) and the people of his earlier life. Even now 'in my own way, I am with you in spite of the distance that separates us'. Knowledge of the feelings of others acquired by means beyond the external exchanges of information or close daily observation is one of the most distinctive features of *The Master Builder*. In this respect it relates very closely to *The Lady from the Sea*, and it is of course from this play that the principal possessor of such knowledge, Hilde Wangel issues. Her relationship with Solness, and with the element of Air which he, for her, represents, is to an important degree a re-enactment (or extension) of Ellida's to the Stranger and to Water (represented there by the open sea). Hilde it was who saw Solness atop the church-tower, in, as it appeared to her, mystic communion with Air, participating in (singing) its special sacred music, which she herself will hear again when he makes his fatal ascent. She alone it was who understood, though herself only very young, that he was going through a crucial experience when up aloft, and that the entire future direction of his life was then at stake. And it is entirely consonant with such powers that when she turns up exactly ten years later 'to claim her kingdom' from him, it is at the very moment when Solness has exclaimed to Dr Herdal: 'Jo, pas De bare på, doktor. Engang kommer ungdommen her og banker på døren – ' (p. 52) (Yes, just you watch, Doctor! One of these days, youth is going to come here beating on the door ... ; p. 375)

No sooner has he spoken than they hear a *literal* knocking on the door: Hilde enters, unannounced, unexpected, and indeed unrecognised, but unquestionably a member of the younger generation. Solness has, it appears, forgotten all about Hilde Wangel – who may well have invented much of her account of their first meeting ten years ago to the day. But as the play progresses, we become convinced that Hilde somehow communicated her expectations to him, her intention that they should be gloriously reunited on this anniversary day. Unconsciously then Solness' own will has assented to her dreams. He is thus as responsible for her quixotic-seeming arrival at his house as she herself is, in the throes of youthful caprice.

Hilde's youth/youthfulness is, of course, of utmost thematic importance; the challenge posed by younger generations than one's own is another major concern of both the letter to Hedvig and the play. Ibsen ponders what it would be like to be 'surrounded by a new generation, all strange to me', comforting himself with the thought that to someone who still feels rooted in his native town, as he does, none of its inhabitants can be exactly a stranger. To Solness all the young – Ragnar Brovik, Kaja Fosli and Hilde Wangel – whether he knows them or not, are threatening like strangers, and while with the women he has, and can develop, telepathic rapport, with the younger man he cannot. His fellow-male eludes him, and brings out what is worst (and most fear-ridden) in his own character. Solness' preoccupation with the young is nothing short of obsessional – destructively so with Ragnar to whom he behaves, for the most part, abominably, and unscrupulously so with Kaja. With Hilde there is fascination, but of an involved and possibly unhealthy kind. His preoccupation connects as much with Thanatos (Death) as with Eros (Love), and will be the cause of his falling off his new tower to his death. Without her very personal instigations he would never surely have mounted it – or rather, these give him the *conscious* reason for his deed. It may well be that only through Solness' death can the young ones, Ragnar, Kaja and even the enamoured Hilde herself, go forward to any kind of self-fulfilment, and that unconscious responsibility for it lies on their shoulders.

Ibsen's letter to Hedvig then is permeated by the sadness of a man in late middle age at the irrevocable disappearance of an intimately known past, of buildings and people alike. *But* – and this is an equally conspicuous aspect of it – it is full of palpable pleasure at the prospect his sister has given him of a rebuilt, rejuvenated Skien, of a community given new outward form, new stimulus to living. He wishes he could be there, enjoying all the entertainments and ceremonies planned. These were to find their way into *The Master Builder* in the consecration festivities for the church at Lysanger, and ten years later, for the Solness' new house. But it is not only the celebrations that appeal to Ibsen. His hopeful belief that the new Skien is not just a welcome triumph of reconstruction, but something admirable and delightful in itself, shines out from his lines: its very newness, its modernity excites him. He feels sure that the Public Festival Hall will be 'fine', that the style in which the town has been rebuilt is 'handsome and beautiful'; Skien will look as it should do, vindicating its ambitious regeneration programme, and paying tribute to its social and economic progress. *The Master Builder* has building, rebuilding, forms of architecture at its commanding imaginative centre. When Ibsen was asked, by Norwegian painter, Erik Werenskiold, whether he were interested in architecture, he answered: 'Yes, it is, as you know, my own trade'.[3] This play proves that remark scarcely an exaggeration.

Hedvig's letter about reconstructed Skien and Ibsen's reply were earnests of the dramatist's own actual experience of Norway after the summer of 1891, when he began to lead a regular life there and to travel more within its borders. He would then have found new buildings everywhere, most conspicuously in Christiania itself, and obviously these reflected changes in Norwegian economic and social conditions and in national – and international – taste. Annoyed by all the questions put to him about whom Solness represented – Bjørnson, politicians of the Right or Left, Bismarck or the author himself? – Ibsen exclaimed: 'The play has absolutely nothing to do with political or social problems!' He was right to dismiss too many literal topical interpretations. But the dismissal is a little disingenuous. No question of it, this first fruit of his permanent return is passionately concerned with the cultural health of the society he had re-joined – a society moreover, for all its mounting nationalist desire for secession from Sweden, more in tune with trends in the rest of Europe, Germany, France, Britain, than at any previous stage of his life. He conceded as much in conversation with Ernst Motzfeldt:

> I draw real, loving people. Any considerable person will naturally be to some degree representative of the generality, of the thoughts and ideas of the age... [4]

And nothing exhibits an age's – or a country's – cultural health more clearly than its buildings, as W. H. Auden wrote:

> Publish each healer that in city lives
> Or country houses at the end of drives;
> Harrow the house of the dead; look shining at
> New styles of architecture, a change of heart.[5]

Architects, master-builders, meet their society's needs and demands, they cater for their tastes and, if sufficiently talented and well-known, can not only foster these but extend them. In turn their work affects lives, simply through its durable presence, contexting or conditioning them, inspiring or antagonising them. We are all the products of the architecture which surrounded us in early years, and we all owe much of our prevailing state of mind to what we find around us now. In making a *Bygmester* the protagonist of his new drama Ibsen was taking a man with more influence on the lives of fellow-citizens than the central character of any previous prose play had had. (Karsten Bernick and Dr Stockmann are the only rivals, but they are very much men of one specific small town; Solness' sphere of operation and influence is so much larger.) Perhaps such a man as this prospering builder of houses could best be compared, as proponent of the *Zeitgeist*, as creator of atmosphere, as shaper of minds and hearts, with a widely-read writer, a much-played dramatist.

Ibsen himself stated that serious work on *The Master Builder* began with a poem he dated 16 March 1892:

> De sad der, de to, i så lunt et hus
> ved høst og i vinterdage.
> Så brændte huset. Alt ligger i grus.
> De to får i asken rage.

> For nede i den er et smykke gemt,
> Et smykke, som aldrig kan brænde.
> Og leder de trofast, hænder det nemt,
> at det findes af ham eller hende.

> Men finder de end, de brandlidte to,
> det dyre, ildfaste smykke,
> aldrig hun finder sin brændte tro,
> han aldrig sin brændte lykke.

> They sat there, those two, in so snug a house in autumn and in winter days. Then the house burnt. All lies in ruins. Those two must rake in the ashes.

> For among them a jewel is hidden, a jewel that can never burn. And if they search diligently, it might perhaps be found by him or her.

> But even if this fire-scarred pair ever do find that precious fireproof jewel – she will never find her burnt faith, he never his burnt happiness.[6]

These elliptical lines present the destruction of a home in its harrowing negative aspect only: no question here of rebuilding, let alone of making something handsome and new to stand in its stead. Intact the house in question was *lunt* – cosy, snug – and the lives led inside it accorded. But when it has been reduced to ruins and ashes, the couple can only reproduce the desolation; deprived of supports they have nothing to give each other, and but little to sustain their individual selves. The jewel that fire can never burn must represent some valued link to the past which could assist them to a shared, brighter future. But in this case, says this strange poem, even if found, it cannot repair the damage done to wife and husband.

For the woman it is her faith that has been impaired. And Aline Solness, who has never recovered from the tragedy, lives by a religion that combines superstitious surrender to Fate (God's will) with a joyless sense of Duty (as Hilde Wangel is quick to perceive). What the man has lost is different – *lykke*, happiness. This implies what I believe to be a truth about the play, that Solness does indeed have a faith, and maybe a less heterodox one than we are apt to assume. But happiness – no, that he lacks, and we will hear him exclaim (*i vill angst* – *in wild anguish*): '*Jeg* – jeg, som ikke *kan* leve livet glædeløst!' (Me ... A man who cannot lead a joyless life; p. 428).

His is the predicament of Captain Alving (according to his widow), of Osvald Alving, Solness' fellow-artist, even of Lyngstrand who so feared dying before he could see the Mediterranean and the joyful art produced by its shores. And no doubt Løvborg would have said much the same thing. It is an interesting and significant attachment of the pleasure principle to the *male* psyche. And the one woman in Ibsen's oeuvre who might have spoken the above sentence, Hedda Gabler, has a male psyche in a woman's body.

Considered together, Ibsen's letter to Hedvig and his lyric poem, written almost exactly one year later, constitute a dialectic. On the one hand the eternal human capacity for self-renewal, whatever the sorrows and deprivations experienced. On the other, the impossibility of restoration if love or mutual regard has been too tainted by self-serving elements. Both possibilities are offered via the image of buildings – buildings not just as shelter but as artefacts that give meaning to existence. After all '[Architecture] is my own trade.'

Indeed in 1858, aged thirty, Ibsen had written a poem to this effect:

BYGGEPLANER

Jeg mindes så grant, som om idag det var hændt,
den kveld jeg så i bladet mit første digt på prent.
Der sad jeg på min hybel og med dampende drag
jeg røgte og jeg drømte i saligt selvbehag.

'Et skyslot vil jeg bygge. Det skal lyse over Nord.
To fløje skal der være; en liden og en stor.
Den store skal huse en udødelig skald;
den lille skal tjene et pigebarn til hal. – '

Mig syntes at i planen var en herlig harmoni;
men siden er der kommet forstyrrelse deri.
Da mester blev fornuftig, blev slottet splittergalt:
storfløjen blev for liden, den lille fløj forfaldt.[7]

BUILDING PLANS

I remember as clearly as if it had been today the evening when, in the paper,
I saw my first poem in print. There I sat down in my den, and with long-
drawn puffs, I smoked and I dreamed in blissful self-complacency.

'I will build a cloud-castle. It shall shine all over the North. It shall have two
wings; one little and one great. The great wing shall shelter a deathless poet;
the little wing shall serve as a young girl's bower.'

The plan seemed to me nobly harmonious; but as time went on it fell into
confusion. When the master grew reasonable, the castle turned utterly crazy;
the great wing became too little, the little wing fell to ruin.[8]

With hindsight the prophetic nature of this poem (for all its wry young
man's humour, its mocking of a neophyte's vanity) is startling, even if
its components are very differently arranged in the later work. Instead of
more conventional constructions the author decides on '*et skyslott*' , a
'cloud-castle' – in the play it is '*et luftslott*' , an air-castle – which will
shine over his own northern homeland. In one part of it will live a
'skald', an immortal artist, in the other a young girl. *The Master Builder*
will bring these two into short-lived, joyful but fatal conjunction. Far
from being immortal, in this, his for me profoundest play, the artist will
die as a result of a fall, which ends with his head smashed in, while the

girl experiences bewildered (and surely temporary) triumph. 'When the master grew reasonable, the castle turned utterly crazy...' Perhaps it took Ibsen thirty-three years to understand what he meant by this mysterious line. In a note for *The Master Builder*, resembling the jottings for *The Lady from the Sea*, he wrote: 'The airship that can be steered. Insight into the life of the inhabitants of Mars'.[9] No castle of fantasy ever turned as crazy as what human beings themselves have gone on to build.

2.

What we see when the play opens is the premises of Solness' firm, inside the house in which he and his wife live: a general office where Kaja Fosli keeps the books, and, opening off from this, a drawing office, where work Kaja's fiancé, Ragnar Brovik, a draughtsman and his old father, Knut, formerly an architect with a business of his own. Their employer is Bygmester Solness, Master-Builder Solness, and it is a pity that English-language versions did not keep the full designation as title for the play, for it offers an important key to his not always easy professional position. Solness himself, in Act Two, when confessing to Hilde the role of the fire in his success, draws our attention to this:

> SOLNESS: Ja, ser De, – som sagt, – den branden, den bragte mig ivejret, den. Som bygmester da.
> HILDE: Hvorfor kalder De Dem ikke arkitekt ligesom de andre?
> SOLNESS: Har ikke lært grundig nok til det. Det, jeg kan, det har jeg for det meste gåt og fundet ud selv. (p. 81)

> SOLNESS: So you see – as I said before – that fire was the thing that made me. As a master builder, I mean.
> HILDE: Why don't you call yourself an architect, like the rest?
> SOLNESS: I never really had the proper training. Most of what I know I've taught myself. (p. 404)

Solness has the paradoxical combination of forceful confidence and blustering uncertainty so often a characteristic of the self-made man, and in itself a means to his further success. The boss of Knut and Ragnar

Brovik and of Kaja, whom he took into his employ four to five years earlier, he is in class provenance humbler than they, and in terms of education and qualifications is most definitely the inferior of the erstwhile architect. In terms of achievement and present-day fame, however, it's quite another matter. Solness is never entirely comfortable with this discrepancy, and it explains much in his awkward dealings with them, which combine in manner swagger and social self-consciousness.

When we see them first, these three employees of his are pursuing their business in the silence of intent application. Just as Ibsen broke new ground in setting the second act of *The Lady from the Sea* in a tourist-spot complete with tourists, so does he do something new here. What other nineteenth-century play begins with people hard at work, with an opening silence that is in itself a statement about what is conditioning their lives – ie their jobs? More, by giving dramatic significance to offices and office-procedures, it is delivering the theatre from the often too close romantic and recreational associations, and links it indissolubly to the everyday world of jobs and money-making.

The silence is broken by the involuntary exclamation from old Brovik: 'Nej, nu holder jeg det snart ikke længer ud!' (p. 33) (Oh, I can't stand this much longer!; p. 357). He means the physical pain of which he has suffered yet another spasm, but the line has a resonance beyond this: the situation of all three of them is intolerable, and has been so for virtually the length of their employment here.

Ibsen's dialectic, his conflict in values, is worked out – and more precisely than, I think, has always been appreciated – through what is going on in these very offices before us. The plot of the play is advanced by the concerns of Solness' firm and so depends on decisions about *buildings*. One of the important things this play demonstrates is that in a world ever more based on industry and commerce people do not forego what quickens or devours them as soon as they enter an office. Office duties can be informed by the tragic sense of life as fully as the rites of more traditional and time-hallowed occupations; dark irrational forces may well have contracts or folders of plans for their instruments, as they do here. And an enterprise as central to society as construction of homes for people is bound to reveal its own truths about human nature.

When Solness makes his bullying entrance, he hears that earlier that afternoon a young couple called. They were anxious that the building of their new villa out at Løvstrand should get underway as soon as possible. Solness is dismissive, accusing the couple of lack of taste, and refuses to be impressed by old Brovik telling him that they are in fact people of substance. Before he goes home ill, however, Brovik lets Solness know that the commissioning couple are members of a family with whom his son is friendly, and that Ragnar has, off his own bat, drawn up plans for the kind of villa that he thinks would appeal to them. Solness, not worried about inconsistency, is far from pleased to hear this. Ragnar, of whom we read in the stage directions that he is 'i tretiårene, velklædt, lyshåret, med en lidt ludende holdning' (p. 33) (in his thirties, well-dressed. Fair-haired, with a slight stoop; p. 358), is, in his view, but a draughtsman, and a still young one at that, who is harbouring unacceptable ambitions above his professional station. The following exchange is crucial to the entire drama:

SOLNESS: Og de tegningerne, de er de fornøjet med? De, som skal bo der?
BROVIK: Ja. Dersom bare De vilde sé dem igennem og godkende dem, så –
SOLNESS: Så vilde de la' Ragnar bygge hjemmet for sig?
BROVIK: De likte så svært godt det, som han vilde ha' frem. De syntes, det var noget så aldeles nyt, dette her, sa' de.
SOLNESS: Åhå! *Nyt!* Ikke sligt noget gammeldags juks, som det, *jeg* plejer bygge!
BROVIK: De syntes, det var noget *andet.*
SOLNESS: (*i undertrykt forbittrelse*). Det var altså til Ragnar de kom her – mens jeg var ude!
BROVIK: De kom her for at hilse på Dem. Og så spørge om De kunde være villig til at træde tilbage –
SOLNESS: (*opfarende*). Træde tilbage! Jeg!
BROVIK: Ifald De fandt at Ragnars tegninger –
SOLNESS: Jeg! Træde tilbage for Deres søn!
BROVIK: Træde tilbage fra aftalen, mente de.
SOLNESS: Å, det kommer jo ud på *et.* (p. 38)

SOLNESS: And these plans, are they pleased with them? The people who are going to live there?

BROVIK: Yes. As long as you're ready to look them over and approve them ...

SOLNESS: And they would get Ragnar to build their home for them?

BROVIK: They liked his ideas very much indeed. They felt they were getting something quite new, they said.

SOLNESS: Aha! *New!* Not the sort of old-fashioned rubbish *I* generally build!

BROVIK: They thought it was somehow *different.*

SOLNESS: (*with suppressed bitterness*) So it was Ragnar they came to see – while I was out!

BROVIK: They came to talk to you. To ask if you might be willing to withdraw.....

SOLNESS: (*flaring up*). Withdraw! Me!

BROVIK: As long as you felt that Ragnar's drawings ...

SOLNESS: I! – Withdraw in favour of your son!

BROVIK: Withdraw from the agreement, they meant.

SOLNESS: It comes to the same thing! (p. 362)

We have learned so much here: that Ragnar is capable of impressing, and therefore of succeeding in, the world outside the office quite independently from Solness: that Solness is terrified that this might be the case, and less for business reasons than for psycho-existential ones; that Ragnar's full professional debut would mark for him the start of his own unstoppable decline, if only because accepting it would deal his *amour propre* such a hard blow. Solness remains adamant in his stance, taking the young couple's satisfaction in Ragnar's designs as some kind of judgement against himself, an indicator that he is – what he dreads more than anything – finally out of date. The words 'new' and 'different' which Brovik has, maybe knowingly, quoted, anguish him. And we should, even at this point, begin to ask ourselves what these adjectives would mean when applied to a villa for a young couple with whom its designer is personally friendly...

Even when Solness (and with genuine feeling) appreciates just how ill Old Brovik is, and how desperately he would like positive proof of his son's abilities, he is obdurate. Ragnar, he says, lacks proper competence beyond his undoubted ability to draw. Brovik is moved to a sarcastic reply:

(*ser med lønligt had på ham og siger hest*) *De* havde heller ikke lært stort af faget dengang De stod i tjeneste hos mig. Men De la' i vej lige fuldt, Ed. (*drager vejret tungt*) Og slog Dem op. Og tog luven både fra mig og – og fra så mange andre. (p. 37)

(*looks at him with suppressed hatred and says hoarsely*) You hadn't learned much about the business either, when you were working for me. But that didn't stop you from launching out. (*Breathing with difficulty*) Or from getting on. You went and left me standing ... And a lot of other people as well. (p. 361)

The history Brovik refers to still causes Halvard Solness discomfort, and it is worth clarifying at this juncture, since it contains the germs of the later action – inside the office and beyond it. It can be seen as a history with only one possible outcome: Solness' final fall from the tower.

He came from a poor, pious, rural background of which he seems proud even now. At some time when still young – his age can't be precisely estimated – he went to work for Knut Brovik in that man's architect's practice. It would seem from the outburst quoted above that he didn't show himself as outstanding in any particular way, though doubtless he was intelligent about what he undertook, and always had energy. At any rate he proved himself competent enough to be entrusted with major church-building, church-restoration projects. And then the watershed event occurred, about which Solness, both tragic victim and triumphant beneficiary, will ever afterwards ask himself: Why? *Why should it have happened to me?*

Socially Solness had made a good marriage, to Aline. The two of them lived in an old house on a hillside above Solness' present property, which they inherited from Aline's mother. Now we are truly entering the world of Ibsen's curious initiatory lyric, though Dr Herdal calls their former home 'den gamle fæle røverborgen' (p. 51) (that ghastly old fortress of a house; p. 374). But it was pleasant and cosy inside. Here the couple lived for five years or so, and here they began a family.

When their babies, twin boys, were only three weeks old, the disaster – fire, Skien's destroyer – struck. It broke out in a cupboard but spread rapidly. The rescue operations were successful; everybody was carried to safety, but Aline soon was running a fever consequent on the bitter cold and the strain. She insisted she went on feeding her babies, who both died from her germ-contaminated milk.

The accident however gave Solness the business opportunity he had for some while been looking for. With the house gone he could divide the land on which it had stood into lots, and sell them, making good money, so much indeed that he could use it to quit Brovik's practice and start out on his own – exactly as Ragnar Brovik now wants to do. And this he did and discovered formidable abilities in himself. Before long he became the locality's leading builder/architect.

But no longer of churches. About two years after the tragedy Solness completed commissioned work on the church of a fjord-town called here Lysanger. A traditional ceremony was staged in which he, as its builder, was asked to place a wreath on top of the tower. Though suffering as usual from vertigo, Solness was able to carry out this ritual to the full because he found the confidence, up there on the church's highest point, to make a solemn vow to the God of his pious childhood:

> Og da jeg stod helt der øverst oppe og hang kransen over tårnfløjen, så sa' jeg til ham: Hør nu her, du mægtige! Herefterdags vil jeg være fri bygmester, jeg også. På mit område. Ligesom du på dit. Jeg vil aldrig mere bygge kirker for dig. Bare hjem for mennesker. (p. 117)

> And as I stood there on high, at the very top, and as I hung the wreath on the weathercock, I spoke to Him: Listen to me, Almighty One. From this day forward, I too will be free. A master builder free in his own field, as you are in yours. Never again will I build churches for you. Only homes for people. (p. 439)

By a sublime and pervasive irony Solness' dedication to his work as builder will be every bit as unremitting as any devotee's to his church faith. Indeed we may find it hard to distinguish between the two. Likewise the opponent of the 'all or nothing' religion of Lammers and Brand (Ibsen himself) applied the same maxim to his writing, to which he gave everything, cutting himself from his blood-family, cutting himself off from his native country, keeping to an awesome daily regimen, always working in his head even when not working on paper – and then going over and over what he'd produced until he felt it was absolutely right.

Whatever the metaphysical implications of his defiance, Solness' choice of houses over churches displayed excellent professional judgement of a kind the more hidebound Knut Brovik would not have dared. (One assumes, then, that church-building and restoration of monuments had been his own firm's main concern.) The economic and social climate was clearly propitious for private dwellings; consequently Solness flourished.

> Ene og alene ved den branden blev jeg sat i stand til at bygge hjem for mennesker. Hyggelige, lune, lyse hjem, hvor far og mor og hele barneflokken kunde leve i tryg og glad fornemmelse af at det er en svært lykkelig ting, det, at være *til* i verden. Og mest det, at høre hverandre til – så'n i stort og småt. (p. 82)

> That fire, and that alone, was the thing that gave me the chance to build homes. Warm, cheerful, comfortable homes, where fathers and mothers and their children could live together, secure and happy, and feeling that it's good to be alive. And more than anything to belong to each other – in great things and in small. (p. 411)

Meanwhile, for all the architect's trained expertise, Brovik's business began to go downhill, descending eventually into bankruptcy. Certainly Solness must have pursued clients and contracts determinedly and won where Brovik lost, equally certainly Brovik resented this. But it's important to note that, grumble though he does, hate him indeed though he surely does, old Brovik never suggests any ethical impropriety on Solness' part, nor does Ragnar, who dislikes him even more strongly. The triumph of the builder and the failure of the older architect are attributable to other factors than malpractice, though the contemplation of these may not be any the less disturbing for this fact. Solness says to Hilde:

> Havde gamle Knut Brovik ejet huset, så var det aldrig i verden brændt så belejligt for *ham*. Det er jeg så sikker på. (p. 88)

> If old Knut Brovik had owned the house, it would never have burned down quite so conveniently for *him*, I'm quite certain of that. (p. 411)

Is he speaking of blind Fortune? Of good luck? Of his own strength of will-power? Of the eventual Darwinian victory of the naturally gifted

over the merely intelligent and industrious? Or of the operation, on
people, on material objects, of components of the psyche, arcane and
undetectable 'hjelpere og tjenere' (helpers and servants) who dwell
within but can act without? (A sort of internalisation of the guardian
angels of the Christian tradition.) Solness pours out his misgivings about
the relationship between self and success more fully to Hilde, emanation
of youth, personification of all in the female that is alluring and
indispensable to the male, than he ever has done to anybody else, even
the valued family doctor. And as he does this, we can't but reflect that he
did not really leave his religion behind on top of Lysanger church.
Rigorous moral self-examination is as habitual to him now, if
compulsively, as ever it was in his pious youth:

> SOLNESS: Hvem ropte på hjælperne og tjenerne? Det gjorde *jeg*! Og så
> kom de og føjed sig under min vilje. (*i stigende oprør.*) Det er *det*, som
> godtfolk kalder at ha' lykken med sig. Men jeg skal sige Dem, jeg, hvorledes
> den lykken kendes! Den kendes som et stort, hudløst sted her på brystet. Og
> så går hjælperne og tjenerne og flår hudstykker af andre mennesker for at
> lukke *mit* sår! – Men såret heles ikke endda. Aldrig, – aldrig! Å, om De
> vidste, hvor det kan suge og svie iblandt. (p. 89)

> SOLNESS: Who called on the helpers and servants? *I* did. And they came
> and did my bidding. (*In rising excitement*). That's what people call being
> lucky. But let me tell you what that sort of luck feels like! It feels as if my
> breast were a great expanse of raw flesh. And these helpers and servants go
> flaying off skin from other people's bodies to patch *my* wound. Yet the
> wound never heals ... Never! Oh, if only you knew how it sometimes burns
> and throbs. (p. 412)

Nor can Solness now appease all these tormenting doubts of his – though
he tries to do just this – by bringing to mind how he came to the rescue
of his former boss in his insolvency, and gave him, and his clever son
Ragnar, regular and well-paid posts. For he is under no delusion about
his daily dependence on them.

> For de er i grunden et par flinke fyrer, de to, ser De. De har evner, hver på
> sin måde. Men så fandt sønnen på at forlove sig. Og så, naturligvis, så
> skulde han til at gifte sig, – og begynde at bygge selv ... Men det kunde jo
> ikke *jeg* være tjent med. For jeg havde jo selv brug for Ragnar. Og for den

gamle også. Han er nu så svært flink til beregninger af bæreevne og kubikindhold ... (pp. 46-47)

Because actually they are both pretty clever, you know. They both have ability, in their different ways. But then the son took it into his head to get engaged. And then., of course, he began thinking of getting married – and of setting up on his own as a builder ... But that didn't suit *my* book at all. I needed Ragnar myself. And the old man too. He's so extraordinarily clever at working out stresses and strains and cubic contents. (pp. 370-371)

The work in which the Broviks excel does not come so easily to Solness himself; he lacks the requisite education. For the Broviks to leave him, a distinct possibility while the son was displaying unmistakable signs of restlessness, would be highly prejudicial to the company. And then Solness had yet another stroke of luck. One day Ragnar's fiancée called in at the office, and the master builder at once appreciated the intensity of their mutual love. If only he could get Kaja to work alongside him, he need not worry about Ragnar's leaving. And sure enough Kaja herself came round to see him the very next day and, strangely, talked as though there were an actual place for her in Solness' offices, book-keeping. It was as if she'd sensed his will and obeyed it. With one difference, however; Kaja had transferred her capacity of devotion onto Solness himself, and to keep her (and Ragnar) where he wants them, the master builder has to play her along.

None of these memories and speculations, none of his angst, makes Solness any more sympathetically inclined to the young man whose present position is so similar to his own past one. If anything they make him *less* sympathetic, so inclined is he to consider himself a unique favourite of Fate. As he tells Hilde '*fortrolig*', '*confidentially*':

Tror ikke De også det, Hilde, at der findes enkelte udkårne, udvalgte mennesker, som har fåt nåde og magt og evne til at *ønske* noget, *begære* noget, *ville* noget – så ihærdigt og så – så ubønhørligt – at de må få det tilslut. Tror De ikke det? (p. 88)

Don't you believe too, Hilde, that you find certain people have been singled out, specially chosen, gifted with the power and the ability to *want* something, to *desire* something, to *will* something ... so insistently ... and so ruthlessly ... that they will inevitably get it in the end? Don't you believe that? (p. 411)

But why should not this apply equally to Ragnar Brovik, long though he has taken to assert himself? And by the end of the play it surely does. Ragnar will surely also think, after his success over the Løvstrand villa, that he has justified his years of figure-stooping patience, that he was in fact all along a favourite of Fortune, destined for success. And, like Solness before him, the Philoctetes legend will apply to him: the bow of his creativity will be activated by the wound of his guilt over the Master Builder's death. For he will half-believe himself to have *willed* this, through his pent-up resentment and his need to be free. He, no less than Hilde Wangel, drove Solness up that tower.

To return to office business.

Solness' attitude to Ragnar's drawings for his friends' villa is so slightingly lofty that we may initially be tempted to doubt the younger man's abilities. Perhaps they're just a fond father's hope. Perhaps any signatory endorsement of the plans by Solness – whether or not he agrees actually to give it – would be primarily a matter of kindness, of his remembering past obligations rather than his being true to his real professional opinion. Any such thoughts disappear the moment Act Two begins – on the morning of the following day. Once again we encounter the silence of concentration; once again we are given the spectacle of an informed mind at work which we can carry with us through the rest of the act. Solness has not only opened Ragnar Brovik's folder of plans for the Løvstrand villa, he is examining the drawings inside it with great care. Thus we know that Ragnar has the needed (and dreaded) talent; the master builder would have quickly tossed them aside if they had been no good.

When Kaja questions him about the designs, he prevaricates – even though it's clear by now that old Brovik is dying. Later, when Hilde, observing the folder, asks about Ragnar, he says merely that he's a useful young man, one of the many who have been through his hands for training-up, not in itself a guarantee of talent. And when Ragnar actually appears and, swallowing his pride, begs for the endorsement that will lighten his father's last moments, then Solness' behaviour exhibits him at his basest (and this in a play permeated by heights and depths). He wants to hear nothing more about the drawings, he declares, will not say whether they're good or not, and yet implores Ragnar to stay on. And even when he makes the concession that Ragnar can tell his father what he likes, he will not utter any encouraging words. In his morally most contemptible moment he roughly tells Ragnar to take his drawings away.

His behaviour horrifies Hilde who witnesses it. And not merely because youth sympathises with youth. Her admiration of him, her elevation of him into hero – which requires a literal assumption of that position – sees this conduct as essentially self-betrayal, the fruit of Solness' mental agony. She intervenes and tells Ragnar to leave his folder where it is; she would like to see its contents. *This intervention is the turning-point of the whole play.*

When Ragnar has left the room, Hilde rebukes Solness in the strongest terms, accusations of deliberate cruelty and hardness of heart that hit home. Moved by them, Solness proceeds to deliver himself of his most painful long-guarded memories and thoughts. The release of these enables him to yield to Hilde's skilled and determined coaxing and finally write the necessary words of endorsement for Ragnar. Having them, the young draughtsman can – and will – start work on the villa out at Løvstrand, and thus begin his career on his own account.

The play, seen as a whole, vindicates Solness in his fear of Ragnar. The endorsement of him triggers an irreversible movement in Solness' psyche which will lead him to that fatal ascent of the tower: Ragnar will take the place Solness once occupied among the architect/builders of the day, and he must dedicate himself to some other ambition.

Why, we legitimately ask ourselves, this fear and, even more pressing, why this vindication of it? What can Ragnar as fledgling architect do that Solness, an energetic man still of experience and esteem, cannot? The answers are all there in the text.

The subject of threat from the younger generation caused contemporary readers and playgoers to draw parallels here with Ibsen's coming under attack from younger writers like Knut Hamsun[10] – from *him* especially! Hamsun had the temerity in the autumn of 1891 to deliver three lectures attacking the revered playwright, which Ibsen attended with interest, later assuring people that he was not in the least afraid of the young. Hamsun's criticism was basically that Ibsen was far too preoccupied with social issues and consequently deficient in understanding of the unconscious mind. Hindsight makes this accusation seem preposterous: with what are *Rosmersholm* and *The Lady from the Sea* concerned if not the unconscious mind, though its interplay with – or against – the conscious life of organised society is always vitally important? Nor is it hard to trace Ibsen's interest in this right back to the early historical plays. Furthermore, to retaliate, when we turn to the novel which Hamsun offered the reading public the following year, *Mysterier* (*Mysteries*, 1892) as a model of what new writing should be, we find the relationship of the central character to the well-delineated coastal community in which he is a stranger to be of pivotal significance. Nevertheless we have to concede that a fair portion of Ibsen's massive reputation at home and abroad, and nowhere more so than in Britain,[11] was that of social diagnostician, and that this aspect of his art seems to have overwhelmed many of his contemporaries. But it does seem possible to say now that with *The Master Builder* the male protagonist, henceforward at the centre of our attentions, experiences tremendous demands from his unconscious which his relationship to society cannot meet, and this to a degree surpassing anything in Ibsen's earlier work. So there was a measure of response to Knut Hamsun after all.

Certainly there was the liveliest public interest in what in *The Master Builder* was personal, not to say autobiographical. These speculating readers and theatre-goers were, however, able to take more or less for granted what we, for obvious reasons, cannot: the architectural dimension of the work. They knew Christiania, its newer buildings and all the plans in progress, from their own daily lives, and therefore, without violence to their understanding of the play, could absorb its dynamic use of architecture even while ferreting out references to the author's own life and situation. Gossip about the spells that various young girls – Emilie Bardach, Hélène Raff, Hildur Andersen – had cast, Hilde-like, over the Norwegians' most senior playwright only seemed to validate biographical inquiries. As further knowledge of Ibsen's private life has continued to do, so that this work has too often been taken as a kind of 'Portrait of the Artist as an Elderly Man'.

But I believe we should look at the play the other way about, that we should take it for what it is, as announced in the title, a study of an architect and the assault on his powers occurring in the Norway of his day. If we do this, the play, so intricately worked, offers a richness of harvest unsurpassed even in Ibsen's own oeuvre. We can apply what we have garnered to Ibsen if we like – to his marriage, his status as a Grand Old Man, his reputation, his friendships with young girls – but we can also apply it more universally, since it is in universals that the play deals.

3.

After discharging his commission in Lysanger, Solness' career radically changed. He must indeed have worked on a good many churches before; there would be little point in his abjuration on the tower were this not the case. About what he did at Lysanger Solness is quite specific; recalling that he has indeed met Hilde Wangel before, he speaks of 'Den sommer, da jeg var der og bygged tårn på *den gamle kirken*' (p. 53) (The summer I was up there building a tower on *the old church*; my italics, p. 376)

As its completion was marked with lavish civic celebrations (a translation surely of those that Ibsen had been invited to, but missed, in Skien), we deduce that Solness was responsible for either the repair of, or an important addendum to, an old building much venerated in the locality. Ibsen scholar Eivind Tjønneland has, in an interesting essay,[12] investigated Norwegian legends about tower-builders on which Ibsen may have drawn, just as he did on fjordland tales about sailors in *The Lady from the Sea*. Tjønneland reminds us that Ibsen's old friend the art-historian, Lorenz Dietrichson,[13] whom he knew in Rome, and with whom, after a long breach, he was reconciled in 1891, brought out later that year his authoritative study of Norway's stave churches; Ibsen, it appears, had already read an article by him on this subject in 1888. And Dietrichson's book had an illustrious predecessor in that of 1837 by the leading Norwegian romantic painter, Johan Christian Dahl (1788-1857). Tjønneland has done us a valuable service in bringing stave churches to our attention in relation to *The Master Builder*. But in addition to the tales that have accrued round them, they have, I believe, an *architectural/historical* significance essential to the work read as a whole.

Their stave churches are Norwegians' most remarkable architectural inheritance, and infinitely precious to the rest of us, since their artistic ambition is realised in *timber*. Christianity coming late to Norway, between 995 and 1030 CE, these churches are, by European continental or British standards, not remarkable in terms of sheer age. But in fact the method by which they were constructed reaches back to (though is a considerable sophistication of) original Viking practice – of splitting logs, ramming them into the ground to form walls, and putting up a roof over these. They usually stand on the sites of Viking holy places, in high, open, prominent spots. The earliest attempts at church-building have not survived: the two earliest intact examples, both in the Sogn and Fjordane district, Urnes and Borgund, date from 1150, but beautiful Rødven in Møre og Romsdal was built between 1150 and 1200.

The staves after which the churches are named are long timber pillars, resting on a stone sill on the ground and serving as corner-posts. A skeleton of wooden planks is placed between them, and some churches have also a high stave, a mast, in the very middle; this supports a tower or spire, which in these cases itself stands at the central point of the building. 'Mast' is an appropriate term, for the Viking transferred boat-building techniques to their more important constructions on land. Looked at from inside, the roof of a stave church resembles nothing more than an upturned Viking ship, its ribbing repeated in the row of arches positioned within the row of rafters. Viking culture is also reflected in the decoration, usually intricate, particularly in the entrance-ways, and often employing a dragon motif; indeed another name for them is 'dragon-churches'. Increasingly, however, the carved-wood illustrations in the churches reflected and represented both the opposition of Viking and Christian religious symbols and the victorious superiority of the latter. Stave churches have been acclaimed 'the West's only temples in wood', and there is something pagoda-like about them. The shingled roofs succeed each other all the way up to a high point, tower or spire, often capped by a weather-vane (as Lysanger church, we know, was), their eaves broad and dragon-adorned. Dahl mentions the dragon as a notable feature in his 1837 study.

At one time Norway had as many as twelve hundred stave churches; now there are only twenty-nine. The eighteenth century had treated them with disregard, and the nineteenth only too frequently chose to replace them with 'modern' churches (on which, of course, Solness may also have worked). Nevertheless in 1844 a Society for the Preservation of Ancient Monuments, still in existence today, was founded with the safeguarding of stave churches in mind. Later men like Dietrichson and the architect Peter Blix did their best to make Norwegians wake up to their priceless heritage, but the fate of that at Ål was only too typical: the stave church there was pulled down in the 1880s to make room for a new church, its fine timber vaulting becoming an exhibit at the University Museum of Antiquities in Oslo.

If we look at the distribution of the surviving stave churches, we note that eleven are in Oppland which includes Gudbrandsdal, the quarry for, and original home of *Peer Gynt*; five, including the two oldest and most famous, in the Sognefjord area, where Ibsen collected folk-tales; and two in his native Telemark. Tjønneland thinks that, during his folklorist expeditions, Ibsen gained knowledge of stories of church-builders who made bargains with supernatural forces to ensure the completion of their work, and who hear on high places the music of the supernatural *huldrefolk*, probably the proto-type of the harp-players that Hilde Wangel hears on both of Solness' ascents. But we have also to remember what we explored in the chapter on *The Lady from the Sea*; that Hilde lived in a town Ibsen based largely on Molde. In Molde's province of Møre og Romsdal there are three stave churches: Grip, which situated on an island, obviously doesn't offer itself as a candidate, Kvernes (which indeed had a tower built on it during the nineteenth century, though as far back as 1810) and Rødven, whose antiquity and loveliness of setting commend it.

If we see 'den gamle kirken', 'the old church', on which Solness has worked as one of these stave churches preserving Viking-style carvings, we surely have a valuable key to what is perhaps the most arresting (and in some respects the most puzzling) feature of his converse with Hilde ten years after his commission had been discharged: their ability to relate to each other imaginatively, in interlinking mental worlds. At a crucial point in their dialogue they enter together the domain of the Vikings. To Solness' confession of inner torment, that he may somehow have connived at the misfortunes which promoted his own success, Hilde replies that maybe his conscience is perhaps a little over-delicate, too prone to strain; shouldn't it be more 'robust'? This encourages Solness to remark that both Hilde and himself have 'trolls' from Viking lore inside them, in league with dark forces and operating beneath the line of ordinary morality. He goes on to ask her whether she has read any Viking sagas, and indeed, when younger, she had done:

> SOLNESS: I sagabøgerne står der om vikinger, som sejled til fremmede lande og plyndred og brændte og slog mænd ihjæl –
> HILDE: Og fanged kvinder – ...
> SOLNESS: Jo, for *de* karene, *de* havde robust samvittighed, de! Når de kom hjem igen så kunde de både æde og drikke. Og glade som barneunger var de også. Og kvinderne da! De vilde mangengang sletikke ifra dem igen. Kan De skønne sligt, Hilde? (p. 91)

> SOLNESS: The sagas are all about the Vikings who sailed to foreign lands and plundered and burned and killed ...
> HILDE: And carried off women ...
> SOLNESS: Ah, yes. Those fellows now – they had robust consciences all right. They hadn't lost any of their appetite when they got home. Happy as children they were, too. As for the women – very often they wouldn't hear tell of leaving them. Can you understand that sort of thing, Hilde? (pp. 413-414)

Yes, Hilde can understand this perfectly. Should we see her in pagan terms, knowing an ecstasy free from ethical considerations? No! One of the keenest and most resonant ironies of the play is that only a minute or so after this interchange, elaborated (like some wooden vault in an old church) by further 'pagan' images – devils, forest-birds and the rising sun – Hilde succeeds in the seemingly impossible, in getting Solness to endorse those drawings of Ragnar's, so undoing his years-long unkindness to his employee as well as the cruelty he had just shown him. He is set free, and, with him, the play's one example of 'a captive young woman', Kaja Fosli (though doubtless Aline had also been this earlier). The robust conscience that puts attainment of one's strongest wishes above all other considerations is not enough to live by, it would seem; it leaves (possibly latent) moral aspirations unsatisfied. And we have already observed that Hilde's words of persuasion are for Solness his Rubicon.

Similarly we may find ourselves in a stave church and be transfixed by what this art-form has conserved of the ancient Vikings, the imaginative boldness, the challenging artistry, the relics of a *Weltanschauung* that gives daring and courage the highest valuation. Nevertheless we are in a Christian building, whatever reminders we have of an earlier religion; it was the Christian faith that brought it into being, and that has sustained it through the many subsequent centuries. And however inadequately realised, however shot through with other more dubious elements and ambiguities, with power-lust, with ideas of divine retribution, the denials of human pluralism, this faith has differed from others in accentuating qualities very different from those Solness has remembered from the sagas – forgiveness, mercy, compassion, love, even self-sacrifice. And though he may sign Ragnar's drawings with great reluctance and give the folder containing them back to Kaja with a regrettable hardness of face, voice and words, it is in fact these qualities that Solness is (knowingly) serving when he performs these actions. Solness may have spurned one of God's faces – his mighty Jehovah's whom Lammers/Brand honoured – but not all of them; denial anyway is never that simple. Nor can any adequate judgement on a religion or culture be so simple either. The Vikings after all, however tougher over some things than ourselves, were not just plunderers and abducters of women, their art was sufficiently sophisticated to be adapted for the beautification of Christian churches. And of course they created the Icelandic sagas, one of the first major prose literatures of the world, presenting people in ways that remarkably anticipate the novelists and dramatists of the modern era, their pasts, their tensions, their daily lives as well as their defining deeds; Ibsen admired them intensely, citing them as one of the greatest influences on his own work.

Annexation of Vikings to Christian tradition preoccupied many nineteenth-century historians and clergymen throughout Scandinavia. Bishop Grundtvig (1783-1872), who was both, and one of the great founders of modern Danish society, stressed the line of continuation between the Norse myths and the Christian world-picture, in a manner which recalls Erasmus' blessing of Greek civilization from a Christian standpoint ('*Saint* Socrates!' Erasmus famously declared). For Grundtvig and other Nordic nationalists pride in the Norse inheritance was a way of further separating their Christianity from any tradition that had come through the Roman Catholic Church; there was felt to be in Northern mythology a sort of Protestantism *avant la lettre*.

If Solness the man combines Viking strength-of-will and stubbornness with a Christian introspection that will always eventually cause him, even if reluctantly, to *re*consider instinctual heroic stances, and pay attention to the feelings and needs of others, Solness master builder/architect also demonstrates this (uneasy but highly individual) fusion of cultures. Here is the first conversation that Solness and Hilde have on the subject of his work:

> SOLNESS: ... Alvorlig talt, – hvorfor er De kommen? Hvad vil De egentlig gøre her?
>
> HILDE: Å, for det første så vil jeg gå omkring og sé på alt det, som De har bygget.
>
> SOLNESS: Da får De mere end nok at løbe om efter.
>
> HILDE: Ja, De har jo bygget så forfærdelig meget.
>
> SOLNESS: Jeg har det. Mest i de senere årene.
>
> HILDE: Mange kirketårne også? Så'ne umådelig høje?
>
> SOLNESS: Nej. Jeg bygger ingen kirketårne nu mere. Og ingen kirker heller.
>
> HILDE: Hvad bygger De *nu* da?
>
> SOLNESS: Hjem for mennesker.
>
> HILDE: (*eftertenksom*) Kunde De ikke gøre lidt - lidt så'n kirketårn over de hjemmene også?
>
> SOLNESS: (*studser*) Hvad mener De med *det*?
>
> HILDE: Jeg mener, – noget, som peger – ligesom frit tilvejrs. Med fløjen så svimlende højt oppe.
>
> SOLNESS: (*grubler lidt*). Mærkværdig nok, at De siger *det*. For det er jo netop det, jeg allerhelst vilde.
>
> HILDE: (*utålmodig*) Men hvorfor *gør* De det så ikke da!
>
> SOLNESS: (*ryster på hodet*) Nej, for menneskene vil ikke ha' det.
>
> HILDE: Tænk, – at de ikke vil det!
>
> SOLNESS: (lettere). Men nu bygger jeg mig et nyt hjem. Her lige over for.
>
> HILDE: Til Dem selv?
>
> SOLNESS: Ja. Det er omtrent færdigt. Og på *det* er der et tårn.
>
> HILDE: Højt tårn?
>
> SOLNESS: Ja.
>
> HILDE: Svært højt?

SOLNESS: Folk vil visst si' at det er altfor højt. For et hjem at være.

HILDE: Det tårnet vil jeg ud og sé på straks imorgen tidlig. (pp. 63-64)

SOLNESS: ... Seriously – why have you come? What in fact do you want here?

HILDE: Oh, first I want to go round and look at all the things you've built.

SOLNESS: That's going to keep you pretty busy.

HILDE: Yes, I know you've built an awful lot.

SOLNESS: I have. Especially in recent years.

HILDE: Many church towers, too? Great high ones, I mean?

SOLNESS: No, I don't build church towers any more. Nor churches either.

HILDE: What do you build now, then?

SOLNESS: Homes for people.

HILDE: (*pensively*) Couldn't you ... try putting some kind of tower on them too?

SOLNESS: (*starts*) What do you mean by that?

HILDE: I mean ... Something pointing ... Right up into the air. With a weathercock on top at a great dizzy height.

SOLNESS: (*muses a little*). Strange you should say that. That's what I want to do more than anything.

HILDE: (*impatiently*) Then why don't you?

SOLNESS: (*shakes his head*). Because people don't want that.

HILDE: Fancy not wanting it!

SOLNESS: (*in a lighter vein*) But now I'm building a new house for myself. Just across the way here.

HILDE: For yourself?

SOLNESS: Yes. It's just about ready. And *it's* got a tower.

HILDE: A high tower?

SOLNESS: Yes.

HILDE: Very high?

SOLNESS: People are sure to say it's too high. For a house.

HILDE: I'll be out first thing in the morning to see that tower. (pp. 387-358)

What he says here to Hilde is strangely ambiguous, almost evasive. He tells her that he has been very productive 'especially in recent years', which means, obviously, *after* he had taken the Broviks into his firm. His doing so enabled him to leave mathematical calculations to them, and concentrate on what he himself could do best – getting commissions from clients with good positions and money, planning the outward appearance of the buildings, for which he seems to have had quite an eye, and attending to the practicalities of their construction. 'Homes for people' has been for ten years his concern; a-top Lysanger church he vowed to build 'warm, cheerful and comfortable' homes, partly because these do not connect to worship of an exigent God, partly to give himself vicarious experience of what had so terribly been taken from him.

'Warm, cheerful and comfortable homes' – it is difficult to associate these with the Solness we know, but ... When telling Hilde about his and Aline's first home he says of it (echoing Dr Herdal's words earlier):

> Det var en stor, styg, mørk trækasse at sé til udvendig. Men nokså lunt og hyggeligt inde alligevel. (p. 79)

> It was a great, ugly barn of a place to look at. But it was pretty cosy and comfortable inside. (p. 402)

'Lunt og hyggelig' – back we go to the lyric poem from which Ibsen dated work on this play. The inference is clear – the ugliness of the exterior is immaterial, the interior expressed the unselfish pleasures and rewards of married love, of bringing a young family into the world, and so was pleasing in itself. The spirit in which a work of art is made, whether church or living-room, is all-determining. Solness' words, with, behind them, a touching longing for the happier past, stand in grim ironic contrast to his present house which does not, well-appointed though it is, manage to be a home. (And this opposition between 'house' and 'home' recurs in *When We Dead Awaken*, in dialogue between Maja and Rubek.) No more of a home will the new villa be, as Aline herself appreciates. Why not? Because of the scale of the tragedy the Solnesses had endured? Maybe so – but if this were the only explanation, Solness would at least have created houses suggesting and promoting happiness, yet successful though he has been, we are given no indication that he has accomplished this. In fact towards the end of the play this is his own opinion of his productions.

The last third of the nineteenth century, with increased prosperity all over Europe, was a period in which *Gemütlichkeit* flourished as never before, in Norway included. The paintings of Gustav Wentzel (1859-

1927) from the 1880s show this; such delightful pieces as 'Frukost I' (Breakfast I, 1881) and 'Frukost II' (Breakfast II, 1885), both now in the Nasjonalgalleriet in Oslo, are studies of the young artist's own family, from the *artisanat*, living simply and amiably, at ease with one another as they sit round the breakfast-table, father reading a newspaper, one schoolboy son giving his lesson-book a final look-over, another drinking coffee from his saucer, while beyond charmingly curtained windows we can see a city street and church. A table-lamp and the early morning sun streaming through the window irradiate a domestic harmony that is neither self-conscious or exclusive. It's hard to see that Solness' work – catering as it would be for people with far more money than the Wentzels – would encourage such a scene.

It is obvious from that conversation with Hilde that Solness' tastes strongly incline towards the decorated, the dramatic, even the florid. He doesn't find Hilde's request for a tower in the least surprising, though he does say that 'people' don't all appear to find his own super-adventurous addendum to his new villa palatable. In fact some of them disapprove. But clearly a man capable of championing and building for himself such a deliberate architectural extravaganza is unlikely to have put his energies to the building of plain homes that work from the interior outwards rather than vice versa.

Here it is important to recall his church-building past. Whatever the words he addressed to God up in Lysanger, he did not leave behind on the church-tower either his sense of a divinity or of the style, Viking and Viking-Christian, which hitherto had served it. In this he embodies the whole move forward of the nineteenth-century aesthetic, above all in architecture, which had to find secular homes for what had formerly been emblems of faith (just as railway stations, banks, libraries, hospitals had increasingly to take the place of the churches themselves). Solness' later account (to Hilde, his only true confidante) of the transition in his career is impressive in its honesty, a quality that will characterise him more and more as he advances towards death.

> SOLNESS: ... De véd jo at det første, jeg begyndte med, det var med kirkebygninger.
> HILDE: (*nikker*) Det véd jeg godt.
> SOLNESS: For jeg, sér De, jeg var som gut gåt ud fra et fromt hjem på

landsbygden. Og derfor så syntes jeg jo at dette kirkebyggeriet, det var det værdigste, jeg kunde vælge.

HILDE: Ja-ja.

SOLNESS: Og det tør jeg nok si' at jeg bygged disse her små, fattige kirkerne med et så ærligt og varmt og inderligt sind at – at –

HILDE: At – ? Nå?

SOLNESS: Ja, at jeg synes, han burde været fornøjet med mig.

HILDE. *Han*? Hvilken *han*?

SOLNESS: Han, som skulde ha' kirkene, vel! Han, som de skulde tjene til ære og pris for.

HILDE: Nå så! Men er De da viss på at – at han ikke var – så'n – fornøjet med Dem?

SOLNESS: (*hånlig*) Han fornøjet med *mig*! Hvor kan De snakke så, Hilde? Han, som gav troldet i mig lov til at rumstére slig, som det selv vilde. Han, som bød dem være på pletten både nat og dag for at tjene mig, – alle disse – disse –

HILDE: Dævlerne –

SOLNESS: Ja, både den ene og den anden slags. Å nej, jeg fik nok føle at han ikke var fornøjet med mig. (*hemmelighedsfuldt.*) Se, derfor var det egentlig at han lod det gamle huset brænde.

HILDE: Var det derfor?

SOLNESS: Ja, skønner De ikke det? Han vilde, jeg skulde få lejlighed til at bli' en hel mester på mit område – og bygge så meget ærefuldere kirker for ham. I førstningen forstod jeg ikke, hvor han vilde hen. Men så med én gang gik det op for mig.

HILDE: Hvad tid var det?

SOLNESS: Der var da jeg bygged kirketårnet oppe i Lysanger. (pp. 116-117)

SOLNESS: ... You know that I first began by building churches.

HILDE: (*nods*) I know that.

SOLNESS: You see, I was brought up in a God-fearing home out in the country. That's why I thought building churches was the worthiest thing I could do.

HILDE: Yes, yes.

SOLNESS: And I think I can say that I built those humble little churches with such honesty and sincerity and devotion that ...

HILDE: Well?

SOLNESS: Well ... that I think He should have been pleased with me.

HILDE: He? Which he?

SOLNESS: He for whom the churches were intended, of course. He, whose honour and glory they were meant to serve.

HILDE: I see! But are you so sure that ... He wasn't ... pleased with you?

SOLNESS: (*scornfully*) *He* pleased with *me*! How can you say things like that, Hilde? He who has let loose this troll within me to rampage about as it will? He who bade them all be ready night and day to minister to me ... All these ... these ...

HILDE: Devils ...

SOLNESS: Yes, of both kinds. Oh no, I was soon made to realise that He wasn't pleased with me. (*Mysteriously.*) In fact, you know, that's why He let the old house burn down.

HILDE: Was that the reason?

SOLNESS: Yes, don't you see? He wanted to give me the chance of becoming a complete master of my craft, so that I could build ever more splendid churches for Him. At first I didn't understand what He was getting at. Then suddenly I realized.

HILDE: When was that?

SOLNESS: It was when I built that church tower at Lysanger. (pp 438-439)

Solness brings with him into his new life as civic architect both the baggage of the religion he has solemnly renounced – not because of doubts about God's existence but because of His nature as generally presented – and its artistic vocabulary as well. Just as the Gothic revival villas of English cities – North Oxford springs to mind – are Puginesque mock-ecclesiastical, their windows and doorways repeating the designs of the medieval church-masons, so Solness will have turned to the old churches for inspiration for the houses he was putting up, and in doing so was consistent with Norwegian colleagues/rivals. The last three decades of the nineteenth century and the early years of the twentieth century saw an ascendancy of the 'dragon' style the earlier proponents of which had been Romantic painters, Johan Christian Dahl, who had drawn attention to the importance of the dragon motif in stave churches, and Johannes Flintoe (1786-1870) who brought the dragon to Christiania, in his 1841 decorations for the Royal Palace. Archaeological finds from the Viking era, and the intensifying nationalism that these stoked, both brought a proliferation of dragons into the decorative arts in Norway – as ornaments in all manner of buildings public and private, in the frontispieces and on the bindings of books, particularly those dealing with antiquities, history and folk-lore, and on flags and banners (such as those Hilde waved at the festivities at Lysanger). The creatures became an emblem of Norwegianness, which accounts for their continuing popularity even after 1905 and the dissolution of the union with Sweden. And their widespread appearance is consonant with the general delight of the times in motifs from earlier cultures for the enhancement of their own.

The Arts and Crafts movement (which turned among other traditions to Japan – as in the work of Walter Crane) radiated out from Britain to influence designers all over the West and helped galvanise those schools of style to be known, somewhat further into the 1890s, variously as Art Nouveau, Jugendstil (this particular term dates from 1896 with the founding of the review *Die Jugend*), and, in Catalonia, as Modernista, where it attracted the flamboyant genius of Antonio Gaudí. Buildings vaunted elaborate ornamentation, were unafraid of Promethean challenge to norms, of stretching the possibilities of resources as far as they could go – Gaudí's audacious soaring cathedral in Barcelona, the wonderful Sagrada Familia, begun in 1884, was never completed. They also celebrated the craftsman's flourish, the beautifying detail included *for its own sake*. In part a reaction against mass-production, against the standardisation that industrialisation had everywhere enforced, these tendencies honoured the labour of human hands (of the old master builders, in other words) without shrinking from modern materials or techniques. Whether in institutional buildings or in private homes, they catered to the growing affluence of the European middle classes, and in their exuberance of invention, in the eclecticism of what they drew on, indicated a future of immeasurable expansion. It was for this reason that Art Nouveau, whatever its guise and name, did not survive the First World War.

There are respects in which Solness can be likened (though no more than that!) to one of the leading Norwegian architects of his day, Henrik Thrap-Meyer (1833-1910). He had studied in Bergen in the early 1860s, and designed churches – in Lillehammer, in Kristiansand (the cathedral) – but moved with the years more towards large-scale private and public works, many of which anticipate Art Nouveau buildings. His Bispegård (Bishop's Palace) built 1883-1884 is indeed a towered edifice. Perhaps Thrap-Meyer's most spectacular legacy to those who know Oslo today is the huge grandiose complex erected under his leadership called Viktoria Terrasse. The area known as Pipervika in which it was put up, had long been a notorious downtown slum much objected to by the haute bourgeoisie as a haunt of the indigent and criminal, and its tremendous façade reared itself up like a material statement by the superior class that order must be imposed on disorder. It was in Viktoria Terrasse, the semi-baronial towers and turrets of which would surely have pleased Hilde Wangel at her headiest, that the Ibsens took lease on a flat in August 1891. The place is thus intricately bound up with the growth of *The Master Builder*, and I would suggest that both its opulent splendour and its surroundings found their way into the play. (Completed later in the 1890s with the cooperation of a group of distinguished Norwegian architects, the building had, unfortunately, the proportions and the prominence that made it an obvious choice for the Nazi occupiers of Norway as headquarters of the dreaded Sicherheitspolizei, so imposing order of a different kind and by fouler means.)

Whatever one thinks of such creations – and our own aesthetic standards have, I think, moved too far away from them, both empirically and ideologically, for us to do them any adequate justice – what they most definitely are not is 'warm, cheerful and comfortable'; indeed they are about as distant from those conditions as – well, a church. As for the surroundings, there is surely no stage direction more significant to the play's overall meaning than that at the beginning of Act Three, dealing with the setting of Solness' new villa. '*I baggrunden begrænses haven af et gammelt pindegærde. Udenfor gærdet en gade med lave, forfaldne småhuse*' (p. 100) (In the background, the garden is bounded by an old wooden fence. Beyond the fence is a street with mean dilapidated cottages; p. 422). So this is what this man from a humble but pious background has achieved! – a stylistically ornate, not to say pretentious structure for the well-to-do with close at hand the inadequate homes of the conspicuously poor. No wonder then that despite his many career triumphs he can justify his wave of despondency to Hilde, shortly before he makes his fateful ascent, by saying of all he has produced :

> Ja, for nu ser jeg det. Menneskene har ikke brug for disse her hjemmene sine. Ikke for at være lykkelige, ikke. ... Se, *det* er hele opgøret, så langt, så langt jeg ser tilbage. Ingenting bygget igrunden. Og ingenting ofret for at få bygge noget heller. Ingenting, ingenting – altsammen. (p. 118)

> Because now I see that people have no use for these homes of theirs. It doesn't help them to be happy ... And now, looking back, what does it all add up to? In fact, I've built nothing. Nor did I sacrifice anything for the chance to build. Nothing! Absolutely nothing! (p. 439)

For how long has Solness held this view, and what made him come to this conclusion? Certainly one senses that this admission of ultimate failure to Hilde comes as an immense purgation to him, after months, maybe years, of pent-up doubts. The answer lies in his own interior world, just as – to be examined presently – the solution to successful home-building will inevitably lie in ensuring that interiors are comfortable and welcoming spaces, at once efficient enablers to harmonious contemporary living, and grateful to all the senses.

The 'fire-scarred' pair of Ibsen's little poem had, it will be recalled, a cosy home until disaster struck. Some deficiency in their relationship, in their outlook on life, prevented recovery from this. So with Solness and Aline. They too are 'fire-scarred'; they have never recovered from their tragedy of twelve-thirteen years before. Of course it was one of such tremendous dimensions that for anybody, irrespective of temperament or *Weltanschauung*, recovery would be hard, painful and never complete; this is why *The Master Builder*, in company with *The Wild Duck*, is one of the profoundest examinations of suffering ever made. But clearly all the evidence surrounding us from our earliest days, from both the natural and the human worlds, tells us that terrible things – even if their distribution is bewilderingly unpredictable and unjustly distributed – are inextricable from existence. Any 'philosophy' embraced to get us through life must fully have taken them into account, have prepared us so that we do not break when calamities, the like of which have visited our fellow-beings every hour of our lives, come our own way at last. The God of pietistic Evangelism, punishing those who have offended Him and rewarding those who have been obedient and 'loved' Him, is an inadequate Being for us to carry around through life, too little susceptible to the demands of human reason, and too aloof from human emotions and our need for affection and assurance. Small wonder then that Solness and Aline could not accommodate Him whom they had worshipped after the destruction of home and children, he turning to repudiation of God and of all outward monuments to Him, she to the crippling and fearful fulfilling of a narrow sense of duty, by which perhaps she may win herself back into His favour and understand why she was, as she doubtless sees it, singled out for such cruel occurrences.

Defiance – or challenge, if that word is more comfortable – is in itself a difficult, indeed a dangerous business, since it is inevitably more complex than those delivering it realise. In his riposte to God Solness is obliged to spurn what (apparently) sustained his own parents, his own community of early years, and beyond that his own country over centuries. In the Freudian terms so appropriate to the late Ibsen it administers such a blow to the Superego that the Ego is destabilised and therefore at the mercy of disruptions from the Id, all those trolls, devils, and maleficent helpers and servers to whose existence Solness so regularly testifies. Lammers at Skien therefore is still under attack in this late play. What he served was not so much a non-existent God as one defined by one of the more morally and psychologically dubious human attributes: the inclination, more, the desire, to serve and obey whatever the virtue or sense of the orders.

For all that it is only after first the fire, and next the episode on the church-tower that Solness knows success, spiritually he, no less than Aline, is destroyed – with the additional and painful burden of being able, unlike his wife, intellectually to appreciate this fact. What he has had recourse to, in compensation for what he has suffered, is his own energy: it is with this that he not only defies but rivals his old God. There would be no point in his turning his energies to 'worldly' achievement if he didn't look to the world of his times and see what it wanted, to find out what would harness his own talents and prove advantageous to him. The kind of building work that would bring him fame and fortune has already been adumbrated. He may indeed have told himself that his task would be now 'homes for people', but what they are, for himself and his clients, is 'homes for success'. This may be splendid for fiscal, material or social reasons, but from the point of view of psychic health it will prove disastrous. At some time or other all those former aspirations and ideals, deliberately suppressed in the interests of furthering status, will return to mock, and so they do to Solness. And so it is too that he will fall to his death off the literal physical acme of his architectural attainment, the one which most appealed to him personally, outdoing all appurtenances to villas of a similar kind, rivalling the churches he had given up on, a construction that has nothing whatever to say about democratic, psychologically satisfying living.

If Solness is of his time in his architectural practices and their uneasy transference of the religious to the secular, so he is in another respect. The years of the emergence and dominion of Art Nouveau were also years of obsessive preoccupation with the paranormal, with extra-sensory communication, spiritualism, visions, table-rappings, clairvoyants, with auras, astral planes, occult visitations, all the way from St. Petersburg (where, already in his masterpiece completed in 1877, *Anna Karenina*, Tolstoy shows Karenin and his circle of government high-ups only too vulnerable to the appeal of mystical arcana) to Boston, Massachusetts (see Henry James' *The Bostonians* of 1886 with its mordantly funny portrait of Verena Tarrant's 'inspirationalism'). Not until the New Age movements of the late 1980s and 1990s were such matters given wider-spread or more intensive attention. The Psychical Research Society was founded by Frederick Myers and Edmund Gurney in London in 1882; in 1875 Madame Blavatsky had inaugurated the Theosophical Society (in New York) and in 1889 teamed up with the Anglo-Irish Annie Besant, to proselytise for a system which saw this world as one beyond which many successive planes extended, of which knowledge, through developed special powers, could be attained. We should, I believe, view Solness in the context of these popular cultural preoccupations – which were those of Suzannah Ibsen and her friends. They throw light on the man *but not on him alone*. He becomes, seen thus, a convincing and individually realised representative of his times. For I think it a mistake to regard Solness' paranormal experiences and powers as anything very out-of-the-ordinary. It is his combination of energy, ambition, and ability to turn desires into concrete achievements that bring in money and reputation which is outstanding; a man of this kind will easily convert the events that have befallen him, the situations he has found himself in, and the wishes he has entertained into meaningful episodes of a unique autobiography. And this is exactly what Solness does, and to an attractive, excitable girl he wishes to impress at that.

Traditional religion converted the motions of the psyche and communications of an extra-rational, extra-sensory nature into manifestations of the Divine that could be ritualised and taken into their daily lives by the faithful. The Bible and all the many stories of the saints abound, after all, in dreams, portents, voices from heaven, miracles, apotheoses. In its pure forms scientific Darwinism could find no more room for these last than for religion itself, thus cutting inhabitants of modern society off from them, leaving them deprived of vital components of human (and, for that matter, animal) experience. (We have all watched animals dream.) It was left to psychoanalysis to find names and make definitions; until this happened it was a territory open for exploration – and appropriation – for all who refused to see existence in strictly materialist terms.

Once we have accepted, as surely everybody in western society does today, telepathic or non-verbal communication as a fact of existence, that it can defy the limits of geographical circumstance and cross the borders between the species, there is nothing that Solness tells us which cannot be paralleled in most lives. It is the size of his own ego, and of the position in society that this has enabled him to hold, which make them seem so significant, even eerie. To anticipate an event in fantasy (the fire), to be able to hold sway over another person, particularly if the dominant figure is a middle-aged man and the subject a young woman (Kaja, Hilde) – these seem remarkable principally to a society which having lost its religious structures needs others to house what in life defies rational explanation. There is no doubt that Solness – the strong man at his most vulnerable – is genuinely frightened, even appalled, as well as excited by the whole paraphernalia of devils, helpers and servants he has created. His psychic pantheon is the exact equivalent of all the dragons, turrets, towers which an age, frightened by its own secularism, sought to impose on public and private buildings, because it no longer had the requisite faith to put up churches or temples.

It is therefore possible to see Solness as, for all the weight of his years, still a seeker, still looking for and needing a framework for both feelings and ideas which external society cannot give him. His is, even though he is in his sixties, a very active mind, indeed a very active temperament, and it seems to him that Hilde can assist him towards what is lacking, even supply it. We must not altogether deny Solness a future, even though he denies himself one. As a builder with only a decade of house-building to his credit he has much still before him, and architecturally he stands, as we have seen, as yet in a vanguard, with the great Art Nouveau figures ahead still to prove themselves. But beyond this yet another future lies, and this Ragnar Brovik will serve. It is always thus: we live with two futures, the one arising out of the year we are living in, the other latent in it, and hidden from all except the most percipient – and the young.

We can be sure that whatever Ragnar designs – from the villa out at Løvstrand forward – will be conspicuously different from Solness' work. The very intensity of Ragnar's dislike of his old boss will see to that. What suppositions does Ibsen want us to make here?

We can but consider Løvstrand. The plans for the villa were something *new*. This was the attribute that appealed to the couple for whom they were made, a *young* couple too, which in itself sets us to thinking about the matter of starting a family and bringing up small children. What they would want would surely embody the ideal of the home in a way that the grandiosity of villas by Henrik Thrap-Meyer or Halvard Solness simply could never do; no room here for towers of any kind (Ragnar is thoroughly contemptuous of the whole consecration ceremony) or for any other appendices not justifiable by their practicality. Mindful of the disturbing contrast with the poor dwellings near Solness' villa, the architect would have comparatively modest plans, certainly ones completely free from ostentation. After all Solness put Ragnar's friends into the category of people that would make do with 'any old thing', in other words who eschewed the sort of vaunted elaborations he went in for.

'Form follows function'; 'architecture must be organic'; houses should work from the interior outwards, and the interiors should blend into the external surroundings of the house; an industrial age cannot turn its back on the machine but must press it into the most imaginative and creative use – these were the ideals of architects in Chicago, and though it is extremely unlikely that Ibsen knew the name Frank Lloyd Wright (1869-1959), he could well have known that of Wright's boss, Louis Sullivan (1856-1924), generally agreed to be the founder of the Chicago School and the first proselytiser of ideals that Wright was to make famous throughout the world, from Chicago to Tokyo to the Arizona desert. When Ragnar Brovik is working for Halvard Solness, Wright was working in Sullivan's firm, preparing designs for the Chicago Auditorium but also for many domestic houses. A year after *The Master Builder* was published, Wright built the famous Winslow House at River Forest which inspired the 'Prairie' houses, thus establishing a pattern for modern American living that spread well beyond the United States. It is, obviously, nothing more than a surmise, but Ragnar Brovik's homes would, I believe, have had much in common with these.

4.

There remains Hilde Wangel and with her the incontrovertible fact that Solness dies through trying to please her: doing her bidding, taking part in a rite more important to her, despite its tradition, than to anybody else on earth. In that poem 'Building Plans' the young Ibsen had imagined himself constructing a 'cloud-castle' in one of which lived a 'death-less' poet (his artists-to-come all the way from Peer Gynt to Halvard Solness?), in the other a young girl. The builder himself grows more reasonable – Apollonian – but as he does, the building itself turns 'crazy' – Dionysian, the great wing proving inadequate for the great poet it housed, the little wing (for the girl) collapsing. The poem reads now as an extraordinary crystallisation of what we find in *The Master Builder*. As in its predecessor *Hedda Gabler* the serene compassionate vision *sub specie aeternitatis* gives meaning and beauty to relationships and conduct that defy reason: a girl driving an elderly man, whose lover she declines to be, on to a deed of mock-Promethean boldness, danger – and foolishness; a distinguished man in late middle age going against common sense, decorum and knowledge of his own vertigo to do what she says. And our last glimpses of the pair reveal orgasmic hysteria and as horrible a death as one could not wish for. The last lines of the play have their own (competing) resonances. Ragnar, who hates Solness and is his successor and supplanter, says: 'Forfærdeligt dette her. Han magted det altså dog ikke' (p. 123) (This is terrible. So in fact he couldn't do it; p. 445). While Hilde who, if she doesn't precisely love him, admires him, believes in him, exclaims:

> Men helt til toppen kom han. Og jeg hørte harper i luften ... *Min, – min* bygmester! (p. 123)

> But he got right to the top. And I heard harps in the air. *My ... my* ... master builder! (p. 445)

Are we then to take our choice? Certainly we know that Solness does hang the wreath over the spire of the villa's tower, and that he does wave his hat at the crowd below, and though our informant in both instances is Hilde herself, Ragnar, who is next to her, offers no contradiction. He does contradict however when she tells him that Solness is engaged in dispute with somebody (God?) just as he was on the height of the Lysanger church, and that music can be heard in the air as the builder stands up there (those *huldrefolk* of Molde legend?). Can there be any doubt though that Ragnar is correct in assuming (confirming Aline's well-based misgivings) that the Master Builder succumbed to his inborn weakness, vertigo – and simply fell, the fall proving impossible to break? He was not a hero, after all, just a mortal human being.

Similarly, Hilde is no princess; all those fantasies of hers come not just from fairy-story but from the cultish work of Maurice Maeterlinck (1862-1949), whose play *La Princesse Maleine* had been one of the literary hits of 1889, all about princesses, castles and imprisoning towers, forests and beautiful deaths, and even a consuming fire. Ibsen detested Maeterlinck's work, even though the Belgian was an admirer of his, and later said that he could not understand how anyone had the patience to read through *Pelléas et Mélisande* (1892). But Ibsen does *not* detest Hilde. We need not here concern ourselves with her original: Emilie Bardach, Helene Raff or Hildur Andersen. It is more important to attend to his words about the play as spoken to Ernst Motzfeldt and cited in Michael Meyer's biography:

> [Hilde and Solness] are not portrayed as extraordinary persons, it is just that they feel spiritually akin, strongly attracted to each other, feel that they belong to each other and that life together would be immeasurably much richer than it would otherwise be, and also that they themselves would be better people (Hilde immediately makes him do for Brovik what he wasn't willing to do before – did his wife ever try to make him do that?) ... And so they decide to build a castle in the air, and to live together in spirit. This lifts him up higher than before, to do things he had not been able to do for a long time (symbolically). But he stakes his life on it – and is killed. But was it so mad if it cost him his life, if he did it for his own happiness and only then, for the first time, achieved it?'[14]

Ibsen wants us to take both Ragnar's and Hilde's interpretation of Solness' end as truths, just as he wants us to join with him in reconciling the Dionysian and Apollonian. In doing this he is asking of us a different and more salutary attitude towards death than the alternately fearful and sentimental ones encouraged by the churches, or the timid shying-away from the whole subject of modern secular societies. He invites us to see it, figuratively and literally, as returning us to a totality fragmented during life, whether we personally experience this or not. The earnest of this attitude came in *Rosmersholm* where it is clear that we need not wholly regret the deaths of Rosmer and Rebekka; its apotheosis will be *When We Dead Awaken*, as the very title of the play suggests. Contradictions when living are of *The Master Builder*'s very essence. Solness is both kindly and selfish, lucky and unlucky, a believer and a God-defier, loving and loveless. All these contradictions are, as I hope to have shown, present in his architectural achievement, just as they are in the oeuvre of any artist. He ascends towards the evening sun – 'sunlit clouds against the evening sky' say the stage directions – that is Apollo's domain carrying the most Dionysian emblem of all, the wreath of poor Hedda Gabler's fantasies. And then he dies. But his death will inspire his survivors, the young, to move ahead to their appropriately different destinations.

When We Dead Awaken
The Artist as Man-With-Woman:
Arnold Rubek

1.

In this 'dramatic epilogue' to his previous plays (however defined) Ibsen takes an artist as the epitome of humanity's needs, aspirations and weaknesses, and makes that man's acknowledged masterpiece an illustration of how even its boldest endeavours must ultimately fail. Humanity's? We have to qualify the word by emphasizing at the outset that the representative plight of the protagonist is inextricable from his masculinity, and to a greater extent even than in *The Master Builder* from the concept of this by which he lives, by others' attitudes towards it.

For this purpose Ibsen took as subject that artist who comes nearest in his procedures to man's own Creator, himself viewed and addressed in orthodox religion as male. The sculptor fashions out of lifeless material – whether the stone or marble he hews or the clay he moulds between his fingers – figures which then stand completely free of him, physical forms sent out into the physical world. And here they elicit response, as if they were not only autonomous but animate as well, as if their maker had inspirited them during his labours. All major arts were male provinces according to general nineteenth-century thinking – with the possible exception of the novel in Anglo-Saxon and Nordic societies. But none more so than sculpture. For one thing the exertions demanded were thought to be beyond a woman's strength, for another – important to recall when listening to the memories of the play's two principal characters – it involved the immodest activity of modelling from life, of first confronting male and female bodies in the nude and then – more morally dangerous still! – reproducing them. Those who were prepared to go in for such things put themselves outside the pale of respectability, would have been more at home in Pultosten among *Kristiania-Bohêmen* than in decent society. Yet there were women sculptors – and one of the most gifted makes herself felt here. We sense her, as I believe audiences of the day did, behind Irene, first model, dedicated assistant and only love of Arnold Rubek, and the character who makes the Creationist nature of his art most plain:

> Men denne støtte i det våde, levende ler, *den* elsked jeg – alt efter som der steg frem et sjælfuldt menneskebarn af disse rå, ufromelige masserne, – for *den* var *vor* skabning, *vort* barn. (HU XIII, p. 260)

> But that statue in wet, living clay ... *it* I loved. As out of that raw and shapeless mass gradually there emerged a living soul, a human child. That was *our* creation, *our* child. (Vol. VIII, p. 276)

These lines reveal a paradox. Sculpture involves in its making enormous expenditure of bodily as well as psychic energy, but in its completed state it can uniquely inspire detachment from the fret of ordinary life, from the flux of time, and this even when its subject is in the throes of passion or pain. Solid, monumental, making their own statements in, and about, space, the masterpieces of sculpture – from Michelangelo's *David* to Rodin's *Balzac* – defy time, and the biology subservient to it. They come as near to time-transcendence as any creation of man's can. Which is to re-affirm that sculpture is the supreme Apollonian art, as so memorably defined by Nietzsche in *The Birth of Tragedy*:

> Apollo, the god of all plastic energies, is at the same time the sooth-saying god ... We might apply to Apollo the words of Schopenhauer [from *The World as Will and Idea*] 'Just as in a stormy sea that, unbounded in all directions, raises and drops mountainous waves, howling, a sailor sits in a boat and trusts in his frail bark: so in the midst of a world of torments the individual human being sits quietly, supported by and trusting in the *principium individuationis*.' In fact, we might say of Apollo that in him the unshaken faith in this *principium* and the calm repose of the man wrapped up in it receive their most sublime expression; and we might call Apollo himself the glorious divine image of the *principium individuationis*, through whose gestures and eyes all the joy and wisdom of 'illusion', together with its beauty, speak to us.[1]

And individuation is, beyond doubt, the primary and very Apollonian business of *When We Dead Awaken*; it even, like *Ghosts*, promises sunrise in its third and last act (even if, again as in the earlier play, the protagonist will never witness it). The course of the play is the movement of an artist, a sculptor, increasingly standing for the human male – in company with the one woman indispensable to his art (there has only ever been the one) – forward from death-in-life, through successive and purging stages of awareness, to a life-in-death: an 'awakenedness' in which they both, passionately together again, encounter the terrifying cataclysm that concludes the play. But we are free to think that the condition they have reached does *not* itself perish. These organically worked rites of passage make of *When We Dead Awaken* something of a *Magic Flute* (1791) for its times, and certainly when we contemplate that final ascent of Rubek and Irene we can't help thinking of the sublime duet Mozart gives Pamina and Papageno:

Mann und Weib, und Weib und Mann,
Reichen an die Gottheit an.

Man and woman, and woman and man,
attain divinity.[2]

But this kinship, which I believe to be a valid one, must not prevent us from recognizing the *dramatis personae* as profound studies in flesh-and-blood human beings. Too much criticism of *When We Dead Awaken* presents the work as proto-Expressionist, a fore-runner of Strindberg, both of *Ett drömspel* (*A Dream Play*), only two years hence (1901) and of such Chamber Plays as *Spöksonaten* (*The Ghost Sonata*, 1907). Or as an essentially Symbolist creation, linking the writer to Mallarmé (who had died the previous year, 1898) or to Maeterlinck, for whom, as we have noted, Ibsen entertained no high regard. The characters of Ibsen's last play do indeed pass into archetypal states and therefore themselves leave their quotidian selves to *become* archetypal – as surely Solness, Aline, Ragnar and Hilde do at the end of *The Master Builder* or the twin Rentheim sisters and John Gabriel Borkman in their play's final act out on the mountainside. But in his last play Ibsen is as attentive to the complexities of his people's pasts and the subtleties of their daily lives as he ever was, and both these are absolutely as essential to it as they were, say, to *The Wild Duck*, and as an individuation ritual it could not operate without them.

In *The Lady from the Sea* Hans Lyngstrand – analogously to any dramatist – sought to capture for posterity moments and moods of emotional stress. There is no particular suggestion of a universalizing process. Anyway Lyngstrand was very much a young man still to discover himself and life, and his intentions for his work also, as we saw in Chapter Three, reached out to the preferred art-form of one of western man's earliest phases of civilization, the Hellenic. In Ibsen's last play, suitably enough, the artist is far from young, and though his best work – maybe indeed his only *genuinely* good work – dates from earlier years, we are asked to consider it in the context of a long, full and successful life, just as we were Solness'. Arnold Rubek is an artist as well-known, with as substantial a corpus to his credit as Ibsen himself, and in his return to Norway, after years away, as a Grand Old Man – he is widely recognized, even by a rough-mannered, half-educated country squire – we can certainly see resemblances to Ibsen's position, to the uneasy, fascinated re-discovery of his own country that he had made since 1891. But the correspondences (the connection with Germany and the Austrian Tyrol, the encumbrances as well as the perks of fame) only go so far and no further, and it seems to me clear that Ibsen is here far less preoccupied with self-portraiture, in any literal sense of the term, even than in *The Master Builder*. Childless, with a younger wife, a *bon vivant* inwardly tormented by a feeling that, for all the plaudits, he has not fulfilled his earlier promise, Rubek impresses us by his *dis*similarities to Ibsen as much as by his similarities. In addition to these facts, themselves significant, Ibsen has, from the start, steered our minds in the direction of another artist than himself.

In this enigmatic, ambiguous, incredibly closely-worked play, which makes such phenomenal demands of readers, directors, stage-designers and actors, one thing is easily apparent and indisputable: that the initials of its sculptor-protagonist A. R., are those of the most famous sculptor of the times, a man already regarded by the discerning as the greatest artist in his medium since Michelangelo himself: Auguste Rodin. People interested in the contemporary arts would surely not have failed to notice this, and, more importantly, it is scarcely likely that Ibsen himself was innocent of the correspondence.

For, though twelve years Ibsen's junior, Rodin (1840-1917), already enjoyed a reputation scarcely less exalted and widespread than Ibsen's own, which extended beyond the parameters of his art-form on account of both the bitter controversies and the intensity of enthusiasm his work aroused. The storms, the contempt of the conservatives, the spiteful attacks such as Ibsen endured over *Peer Gynt*, *Ghosts*, *Rosmersholm* and, incredible as it seems today, even over *Hedda Gabler* and *The Master Builder*, had long been part of Rodin's life too. Substitute for the nervousness of theatres the nervousness (and bewilderment) of the commissioning bodies when faced with the bold originality of the sculptures that their protégé had come up with. Neither *The Burghers of Calais* nor *Balzac*, without which the history of sculpture seems today unimaginable, pleased when first exhibited, and provoked many days of heated talk and many reams of indignantly covered paper. When Ibsen read about Rodin, or heard about him in conversation, or when, as we shall see is more likely than not, he actually looked at the Frenchman's creations for himself, he must have felt strong fellow-feeling (as he did for Munch, when under conservative attack). He must also have thought hard about the very considerable differences between them.

Interestingly Ibsen arrived at his central character's name at a late stage of work on the play, though it must also be admitted that this was not a rare occurrence, as examination of many of his drafts for plays will reveal. Even in July 1899 (final fair copy went off to the publishers in the November of that year, to be issued to the public on 19 December), he was Professor (Arnold) Stubow, amended to Stubeck and Stubek before the decisive change to Rubek.[3] It could be that in the end Ibsen realized that the parallels between fictitious and real-life artist were too strong for the first to be hidden behind a name which made no acknowledgement of the second. Not that there can be any question of Ibsen's wanting us to make a thorough-going identification of the one with the other. No more than Ibsen was Rodin ever characterized by the indolence of Rubek; in fact he was a by-word for compulsive industriousness, something to which the enormous quantity and range of his productions attest to this day. But the 'A. R.' indubitably announces a connection which, once seen, illuminates much that to us seems difficult, arcane.

His first title for his play was *Oppstandelsens dag*, (Resurrection or Judgement Day). This is the name of Rubek's best-known work and acknowledged masterpiece: '... dit store mesterværk ... "Opstandelsens dag" ... det, som er gået hele verden over' (p. 219) (Your big masterpiece – Resurrection Day – which went all round the world; p. 243). Inevitably we think of the living A. R.'s intended master-work whose name could scarcely chime in with Rubek's more closely: *La Porte d'enfer* (*The Gates of Hell* in English). This – though commissioned as early as 1880 – had not, by 1899, been completed; indeed it was *never* to be completed. But sculptures that had been wrought as part of the great design but were in fact well able (possibly *too* able) to stand by themselves, had been widely exhibited and applauded – among other places, in Christiania. Rodin's extraordinary creation is sufficiently similar to Rubek's in its history as well as in over-all theme and individual preoccupations as to be wholly germane to Ibsen's play. Knowledge of it illuminates the work's pivotal scene, so powerful and yet so elusive, between Rubek and Irene in Act Two, so much so that it becomes impossible to banish the idea that Ibsen did not have pictures of specific works of Rodin in mind while he wrote.

2.

It was the eighteen-year-old James Joyce who pointed out in his still remarkably fresh and percipient review of *When We Dead Awaken* (in *Fortnightly Review*, as early as 1 April 1900) how all 'the three acts are *al fresco*'.[4] This links it most closely to *The Lady from the Sea*, where, as we have observed, this is true of four out of the five acts, and half-true of the remaining one (Act Four). The reason for this is the part that the landscape (around Molde) has already played in shaping both the lives and the sensibilities of the main characters, and the continuing significance of place in determining what they do next (Ellida settling for fjord-town rather than open sea, the Stranger leaving by the English steamer, Lyngstrand following the southward drift of tourists and patients).The contrasting settings of each act in Ibsen's 'dramatic epilogue' show him at his most imaginatively (and theatrically) adventurous, and his prose-style at its most incisive and poetic. Taken in succession, they constitute a paradigm of the cultural health of Norway (and, beyond Norway, of western societies generally) and also of the proper progress of the psyche towards that full individuation integral to Apollonian art.

Act One of *When We Dead Awaken* continues what Acts Two and Five of the earlier play established: we are in a Norway ever more determinedly and successfully putting itself on the tourist map. Indeed it is possible to take the resort in which it is set as the Molde-based fjord-town of *The Lady from the Sea*. Norwegians themselves are, of course, beneficiaries of all this opening up of their country, able at last to visit in comfort and ease remote areas of wild terrain previously hard of access. The long train journey through sparsely populated land up to this particular place is beautifully evoked at the very opening of the play, in the talk of the two Norwegians with whom we are concerned. Like the Ibsens they have been living abroad – indeed we can deduce that their domicile has been Munich, as the Ibsens' was for years; from what other big town, where it is possible to own a fashionable house and lead a fashionable life, could you weekend by a Tyrolean lake? – and they confess themselves disconcerted by the atmosphere – 'lydløsheten', 'the stillness' – all around them. Even the resort itself, compared to what they've been used to in mainland Europe, lacks proper life.

Nevertheless Professor Rubek (Ibsen calls him this throughout the play; he is an academic as well as a world-renowned sculptor) and Maja, his younger wife, have elected to stay in the de luxe hotel here, finding it appropriate to their social status. It is the kind of establishment where, after lunch, you sit out on the lawn in basket-chairs and drink champagne and seltzer. The Spa Hotel has an extensive garden containing a pavilion where, we learn, the Woman Traveller and the Nun have been staying for a fortnight, and affords a delightful view of the fjord which with its many promontories and islets cannot but remind us of Romsdalsfjorden. It is, in other words, offering up the landscape for the delectation of the European affluent, and the only discordant note in this arranged symphony of serenity comes from the bursting in on his annual hunting trip of the local squire, Godseier Ulfheim, a coarse-grained man who simultaneously boasts of his great wealth and refers to himself as a 'bondekjøter' (peasant-cur). (Is there a hint here that this is a truth about Rubek's own social origins, that, in distinction to the uncouth but well-born Squire, he, so famous and so sophisticated, is really a country bumpkin, just as Solness had been?) Repellent though he may be, Ulfheim's intrusion on the discontented hotel guests and the fawning Spa Superintendent, made in the company of his silent servant Lars and the dogs (his nearest and dearest, he says), is salutary: now the land around appears in a new light – and it is not a tourist's or an aesthete's. It can be owned and worked and explored, there are animals living in it, and some of them Ulfheim ferociously hunts (he even has the audacity to liken Rubek's sculpting to his own bloody wrestling with bears), in other words Ulfheim is rendering it back in atavistic terms for us. His atavism is of the crudest kind; there is another purer kind, and into that Irene will lead Rubek. Either way his entrance – which casts such a spell on Maja, only too obviously at a loose end – puts an end to our seeing the resort in terms of international holiday-makers and drifters, who seem to presage the rootless crew we encounter in the first part of T. S. Eliot's *The Waste Land*.

Obviously in the eyes of the Spa Hotel mountains and sea are both to be thought of in terms of trips guests can make. Rubek and Maja have been intending to go north by the steamer, perhaps even up into the Arctic waters as far as the North Cape, but more because it would cure their boredom than out of any real interest in the places. During the course of the act the mountains take over as their proper destination. Their slopes – though not the highest peaks – are Ulfheim's hunting-ground; he would like to show the wild territory he knows so thoroughly to Maja. But they are also a magnet for Irene and she wants it to draw Rubek too.

> Rejs heller højt op mellem fjeldene. Så højt op, du kan komme. Højere, højere, – altid højere, Arnold. (p. 239)

> Go high up into the mountains instead. As high as you can get. Higher, higher ... Ever higher, Arnold. (p. 260)

The setting of Act One then gives us the artist as pleasure-giver (and pleasure-seeker), and in social terms, as member of the class that can afford to eat and drink well, buy pictures, take rooms in first-class hotels, build attractive new houses, keep up villas abroad. This is the class that has commissioned from Rubek those portrait busts that have kept him well-paid these last years, but into the execution of which he allowed his residual resentful mockery of its members to enter: their sculpted heads, carefully looked at, reveal them as kin to stupid farmyard animals. In Kierkegaardian terms – those of *Enten-Eller* (*Either/Or*, 1843) – the hotel and its adjacent park provide a potent simile for the Aesthetic stage of life, and the blandness, the soothing artifice of the scene are brought home by the opposing dissonant spirits who entice respectively the wife and the husband Rubek away from it. On the one hand there is the anti-civilization Ulfheim of whom in the next act Maja will say: 'Han er ikke spor af kunstner, han' (p. 245) (No trace of the artist about *him*!; p. 264). On the other there is Irene, with her Nun-attendant, standing for supra-civilization, for spiritual forces, pursuing a path away and up from such this-worldly snares. Anyway Irene – like Rebekka West, like the Stranger in *The Lady from the Sea* – is from Nordland, from a sparsely populated region famous for its ancient Sami/Finnish magic wisdom acquired through co-existence with the elements in a wilderness environment. She needs something more austere to feed on, more challenging than these pleasant anodyne grounds with plashing fountain and basket-chairs.

A caveat must be made here. If we acknowledge, in these three successive acts, a correspondence to the three Kierkegaardian stages of existence, and see them as a vertical structure, as constituting an ascent, as they do literally in the play, we must see this progression as *un*doing what western civilization has erected. The 'aesthetic' is the latest phase of man's achievement: the stage of the over-pampered late nineteenth century. Away from it things can only be better, a purity of movement and mind is again within our grasp. This is not at all to say that the play praises primitivism, as that spokesman of the young anti-Ibsen faction in Norway, Knut Hamsun, had already begun to do. On the contrary Ulfheim with his cruel slaughter of bears is to be deplored. The way out of a decadent culture, out of the hotel parkland, and up onto the mountainsides, will be, indeed, into a greater, a truer kindness, a compassion that can embrace the whole created world and be prepared for even its starkest, most dangerous aspects.

In Act Two we have reached 'et højfjeldssanatorium. Landskabet strækker sig som en træløs, umådelig vidde indover imod et langt fjeldvand. På den anden side af vandet stiger en række af højfjeldstinder med blånende sné i kløfterne' (p. 243) (a sanatorium up in the mountains. A vast expanse of bare treeless wasteland stretches away towards a long mountain lake. On the far side of the lake rises a range of mountain peaks, the snow in their crevasses tinged with blue; p. 263). It is not noon-tide any longer, but evening – 'near to sunset'. The hedonistic hotel-world lies far below, and here is a sanatorium – designed to make sick people better – with some kind of school attached to it, for beyond the stream we find children at play, and throughout the act hear their 'merry laughter'. Some of the children bespeak the town in their clothes, others the country, dressed as they are in folk costume, surely dearer to the Norwegian national identity than to that of any other people of Western Europe; in other words they represent both divisions of a country with an ever more confident sense of itself. Health, Education, Folk-Culture, as superior to the champagne-and-seltzer life of the Spa as the sanatorium is higher above sea-level. We have ascended to Kierkegaard's Ethical stage of human life. Only when it has been reached can the third, the spiritual or religious – a necessity for at least some of us – be a possibility.

Sanatoria and appointed institutions where children can play and learn – these establish a context for facing up to serious matters, for talking them through until mistakes have been undone and clearer vision attained. (Ibsen was not dear to Freud for nothing!) What Ibsen in his notes called the 'big scene' between Rubek and Irene, in which she makes him acknowledge all the many evasions and betrayals of his long, outwardly approbation-studded career, is played out in this mountain spot, and certainly it involves for Rubek the most strenuous moral re-adjudication. In Christian eschatology Resurrection Day is consequent on the Last Judgement. To enjoy the blessings of eternity it is necessary for us, after lives of error and wrong-doing, to be forgiven first, a process in itself dependent on our recognition of ethical priorities and how we have failed them.

In terms of contemporary civilization decadence has been abandoned for a 'realer' culture, and the artist is no longer a mere beautifier, a decorator or embellisher, who, thanks to his ability to please, takes his place among the privileged and well-off. He is once more a moral being, one with instructors, carers, therapists, and essential to society's well-being. For this a sound value-system is a pre-requisite. As Rubek will tell Maja here, he can't live just for pleasure; he was born to work, and ultimately work takes him beyond the reductive pleasure principle ... It is close to the sanatorium and beside a stream that Rubek re-appreciates Irene and her one-time meaning for him and his art, and discards Maja (her name comes from Schopenhauer's use of the Sanskrit word for 'illusion') and her trivial approach to living. Though he has undoubtedly colluded with it, her preferred life-style has always gone against his profoundest convictions:

> Jeg er ble't ked, – uudholdelig ked og træt og slap af samlivet med dig! ... mig, som nu igen har undergået en omvæltning – ... en opvågnen til mit egentlige liv. (p. 253)

> I'm tired – sick and tired and unendurably bored with living with you! ... I am going through another upheaval ... An awakening to the life that is really mine. (p. 271)

Maja is now in the company of the bear-hunter, Ulfheim, whose uncouth ways delight her, his very thirst for violence a source of appeal. It is significant that the happy young children irritate her (there may be a personal reason for this) whereas Irene (who is also literally childless) is thoughtful and kind in her dealings with them. In this context Maja appears the pattern of decadence, a forerunner of all those disenchanted idle women of Fitzgerald and Hemingway, of Daisy Buchanan and Lady Brett Ashley, with their need for kicks, and their infatuation with men such as bull-fighters. Yet, unlike them, she will dislike and protest against the behaviour of her chosen man, his rough handling of her, his boasts about his whoring, though in the face of the storm she will be happy enough to let herself be carried away from it in his arms.

Beyond the quartet – a quintet if we count the Nun forever trailing Irene – behind the lake, the mountains rise higher still, to end in snow-capped peaks. The Dalai Lama in a letter to Peter Goullart wrote,

making a distinction between 'soul' and 'spirit', and drawing on the
mountainous landscape of his own Tibet:

> Spirit is land of high, white peaks and glittering jewel-like lakes and
> flowers. Life is sparse and sounds travel great distances ... When the soul
> triumphed, the herdsmen came to the lamaseries, for soul is communal and
> loves humming in unison. But the creative soul craves spirit. Out of the
> jungles of the lamasery, the most beautiful monks one day bid farewell to
> their comrades and go to make their solitary journey toward the peaks,
> there to mate with the cosmos ... People need to climb the mountain not
> simply because it is there but because the soulful divinity needs to be mated
> with the spirit.[5]

And Act Three takes us right up to those white peaks where mating with
the cosmos can be accomplished: 'snédækte tinder rejser sig til højre og
taber sig i drivende tåger højt oppe. Til venstre i en stenstyrtning ligger
en gammel, halvt sammenfalden hytte. Det er tidlig morgen. Dagen gryr.
Solen er endnu ikke oppe' (p. 272) (snow-covered peaks tower up, right,
vanishing into drifting mist. Left, among a fall of rock, stands an old
broken-down cottage. It is early morning. Dawn is breaking. The sun has
not yet risen; p. 287).

Maja stands for 'soul' not spirit, and Ulfheim possibly not even for
that – for the instinctual life of Lars and his dogs: they will leave the
rocky heights to which Rubek and Irene have ascended. At the time
theirs seems the wiser course, so fierce is the storm whipping up – but
the pair with whom we're asked to identify are concerned with wisdom
of far profounder import than mere common sense and the search for
safety can comprehend. The 'hytte', the 'mountain-cottage' belongs to
man not as builder of societal institutions, let alone as holiday-maker, but
as hunter-gatherer glad of a minimalist roof over his head. (Though
Ulfheim has brought girls up here for his sexual enjoyment.) The artist,
the male human, looking up here into the emergence of morning on
virginal mountains, has risen – or returned to a state of purity, of oneness
with the forces behind the world, towards which all his work should
have been tending, and, most importantly of all, has the woman dearest
to him at his side; indeed they are holding hands when the avalanche
overtakes them. Irene has once seen a beautiful sunrise before: Rubek
always promised he would show her the whole world from the top of a

mountain (a promise he almost blasphemously repeated with Maja), and now there is consummation of these wishes. Compared with the peace of their union – a peace affirmed by the Nun who has sleuthed them right up to these heights – what avail the catastrophe, what avail the death it brings! We have always known that there is turbulence in the universe, that death is an inevitability for every one of us – though we may well have chosen to banish these realities from our minds and screen them with superficialities. We also may not have been constant to the innate human desideratum of male-female partnership with love as its necessary instrument. But Rubek and Irene at the play's very end bear heroic witness to this.

Something of what they experience before being engulfed by the fall of snow is analogous to what Alfred Almers recounts in *Little Eyolf* of his walks in the mountains:

Fik sé solopgangen lyse over tinderne. Føle mig nærmere stjernerne. Næsten som i forståelse og i samfund med dem.[6]

Saw the sun rise over the mountain peaks. Felt myself nearer the stars. Almost as though I understood them, belonged with them.[7]

In his last play Ibsen revisits and re-presents the epiphanies of earlier work. If the final moments of *When We Dead Awaken* recall the terrifying concluding cataclysm of *Brand*, he was also surely remembering Alfred Almers' description of how he lost his way in a desolate tract of mountain-country, but, clambering about precipices, felt all capacity for fear leave him: 'Jeg syntes at der gik jeg og døden som to gode rejsekammerater' (p. 263) (I felt that Death and I walked side by side like two good travelling companions; p. 101).

Behind the three scenes of the three acts there is another place which we never see but which is palpable and resonant throughout the drama: the Taunitzer See. The lake cannot be found on a map, but may well stand for the Toplitzsee in Austria's Salzkammergut, a region Ibsen knew and loved. This has a legend of buried treasure which is a draw for visitors. Right at the beginning of Act One Rubek reminds Maja how fortunate she is in being married to so well-off a man, and alludes to the See:

Og en villa ved Taunitzer See, hvor det jo nu er ble't aller finest – . Ja, for
fint og prægtigt er det alt sammen, Maja, det tør jeg nok sige. (p. 217)

And a villa on the Taunitzer See where everything's now so grand ... In fact,
Maja, I'd say the whole thing's a bit too fine and splendid. (p. 241)

We sense bitterness behind these sentences, the reasons for which
become clear enough later. For in the years when Rubek was a hard-up
emergent artist, presumably practising his art in Munich as a more
culture-minded city than Christiania, and Irene his hard-up, selfless
fellow-Norwegian model, Taunitzer See was a place that gave them
refreshment and which they found conducive to an intense shared
imaginative life contributing to the *Weltanschauung* of his best work –
which he betrayed.

> PROFESSOR RUBEK: ... Kan du huske den sommer vi sad udenfor det
> lille bondehuset ved Taunitzer See?
> IRENE: (*nikker*) Lørdags aftnerne, ja, – når vi var færdige med vort arbejde
> for ugen – (p. 266)

> RUBEK: Can you remember the summer when we sat like this outside that
> little farmhouse on the Taunitzer See?
> IRENE: (*nods*) On Saturday evenings, yes ... when we'd finished our work
> for the week? (p. 281)

However for Rubek the Taunitzer See has not been confined to idyllic
memories. It became a focus of his ambition, of how the life of a
successful man should be, and plays a part in his present as well as his
past. He has to make an admission to Irene that cannot but remind him
of how much he has debased his earlier self, their relationship, their
shared artistic and human ideals:

> PROFESSOR RUBEK: Du Irene, – jeg har købt det lille bondehuset ved
> Taunitzer See.
> IRENE: Har du købt det nu? Du sa' så tidt at du vilde købe det, hvis du
> havde råd til det.
> PROFESSOR RUBEK: Siden fik jeg nokså god råd. Og så købte jeg det.
> IRENE: (*skeler hen på ham*) Bor du da nu derude – i vort gamle hus?
> PROFESSOR RUBEK: Nej det har jeg ladt rive ned for længe siden. Og så
> har jeg bygget mig en stor, prægtig bekvem villa på tomten, – med park

omkring. Der er det, vi plejer – (*standser og retter udtrykket*) – der plejer
jeg holde til om sommeren –

IRENE: (*betvinger sig*) Så du og – og den anden holder til derude nu?

PROFESSOR RUBEK: (*lidt trodsende*) Ja. Når min hustru og jeg ikke er
på rejser, – som nu iår.

IRENE: (*sér vidt frem for sig*) Dejligt, dejligt var livet ved Taunitzer See.

PROFESSOR RUBEK: (*sér ligesom tilbage i sig selv*) Og alligevel, Irene –

IRENE: (*udfylder hans tanke*) – alligevel så slap vi to al den livets dejlighed.
(pp. 266-267)

RUBEK: Irene ... I bought that little farmhouse on the Taunitzer See.

IRENE: Bought it, have you? You often said you'd buy it if you could afford
it.

RUBEK: Later I found I could nicely afford it. So I bought it.

IRENE: (*glancing at him*) Do you live out there now ... in our old house?

RUBEK: No, I had it pulled down long ago. Then I built myself a big, fine,
comfortable villa on the land ... surrounded by parkland. That's where
we generally ... (*Stops and corrects himself*) ... where I generally go for
the summer ...

IRENE: (*controls herself*) So you and ... that woman live out there now?

RUBEK: (*somewhat defiantly*) Yes. When my wife and I aren't travelling ...
as we are this year.

IRENE: (*looks unseeingly into space*). Beautiful! Life on the Taunitzer See
was beautiful!

RUBEK: (*as though looking back within himself*) And yet, Irene ...

IRENE: (*completes the thought*) And yet we let that life and all its beauty
slip through our fingers. (p. 282)

The history of Rubek's relation to the Taunitzer See is, like the
succession of scenes for each act, a succinct, condensed history of
European culture as it has evolved over two/three decades and as we are
witnessing its more recent manifestations in this very corner of Norway
– the growth of an affluent class with an ability to transform the land
for its own interests and pleasures. But it is also, of course, a history of
Rubek himself, and of many an artist, many a man of purpose like him,
who has started out living simply, honouring the people and places that
he responds to, and then, through the ambition fostered by the
prevailing culture, and through the greed that is its concomitant,
dishonours them. Rubek's life moves away from Irene, and the little

peasant farm associated with their love, (even if in literal terms it was she who left him!) and therefore he abandons the original version of *Resurrection Day*. He not only purchases the place as a second house (converting love into property) but has it pulled down so that an imposing (pretentious?) new villa – suitable for one of what he judges is his social standing – can be built in its stead, a destiny by no means confined to peasant-houses in the nineteenth century Salzkammergut. (There is carry-over here from *The Master Builder* where Solness builds expensive new homes for people on the site of the burned-down house of Aline's inheritance. Social advancement, a turning of the back on an early love, a need to have concrete symbols of progress – these are common to both.)

Taunitzer See was where the younger Irene and Rubek rejoiced in an imaginative game which holds the key to the communion possible between them now. This game therefore acts as something of the nature of a prelude to the work proper, in which we hear, if only embryonically, the *leitmotif* connected with fidelity that will expand for us later on. Such a musical analogy is, for once in Ibsen, not inappropriate, for the couple's game derives from *Lohengrin*. While it was the legend behind the opera that occupied the pair, it is hard to believe that Ibsen did not intend us to think about Wagner himself also. *Lohengrin* dates from 1850, the very year of Ibsen's first play *Catiline*, and was a watershed in the career of its composer, who called it a 'Romantic' opera, in distinction to the grand 'historical' ones he had essayed before. Though corresponding far more closely in structure to earlier opera models than did his later and yet better-known work, it is nevertheless intensely characteristic of its creator, exalted, impassioned, chromatic. Imbued with the revolutionary moments of 1848/49 which Wagner had supported, most of all in Dresden, city of the Ibsens' later residence, it speaks of the future even while transporting us to the Brabant of 932 CE. But if Nietzsche in *The Birth of Tragedy* hailed Wagner as Dionysian master of the most Dionysian art-form, dedicating the book to him as his 'sublime predecessor on this path [of art]'; by the time of its later re-issue he had nothing but contempt for Wagner, and was two years later (1888) to publish *The Case of Wagner* putting forward his revised opinion in the strongest terms:

> Bayreuth is large-scale opera – and not even good opera ... the theatre is a
> revolt of the masses, a plebiscite *against* good taste; *This is precisely what
> is proved by the case of Wagner*: he won the crowd, he corrupted taste, he
> spoiled even our taste for opera! – [8]

Wagner, Nietzsche felt, had adapted his early noble ideas and artistic
originality for the gratifications of his own ego and of the appetites for
spectacle, novelty and luxuriousness of the *haute-bourgeoisie*. This
surrender, as we shall be examining more closely, is essentially what
Rubek comes to accuse himself of, a *trahison des clercs*. Richard
Wagner, Henrik Ibsen, Auguste Rodin – all radical masters who became
household names, whose works, once dismissed, attacked, pronounced
socially dangerous, obscene or blasphemous or both, went on to attract
both the fashionable and the respectable, to be played in state-of-the-art
theatres or commissioned by eminent public bodies and rich people of
influence, and just about everywhere – making the men themselves feted
and rich! Arnold Rubek is of their number.

Lohengrin, Knight of the Swan, is the son of Parsifal, Knight of the
Grail. Borne by swan down the river Scheldt to Antwerp, he arrives, a
complete stranger causing consternation among all onlookers, in answer
to the prayers of Elsa, daughter of the late Duke of Brabant now falsely
accused of fratricide. The only condition he gives for the aid he now
offers her against her enemies is: 'You must never ask me, or be at pains
to discover, from whence I journeyed here, not what is my name and
lineage!' Lohengrin goes on to fight and defeat Elsa's principal accuser,
but nobly spares his life. Having fallen instantly in love, Lohengrin and
Elsa decide to marry, and preparations get underway for their wedding.
However the machinations of Elsa's enemies continue; deliberately they
taunt Elsa for not knowing either the name or the identity of her
husband-to-be and systematically undermine her confidence in him. So
eventually she *does* put the forbidden question to him. But, before he can
reply, he is violently assailed by the very foe whose life he spared. They
fight again, and now Lohengrin does kill him, proceeding to confess to
Elsa who he really is. Now that he has done so, he has to submit to the
power of the Holy Grail, and leave. But he will do one more thing for
her. The swan now ready to draw him back homewards is none other
than Elsa's brother, transmogrified. Lohengrin will revoke the spell, and

Brabant will have not only a restored missing son but a new and promising leader. The Knight departs, in a boat now pulled along by a dove. But the double shock has been too much for Elsa, and she dies in her re-found brother's arms.

In a play as spare, as tautly constructed, as *When We Dead Awaken*, Ibsen would not have made Irene and Rubek refer so pointedly to their Lohengrin game, if he hadn't wanted us to absorb it in the meaning of the whole. Also something of the opera's ravishing prelude (music praised in verse by Swinburne) and of the rapturous duets of Lohengrin and Elsa's love permeates the beautiful recollections of Ibsen's pair in Act Two, and suggests some quality we should now re-impose on their present selves, victims both of years of unsatisfactory, sterile living. The recollections have in part been prompted by the gulls the two of them see swimming on the mountain stream they are now sitting beside, and into which Irene has thrown the petals of a mountain-rose:

PROFESSOR RUBEK: ... Da lod du også fugle svømme i bækken. Det var vandliljer, som du –
IRENE: Hvide svaner var det.
PROFESSOR RUBEK: Jeg mente svaner, ja. Og jeg husker at jeg fæsted et stort loddent båd til en af svanerne. Det var endda et skræppeblad –
IRENE: Så blev det til Lohengrins båd – med svanen foran.
PROFESSOR RUBEK: Hvor glad du var i den leg, Irene.
IRENE: Vi legte den ofte om igen.
PROFESSOR RUBEK: Hver eneste lørdag, tror jeg. Hele sommeren udover.
IRENE: Du sa' at jeg var svanen, som trak din båd.
PROFESSOR RUBEK: Sa' jeg det? Ja, det kan godt være. (p. 266)

RUBEK: You made birds swim in the stream then, too. They were water-lilies ...
IRENE: They were white swans.
RUBEK: Yes, I meant swans. And I remember I fastened a big hairy leaf to one of the swans. It was a dock-leaf ...
IRENE: Which became Lohengrin's boat ... drawn by the swan.
RUBEK: How you loved that game, Irene.
IRENE: We played it over and over again.

RUBEK: Every single Saturday, I think. All through the summer.
IRENE: You said I was the swan drawing your boat.
RUBEK: Did I say that? Yes, I might well have. (pp. 281-282)

Swans and water-lilies are both symbols of purity. The swan is constant
to his partner, and thus an appropriate emblem for medieval knights
dedicated to the Virgin Mary or their own particular 'Lady', and the
beauty of his song at death has long suggested the existence of a spiritual
domain beyond the physical world. The lily supposedly sprang up from
the tears of Eve as she repented of her sin, and the *water*-lily is a favourite
symbol in Eastern mysticism because while its roots are in mud its stalks
reach through water to greet light with white cup-like flowers. Fidelity
then was the virtue Irene and Rubek's games celebrated, fidelity of man
to woman and vice versa, and to their 'child', the great sculpture
demanding so much of them but which, when completed, would address
the entire world for its own betterment. Irene was the swan that drew her
own knightly Lohengrin to his appropriate destination in time and place,
when he could present to the world a true new masterpiece.

Their Lohengrin game honoured faithfulness to the inner self
(represented here by the Knight's vow to the Holy Grail) and to all
ideals, especially Love. If Irene in leaving Rubek was the literal breaker
of their union, she did so because he had already been disloyal to her,
speaking of their time together as an 'episode'. Such a betrayal presages
his later one of the sculpture itself.

3.

In the marvellously taut and rich opening exchange between Rubek and
Maja, we receive an overwhelming and disquieting sense of ennui. This
married couple, obviously comfortably-off, on holiday in a beautiful
place, are not at ease with each other or themselves. The man is restless,
while hoping that the boat-trip north may yet do something for him, the
woman, who realises that it won't, is indolent, incurious (until the arrival
of Ulfheim). They bicker, exchange reproaches, neither showing a
particularly attractive personality, yet it is Maja who understands what is
really the matter with her husband (and consequently with herself). He

can't get on with his work, and hasn't been able to – despite all those portrait-bust commissions – since, three or four years before, he completed the sculpture universally acclaimed his best and an achievement of real distinction: *Resurrection Day*. But is 'completed' the right word? Conversationally trapped into momentary honesty, Rubek does not think it is:

> PROFESSOR RUBEK: Det er kanske ulykken det, Maja.
> FRU MAJA: Hvorfor det?
> PROFESSOR RUBEK: Da jeg havde skabt dette mit mesterværk – – (*slår i hæftighed ud med hånden*) – for 'Opstandelsens dag' er et mesterværk! Eller *var* det fra først af. Nej, det *er* det endnu. *Skal, skal, skal* være et mesterværk! (p. 219)

> RUBEK: Perhaps that was the tragedy, Maja.
> MAJA: How?
> RUBEK: When I had created this masterpiece of mine ... (*with a violent gesture*) ... For *Resurrection Day* is a masterpiece! Or was to begin with. No. Still is! It must be ... shall be a masterpiece. (p. 243)

What do all these hesitations, shifts in tense, involuntary body movements mean? Why does a work praised by everybody not satisfy its maker? (We can't but be reminded of Rodin's dictum here: 'A work even when finished is never perfect.') What is amiss with the many subsequent commissions that he has carried out? And inevitably our minds move to the personal, the intimate domain. What *kind* of marriage is that of Maja and Rubek? If we know this, haven't we progressed just a little towards understanding the *in*completion of Professor Rubek's famous piece?

The elliptical dialogue of this scene has spaces filled, with consummate artistry on Ibsen's part, by sometimes quite casual-sounding references to long years stretching back behind this idle summer lunch-hour in which it occurs. One such deserves commenting on now, so resonant is it. Maja, we hear, was partly drawn to marry this much older man by his telling her that he would take her to the top of a high mountain and show her the glories of the world. Rubek starts. Had he really said that to *her*? (We will later find out that he said it in the past to Irene also.) Why, as a boy, Rubek confesses, he would persuade the other children to play with him, in the forest or on the mountainside, by making them bold, outrageous promises: he would, he'd say, take them to the top of a high mountain and show them the world. Outside *Brand* and *Peer Gynt* Ibsen has never supplied us with a cameo so illustrative of the kind of boy he himself had been, aloof, unpopular, disdainful of the amusements of most others yet wanting to win them over by 'magic' games, usually in his case with cardboard cut-outs and puppet-theatre. This exact boastful promise, with its parody of the temptation of Christ, is something Rubek has used in maturer life for the purpose of exercising male mastery over the female. So the little memory not only makes us see Rubek as the friendless but strangely self-confident boy he was, it gives us a key to his adult self, in which both these two attributes are still apparent. Preoccupied as he is with his art and, through this, his ascent in life (of which his offer of showing others the world from a mountain-top is mimetic), he can't separate personal relationships, for which he has little instinctual aptitude, from the gaining of power – something he abuses. Indeed *is* still abusing when we meet him, for, however trivial-minded we might deem her, Maja surely deserves a little more kindness and respect than he shows her. Moreover there is another way in which he has not really outgrown boyish play; he prefers it to adult commitment. Maja herself realizes this. When Rubek makes his admission, she observes somewhat tartly: 'Vilde du kanské bare ha' *mig* ud og lege også?' (p. 222) (Perhaps all you wanted was to get *me* to come out and play?; p. 245). Rubek has not had the courage of his own seriousness.

And later we will be given another instance of this – in Act Two, again in conversation with Maja, when he justifies his abdication of work like *Resurrection Day* for less demanding and better-paying requests. He makes the old stale claim, used by many an artist who has pandered to the commercial, that he rates life above art:

> Ja er da ikke livet i solskin og skønhed noget ganske anderledes værdifuldt end det, at gå her til sine dages ende i et råt, fugtigt hul og mase sig dødsens træt med lérklumper og stenblokke? (p. 252)

> Hasn't life in sunlight and beauty a value different from toiling away to the end of your days in some cold damp cellar, wrestling with lumps of clay and blocks of stone? (p. 270)

To which she replies: 'Jo, det har jeg rigtignok altid syntes' (p. 252). (Yes, I've always thought that; p. 270). And, especially in contrast to the proclaimed past fervours of Irene, condemns herself out of her own mouth. Nothing could be more revealing than this exchange of the flaw in their marriage, and the flaw in Rubek himself which has allowed, not to say encouraged, it. Though in his young manhood capable of truly exacting labour, something in him also recoiled from it, from the hardships, the consumption of time, art of necessity imposes. An easier way of using his gifts first appealed to, and then seduced him. This can be attributed – as in the case of Solness – to the self-made man's ceaselessly coveting more, requiring as measures of his success the sweets of the affluent: indeed the idea of their eventual attainment may in previous years have been what spurred him on. Ibsen, who by old age was a man of considerable substance, did not really share the provenance he ascribes to these heroes, but it would seem that, by now, he could not subtract a journey from provincial obscurity from his self-image. His reunion with his sister Hedvig may have endorsed this; *The Master Builder* and *John Gabriel Borkman* are its testimonies, while behind both works stands the unfortunate Jon Gynt's son, Peer.

The Hotel Superintendent now breaks into their self-dissecting talk, sycophantic to this celebrity patronising his smart establishment. Through this lackey (whom again James Joyce had the insight to praise as yet another example of Ibsen's never-ending creativity), we learn that the strange figures Rubek saw during his virtual *nuit blanche*, a woman in shining white and her attendant in black, are not figures of his fantasy or dream, but visitors to this spa such as themselves. The audience then sees them – indeed their sudden entrance on the scene is comparable with the arrival of Hilde in *The Master Builder* and the eruption of the Rat Wife in *Little Eyolf*, interesting in their mysterious selves of course, but also as emanations from the unconscious of the central character.

We now apprehend – though the very precise connection between Rubek and the Woman in White is unknown to us – that below the disturbed (and disturbing) surface of the situation we have been given, with tantalizing economy, lie depths for the greater part unplumbed, out of which will surely arise those whose secret existence enables them to break – possibly creatively, possibly not – all the tense but amiable superficie of contemporary living. It is worth noting here that Ibsen was as adamant that Irene should be referred to in the cast-list only as 'en reisende dame', 'a woman traveller', as he was that the Stranger in *The Lady from the Sea* (whose function is not dissimilar) should be given no further designation.

Already we realize that in its last stages the *Resurrection Day* that went out so triumphantly into the world and which does not please its maker was worked on during Rubek's relationship/marriage to Maja. How did it differ from the original conception, and why? Already our minds may be moving towards the real A. R.

During their first meeting after many years, Rubek hears from the mentally unbalanced Irene of her unhappy promiscuous past, of her loveless marriages, and is made to feel that he himself is significantly responsible for them. Not the least of the accusations that she levels at him is that never once in their association did he touch her. This surprises him; it was reverence for her that compelled this abstention, and his reverence was profound and informed by gratitude:

> PROFESSOR RUBEK: Irene, forstod du ikke at mangen gang var jeg som sanseforvildet af al din dejlighed? ... Jeg var kunstner, Irene ... Først og fremst kunstner. Og jeg gik der syg og vilde skabe mit livs store værk ... Det skulde kaldes 'Opstandelsens dag'. Skulde fremstilles i lignelse af en ung kvinde, som vågner af dødssøvnen ... Det skulde være jordens ædleste, reneste, idealeste kvinde, hun, som vågner. Så fandt jeg *dig*. Dig kunde jeg bruge i et og alt. Og du føjed dig så glad og så gerne. Og du gav slip på slægt og hjem – og fulgte med mig ... Just derfor kunde jeg mest bruge dig. Dig og ingen anden. Du blev mig en høj-hellig skabning, som bare måtte røres ved i tilbedende tanker. Jeg var jo endnu ung den gang, Irene. Og den overtro fyldte mig, at rørte jeg dig, begærte jeg dig i sanselighed, så vilde mit sind vanhelliges, så at jeg ikke kunde skabe færdig det, som jeg stræbte efter. – Og jeg tror endnu at der er nogen sandhed i det.
>
> IRENE: ... Først kunstværket, – siden menneskebarnet. (pp. 237-238)

> RUBEK: Irene, didn't you realize that many's the time I was nearly driven out of my mind by all your loveliness? ... I was an artist, Irene ... Above all else an artist. And there I was sick with desire to create the great work of my life ... It was to be called Resurrection Day. It was to take the form

of a young woman waking from the sleep of death ... This waking girl
was to be the world's noblest, purest, most perfect woman. Then I found
you. I knew I could use you, wholly, entirely. And you agreed so readily,
so gladly. You left your family and your home ... To go with me ... That,
above all, was why I was able to use you. You, and nobody else. For me
you became a sacred being, untouchable, a thing to worship in thought
alone. I was still young then, Irene. I was obsessed with the idea that if
I touched you, if I desired you sensually, my mind would be profaned
and I would be unable to achieve what I was striving to create. And I still
think there is some truth in that.

IRENE: ... The work of art first ... the human being [child] second. (pp. 258-
259)

What Irene is in effect saying here is that with these priorities of Rubek's
the work of art paradoxically becomes itself second-rate. No great
achievement in the arts, from Michelangelo to Shakespeare, from
Goethe to – Ibsen himself, has ever downgraded the human being in its
own interests. Great art comes from intensity of human concern. This
amounts to a refutation of the 'art for art's sake' dogmas of the 1880/90s
while never straying in the opposite direction, of implying that the
difficulties of a serious work of art should be jettisoned in favour of the
quest for immediacy of more popular productions. And the act of
renunciation Rubek prides himself on having made is in fact a form of
pandering to, of swelling his own egotism, which wreaks its own
revenge accordingly on his creations.

In Act Two, up by the sanatorium, Irene tells Rubek further why she
left him, why she disappeared from his life with the completeness of
Lohengrin quitting Brabant.

IRENE: Da jeg havde tjent dig med min sjæl og med mit legeme, – og
billedstøtten stod færdig, – vort barn, som du kaldte den, – da lagde jeg
for din fod det dyreste offer – ved at udslette mig selv for alle tider.
PROFESSOR RUBEK: (*sænker hodet*) Og lægge mit liv øde.
IRENE: (*blusser pludselig op*) Just det var det jeg vilde! Aldrig, aldrig
skulde du få skabe noget mere, – efter at du havde skabt dette vort eneste
barn. (p. 258-259)

IRENE: After I had served you with my soul and body ... and the sculpture
was complete – our child, as you called it – I laid at your feet the dearest

> sacrifice I could make. I removed all trace of myself for ever.
>
> RUBEK: (*bows his head*) And made of my life a desert.
>
> IRENE: (*suddenly flares up*) That's exactly what I wanted! Never were you to create anything again! Never! Not after you had created this child, our only child. (pp. 275-276)

Such absolutism is not by any means appealing, and maybe just as Rubek has done, Irene, by the time of her final ascent of the mountain, will have won through to a more inclusive approach to existence. For once again we are encountering sacrifice – as a perhaps necessary but inevitably destructive element in the creation of art, and representing major aspects of the relation of man and woman in our unreconstructed society. We have not yet arrived at Ejlert Løvborg's future society of equal companionship by a long chalk, and Irene in her younger years was only repeating Agnes' submission to Brand, Solveig's patience with Peer, Nora's prostration before Torvald prior to her self-realisation, Helene Alving's denial of her own instinctual and intellectual selves for the sake of Osvald, even Aline's dedication to duty while Solness forges ahead to success and riches. Cut off from Rubek, wandering, modelling and then wretchedly married, Irene consoled herself with the thought of the masterpiece in which she participated and for which she sacrificed her happiness. Now Rubek must tell her the painful truth of what happened to the work whose completion she'd not stayed to see.

For it is a two-way process, this sacrifice, this taking advantage. And if the lion's share of the guilt is Rubek's, Irene is not wholly guilt-free. She will presently reproach Rubek for 'using' her, unapologetically, as his right, as material for his great work, thus robbing her of a part of her self, violating her womanhood without physically honouring it, and eventually only to serve his reputation. But in his defence he does make a very valid point:

> IRENE: 'Opstandelsens dag' kaldte du dit livsværk. – Jeg kalder det 'vort barn'.
>
> PROFESSOR RUBEK: Jeg var ung dengang. Uden al livserfaring. Opstandelsen, syntes jeg, måtte skildres skønnest og allerdejligst som en ung uberørt kvinde, – uden et jordlivs oplevelser, – og som vågner til lys og herlighed uden at ha' noget stygt og urent at skille sig af med.
>
> IRENE: (*hurtigt*) Ja, – og således står jeg jo nu der i vort værk?

PROFESSOR RUBEK: (*nølende*) Ikke egentlig ganske således, Irene.

IRENE: (*i stigende spænding*) Ikke ganske – ? Står jeg ikke således, som jeg stod for dig?

PROFESSOR RUBEK: (*uden at svare*) Jeg blev verdensklog i de årene, som fulgte efter, Irene. 'Opstandelsens dag' blev noget mere og noget – noget mere mangfoldigt i min forestilling. Den lille runde plint, hvor dit billede stod rankt og ensomt, – den gav ikke længer rum for alt det, jeg nu vilde digte til –

IRENE: (*famler efter kniven med lader være*) Hvad digtet du så til? Sig det!

PROFESSOR RUBEK: Jeg digted det til, som jeg rundt omkring mig i verden så med mine øjne. Jeg måtte ha' det med. Kunde ikke andet, Irene. Plinten vided jeg ud – så den blev stor og rummelig. Og på den lagde jeg et stykke af den buede, bristende jord. Og op af jordrevnerne vrimler der nu mennesker med dulgte dyreansigter. Kvinder og mænd, – slig som jeg kendte dem ude fra livet.

IRENE: (*i åndeløs forventning*) Men midt i mylderet står den unge kvinde med lysglæden over sig? – Gør jeg ikke det, Arnold?

PROFESSOR RUBEK: (*undvigende*). Ikke ganske i midten. Jeg måtte desværre rykke den statuen noget tilbage. For helhedsvirkningens skyld, forstår du. (pp. 261-262)

IRENE: The work you called *Resurrection Day*. And which I call 'our child'.

RUBEK: I was young then. With no experience of life. *My* vision of Resurrection – the loveliest, most beautiful image I could think of – was of a pure young woman, untainted by the world, waking to light and glory, and having nothing ugly or unclean to rid herself of.

IRENE: (*quickly*) Yes, ... and that's how I now stand in the work.

RUBEK: (*hesitantly*) Not quite like that, Irene.

IRENE: (*with mounting tension*) Not quite ...? Do I not stand there as I stood before you?

RUBEK: (*not answering her*) In the years that followed, Irene, the world taught me many things. I began to conceive 'Resurrection Day' as something bigger, something ... Something more complex. That little round plinth on which your statue stood, erect and lonely ... no longer provided space for all the other things I now wanted to say.

IRENE: (*reaches for the knife, then stops*) What other things? Tell me!

RUBEK: Things I saw with my own eyes in the world around me. I had to bring them in. I had no choice, Irene. I extended the plinth ... Made it broad and spacious. And on it I created an area of cracked and heaving earth. And out of the cracks swarmed people, their faces animal beneath the skin. Women and men ... as I knew them from life.

IRENE: (*breathless and expectant*) But at the centre of the throng stands the young and radiant woman? I do, don't I, Arnold?

RUBEK: (*evasively*) Not quite in the middle. I'm afraid I had to move the figure back a little. For the sake of the total effect, you understand. (p. 278)

Rubek's self-defence asserts that a work of major intellectual and emotional reference is born of maturity – maturity of spirit and probably of literal years as well – and that there was a vitiating callowness about his own youthful attempts, however inspired and ambitious. Callowness has been, we have seen, a feature of both Osvald Alving and Hans Lyngstrand, and possibly of Ejlert Løvborg too, sophisticate though he saw himself to be, signifying the difficulty of the male (especially when cosseted by female admiration) in growing up. The cracks swarming with people that accosted him as he went on working at *Resurrection Day* represent the prolixity of possibilities that occur to any true artist when he tries to square the work he has embarked on with the diversity of the actual outside world (and we shall presently see how this happened to the other A. R. also). Nevertheless – that bitter lesson from what happened in the Lohengrin game! – Rodin has sinned against Irene and their relationship inside and out of art by what he went on to do. In truth he has moved the figure of her, confronting the universe, more than just a little, so that far from standing out in her innocence and fineness, she now competes with many another, often of a very different stamp. Truly the *Resurrection Day* that the world now knows and admires is not the sculpture to which she dedicated herself and for which she seemingly lost her own soul. What stands at the centre of the piece now could not be more unlike the ardent young girl she has believed, all these years, commanded the gaze:

> Ja men hør nu også, hvorledes jeg har stillet *mig selv* hen i gruppen. Foran ved en kilde, ligesom her, sidder en skyldbetynget mand, som ikke kan komme helt løs fra jordskorpen. Jeg kalder ham angeren over et forbrudt liv. Han sidder der og dypper sine fingre i det rislende vand – for at skylle dem rene, – og han nages og martres ved tanken om at det aldrig, aldrig lykkes ham. Han når i al evighed ikke fri op til opstandelsens liv. Blir evindelig siddende igen i sit helvede. (p. 263)

Yes, but listen now how I have placed myself in the group. In the foreground, beside a spring – as it might be here – sits a man weighed down with guilt. He cannot quite break free from the earth's crust. I call him remorse for a forfeit life. He sits there dipping his fingers in rippling water – to wash them clean. He is racked and tormented by the thought that he will never, never succeed. Never in all eternity will he win free to achieve the life of the resurrection. He must remain forever captive in his hell. (p. 279)

Is this not an extremely vivid description of the emotional presence in bronze that is Rodin's celebrated 'The Thinker', reposing his head on the knuckle of his muscular right hand, as if it has entertained too many hard speculations for it adequately to hold together? (And later we shall see that critics Daniel Haakonsen and Frode Helland justify this mental picture.) The back of the neck hauntingly suggests the man being 'weighed down by guilt'; his fingers, though not dipped into water, are strong, nervous adjuncts of the contained anguish that is the work's subject. Sitting there naked, inhabiting his own mind, and outside time, he does truly seem some prisoner of eternity, for what resolutions can there be for his existential troubles, what credible possibility of resurrection? And yet he was originally part of a great whole – that somehow never properly came about.

4.

In 1880 Auguste Rodin received a state commission, in part through his friendship with the then Minister of Fine Arts, Antonin Proust: to make a doorway in decorated bronze for the new Musée des Arts Decoratifs. This was truly a breakthrough for him; his career had been slow to take off, had entailed poverty and academic neglect, and when attention came, it was often so pejorative as to be more harmful than otherwise. Even an early masterpiece like 'The Age of Brass' (1876) with its heart-stirring Rousseauesque representation of primitive man awakening to fuller possibilities of life had brought him as much carping criticism as praise. He must, said a jury perplexed by its amazing fidelity to the body, have used a mould on a living person. Rodin was immensely excited at the prospect of the work now asked of him, and suffered from a virtually

immediate superfluity of ideas, soon covering note-books with sketch
after sketch. He decided to take as his model Lorenzo Ghiberti's doors
for the Baptistery at Florence – not inappropriately, for Ghiberti, chosen
above distinguished competitors, was an appointee of the humanist
forward-looking Florentine Republic, conscious, as his writings testify,
of his duty to give visual expression to its ideals. Rodin saw himself as
similarly manifesting ideals for the comparatively new Third Republic.

In literal fact Ghiberti was responsible for *three* of the Baptistery
doorways, but it is his third, the East door that is generally
acknowledged to be his masterpiece. Rodin would perhaps have done
well to have given more consideration than he did to the length of time
on which the Florentine worked on *his* commission: twenty-seven years,
from 1425 to 1452. Each door portrays five scenes from the Old
Testament, in bronze relief remarkable for its perspective, so that Cain
and Abel and Jacob and Esau are figures with depths behind them, and
events like the Arrival of the Queen of Sheba appear to take place in a
three-dimensional world. All round the rectangles of these biblical
scenes goes a continuous procession of heads, symbolic motifs, and
niches with images of the prophets in them. Before long Florentines
were calling the decorated pair The Gates of Paradise, and later,
according to Vasari, Michelangelo pronounced them indeed 'worthy of
Paradise itself'. The title obviously suggested to Rodin its dark opposite,
The Gates of Hell, and his mind turned to the great poet – whom he
would sculpturally portray – who had charted Hell, Purgatory and
Paradise, and in doing so conducted explorations through all humanity
as, in Florence, he had witnessed it: Dante Alighieri.

Ideas continued to proliferate in Rodin's mind, and sculptures
emerged from many, though not all, of them – beginning life as fairly
small-scale maquettes, often little clay models he could hold within one
hand-span: 'The Three Shades', a disturbing trinity of identical figures
in complex but organic union, intended to look down, weary and
experience-battered, over first a sculpted scroll bearing Dante's famous
words: 'Lascate ogni speranza, o voi ch'entrate' (Abandon all hope you
who enter!) and then over the entire portals; 'The Poet', based on
Rodin's conception of the Dante he so admired, its title later amended to
'The Thinker'; 'Eve', that beautiful bronze tribute to womanhood,

pregnant with her arms folded over her breast as if cradling all future humanity, and trying to protect it from the pains it will indubitably suffer. All these are from 1880-1881. Directly from the *Inferno* came the terrifying 'Ugolino' (1882), a representation of man's ingenious capacity for inflicting misery on his fellows – and the appalling challenge of trying to bear it.

It's hard to think of any sculptor since Michelangelo who had embarked on quite so noble and grandly ambitious a project. A state stipend was fixed – 30,000 francs of which Rodin received fees amounting to 27,000 francs over a seven-year-period. A further 35,000 francs was allocated for the expenses of casting. The state also made two studios available to him. Interestingly Rodin was at much the same point in his life as Ibsen was in his when, after *Brand*, he was awarded a state pension (Rodin forty, Ibsen thirty-eight – and in both instances the remuneration was welcome not just for itself, though it certainly was that, but as a vindication of self-belief adhered to not always without strain and too often in the face of uncompromising hostility.)

There was one major distinction, however, between, on the one hand, Dante, Ghiberti and Michelangelo (even though each belonged to a separate cultural phase) and Rodin and his associates on the other. The Florentines were believers, Rodin was not. He had grown up in a devout family from the upper working-class, and his elder sister, Maria, to whom he was extremely close, and who was supportive of him during his difficult boyhood and student years, became a novitiate in a nunnery. Two years later, in 1862, she had to leave because she had contracted peritonitis. Rodin helped to nurse her, but in vain: she died, leaving him emotionally desolate. For a time he himself turned to religion, and went so far as to enter a community led by an outstanding individual dedicated to the relief of suffering everywhere, but especially among the urban derelict of Paris: Father Eymard, later canonised by Pope John XXIII. Father Eymard, the subject of Rodin's magnificent early bust of 1863, understood with great perspicacity not only that Rodin was unsuited to the life of the cloister, but that what already he lived for was to express his awareness of life in sculptural terms. In the end the tragedy of his sister's death, which he took years to get over, became one of those far from uncommon experiences in the histories of human beings:

an event after which the belief in an all-powerful, all-loving God ceases to be a possibility.

The longer he worked on *The Gates of Hell* the more Rodin sought to sever it from the Christian orthodoxy implicit in its Dante-esque inception. It was to be a panorama of humanity – 'fallen' humanity if you liked to call it that, unable to realise its hopes, its visions, and all too often devoured by the very desires that had urged it on. His own complex vision of humanity – and he was himself a reader, a thinker – was compounded by the upheavals of his turbulent sexual/emotional life, which naturally in turn informed his bronze or marble depictions of human beings often possessed by passion, jubilantly or despairingly or bewilderedly, but always whole-heartedly. Anatole France was later to comment, rescuing Rodin's creations from the appalling notion of eternal punishment that his title proclaims :

> These couples who 'pass so lightly on the wind' cry to us: 'our eternal torments are in ourselves! We bear within us the fire that burns us. Hell is earth, and human existence, and the flight of time; it is this life, in which one is incessantly dying.' The hell of lovers is the desperate effort to put the infinite into an hour, to make life pause in one of those kisses which, on the contrary, proclaim its finality. The hell of the voluptuous is the decay of their flesh in the midst of the eternal joy and triumph of the race. The hell of Rodin is not a hell of vengeance, but one of tenderness and pity.[9]

Rodin was twenty-four when he met Rose Beuret, five years younger than he and from a poor rural family, and she moved in with him as a wife (their first child was born in 1865). They were not officially to marry until January 1917, the opening month of the last year of Rodin's life: Rose survived him by only a few months. If it partakes of a history of devotion, it is also the story of a severe and near-continuous imposition, often taking no account whatever of her feelings or her needs, of the sculptor looking on her when she was still a young woman as primarily as the most accessible and intimate of models and the most convenient of servants. Well could Rose Beuret say, with Ibsen's Irene, as she gazed at herself in marble or in bronze, that she had been robbed of her young womanhood, unsparingly sacrificed on the altar of art. Infidelity – though it might be thought consonant with his personal arrogance and vanity – does not enter the picture of Rubek's life with Irene, but it was the constant companion of poor Rose Beuret. Of Rodin's innumerable relationships – some with models acted out in the many rooms he rented as secret studios with that very purpose in mind, some with housemaids and girls encountered completely casually, others, especially later, with women of fashion, wealth and high society – none plays as important a part in the story of his art, and therefore in that of *When We Dead Awaken*, than Camille Claudel, by common consent the greatest passion of his life.

Camille was born in 1864 into a Catholic farming family in Aisne, who moved to Montmartre in 1881. Her younger brother was Paul Claudel, the distinguished diplomat, poet and dramatist (1868-1955), to become one of the leading Catholic apologists of his generation, in such works as the play *L'annonce faite à Marie* of 1912. Long fascinated by the stones of her native region, Camille joined the Paris studio of the sculptor Alfred Boucher, still at the time an adventurous thing for a young woman to do. Boucher then won the Prix de Rome, but before he took off for Italy to fulfil its terms, asked his friend Rodin to be Camille's adviser. By 1884 she was working in Rodin's studio, acting as assistant to him the following year, modelling for him, using nude models for her own burgeoning work, and entering a relationship of the greatest and most demanding intensity for both partners. We know for certain that Camille became pregnant once, losing the child in an accident, but it is possible that she actually gave birth to two other children by him. The casual adventures that Rodin enjoyed with other women did not unduly disturb her – she obviously knew he was something of a satyr, possessing not only formidable energy but a rarer spiritual hunger for women which only the physical could appease – but she was jealous to the point of unbalance of his relationship with his *de facto* wife. Rose's jealousy of her was correspondingly bitter and unremitting – no previous lover had troubled her in the same way – and she made Rodin's life a hell with her nagging and her usually justified suspiciousness. Rodin was, for example, more than capable of saying that he would be away from home for a night and staying away, with Camille, for a month (he did this in the Touraine, reading Balzac and refurbishing his mental stores – to advantage since out of this came what is surely his greatest single work).

Camille Claudel is integral not only to Rodin's oeuvre as we now have it but to some of the finest individual pieces for *The Gates of Hell* itself. He sculpted her as 'Eternal Springtime' (1884) as 'Aurora' and 'Danaid' (1885), as 'Thought' and 'The Kiss' (1886). These works constitute the final triumphal entrance of the procedures of loving between man and woman into the plastic arts. The marble of 'Aurora' has an extraordinary luminosity that penetrates the very being of the onlooker, while that of 'Thought' disseminates the tranquillity of contemplation, the ability to preserve oneself above the fret of existence while staying true to one's innermost ideals. For this Camille wore a cap over her hair, giving her face, indeed her whole head, a kind of poignant austerity. Of even greater interest to students of Ibsen, however, is 'Danaid'. This illustrates the story of a young woman condemned to Hell (Hades) because, at her father's behest, she murdered her husband on her wedding-night; her punishment was to be eternally filling a jug full of holes with water. But the erotically stirring cast-down attitude of the subject, beside a stream, may have been one in which he wanted to portray Camille anyway, even before deciding on a legend suitable for the pose. It was later exhibited, as 'Kilden' ('The Spring') in Oslo, where it earned much enthusiastic praise, and we can surely see, in the graceful but depressed body-lines, Irene at the stream with Rubek in Act Two, and, as importantly, Irene as Rubek's young sculptor's assistant, model and lover, by the waters of the Taunitzer See on those distant Saturday evenings of summer.

In the tempestuous relationship of the other A. R. and his lover there were breaks – in 1891, in 1893 (more severely), and then the final one, in 1898. Camille's demands that Rodin should leave Rose had become yet more violent, yet more frequently accompanied by suicide threats and hysterical accusations that he had stolen from her own creative work. For, initially under Rodin's tutelage, but soon displaying her inherent originality, Camille had developed into a fine sculptor herself; this was something Rodin always recognised. And her sculptures were known in Oslo; in 1897 Fritz Thaulow, friend of Werenskiold and Krohg, presented the Nasjonalgalleriet with a child's head of hers. The truth was, insofar as truth on such a matter can be decided, that Camille's mental stability had long been precarious, that she lacked the necessary capacity to adjust her sensitive, ardent and sensual temperament to any of the exigencies of life among others, let alone in society. Such too is Irene's position. We must not, even while appreciating how much she has been victimised, underplay the disturbance of her mind, her literally murderous paranoia that makes her always carry a knife which, it seems, she is prepared to use.

Was a strained relationship to the outer world, an inability to feel comfortable outside a *solitude à deux* an essential component of Camille's productive early life, even of her work for all its combination of strength and delicacy – as almost certainly is the case with Irene, who moves from Rubek into a life of promiscuity and destructive marriages? Camille's history after the break with Rodin could scarcely be more ghastly. Her paranoid accusations of having been plagiarised by her one-time lover grew more voluble, bouts of derangement occurred more frequently. After the death in 1913 of her father, her greatest supporter, her family had her committed, and she lived for thirty years in an asylum, unvisited by them, including eventually even by her brother Paul, who nevertheless unequivocally and publicly blamed Rodin for her sustained collapse. Her very last days, when in the German occupation she faced the starvation that was the lot of so many asylum inmates, were ones of appalling, unrelieved suffering. Though they take us in time far beyond the years when *When We Dead Awaken* was launched on the world, these lines of Irene's from the play seem disconcertingly prescient:

> Jeg var død i mange år. De kom og bandt mig. Snørte armene sammen på ryggen – . Så sænkte de mig ned i et gravkammer med jernstænger for lugen. Og med polstrede vægge, – så ingen ovenover på jorden kunde høre gravskrigene – . (pp. 235-236)

> I was dead for many years, they came and bound me. Tied my arms behind my back ... Then they lowered me into a tomb with iron bars over the opening. And with padded walls ... so that nobody up above ground could hear the shrieks from the grave ... (p. 257)

Were the convulsions of his long love-affair with Camille responsible for Rodin's inability to complete *The Gates of Hell*? Among other things, almost certainly. The distinguished Rodin scholar Ruth Butler in her *Rodin: The Shape of Genius* (1993) rightly argues on behalf of Rodin's great feeling for women, his refusal to put them into any subsidiary role in his existence. The passion of the relationship between these two outstanding people and artists, forcing itself into every area of Rodin's own life, dictated the nature of many individual works, and the very intensity of these was increasingly responsible for their resistance to incorporation – and subjugation – in the original grand and singular scheme. Without the commission for so mighty and wide-ranging a work Rodin might never have created those masterworks which already are some of western man's best-known artefacts: 'The Thinker', 'Paolo and Francesca'. But militating against its completion was the very fertility of his mind, particularly when under the pressures of his love-life – and of other equally taxing commissions also. There was *The Burghers of Calais* (1884-1886), there was the controversial *Balzac* (1897), surely his supreme creation. Significantly *The Gates of Hell* came to seem unfinishable to the artist himself who had once hoped so much of it, and his paymasters grew understandably impatient. Rodin put what he had accomplished so far on exhibition in 1900, when it was not well-received (or well-understood), and in 1903 set about reimbursement. '*The Gates of Hell* venture was doomed from the outset,' wrote Rodin scholar and critic, Bernard Champigneulle. 'It had to fail, not because a subject of such magnitude was beyond Rodin's scope, but because – and this was the obverse of his genius – the Dante-esque theme which he had chosen ... was beyond his power to control.'[10]   Nevertheless he quotes approvingly the comment of Rodin's fellow-sculptor Antoine Bourdelle who had sensed the difficulty of ever bringing the piece to completion: '*The Gates of Hell* is full of masterpieces.'And as one confronts it now in the grounds of the Musée Rodin, it is hard not to agree with Kenneth Clark's personal judgement:

> I find that the total effect of the gates, the continuous swirling and floating in Art Nouveau rhythms, makes me feel slightly sea-sick; but the individual figures are saved by the force and freedom of their modelling, every form (as Rodin said) thrusting outwards at its point of maximum tension.[11]

The individual figures are indeed rescued just as Clark says, but the truth is that we know them – have long enjoyed relationships with them – *in isolation* rather than as components of a large-scale work, and so will always be unable to return them to any whole. This of course goes to the very heart of the real problem for Rodin:

Lacking faith, indeed morally opposed to, the controlling idea behind his work, he could not provide that ultimate unity for it; he tried to and it receded from him. In letting this happen he was being true to his profoundest conviction, that the age of religion as generally defined had ended, and humankind was accordingly fractured – splendidly and movingly so, but irreparably also.

And no individual sculpted figure – by Rodin or anybody else – is more familiar to a wide range of people than 'The Thinker'. We are all now indebted to Daniel Haakonsen who in *Henrik Ibsen: mennesket og kunstneren* (Henrik Ibsen: Man and Artist, 1981) established that in 1898 Oslo's Nasjonalgalleriet bought two Rodin pieces, 'The Thinker' and 'Danaid'.[12] Both had been already shown at Blomquist Kunsthandel, an establishment Ibsen used to visit, exhibited however under names other than those by which they are called today. 'Danaid' was, as we have just noted, 'Kilden', the 'spring of fresh water' for Camille/Irene perpetually to fill her jug by, 'The Thinker' bore the label of its first Dante-honouring title of 'Dikteren' ('The Poet'). No piece of evidence is more helpful to us than this in our attempts to comprehend the most difficult passages of the play (inevitably the most emotionally charged and poetically worked) between Irene and Rubek, and their contribution to its overall meaning.

The crime against her that Irene only learns about in the course of the play (Act Two) is that demotion of the representation of herself and the consequent elevation in 'Resurrection Day' of that sculpture in which Rubek portrayed himself. At the end of his heart-felt description of this last, quoted above, with its piercing admission 'I call him remorse for a forfeit life' – forfeit because spent too much with the 'false', the 'unreal', the domains of money and high society rather than the instinctual and creative such as he'd earlier inhabited – Irene makes a strange comment, which baffles Rubek – at least momentarily:

IRENE: (*hårdt og koldt*) Digter!

PROFESSOR RUBEK: Hvorfor digter?

IRENE: Fordi du er slap og sløv og fuld af syndsforladelse for alle dit livs gerninger og for alle dine tanker. Du har dræbt min sjæl, – og så modellerer du dig selv i anger og bod og bekendelse, – (*smiler*) – og dermed er dit regnskab opgjort, mener du.

PROFESSOR RUBEK: (*trodsende*) Jeg er kunstner, Irene. Og jeg skammer mig ikke over den skrøbelighed, som kanske klæber ved mig. For jeg er *født* til kunstner, sér du. – Og blir så aldrig andet end kunstner alligevel.

IRENE: (*sér på ham med et fordulgt ondt smil og siger mildt og blødt*) Digter er du, Arnold. (*stryger ham lindt over håret*) Du kære, store, aldrende barn, – at du ikke kan sé *det*!

PROFESSOR RUBEK: (*misfornøjet*) Hvorfor blir du ved at kalde mig digter?

IRENE: (*med lurende øjne*) Fordi der ligger noget undskyldende i det ord, min ven. Noget syndsforladende, – som breder en kåbe over al skrøbeligheden. (*slår pludselig om i tonen*) Men *jeg* var et menneske – dengang! Og *jeg* havde også et liv at leve – og en menneskeskæbne at fuldbyrde. Sé, alt det lod jeg ligge, – gav det hen for at gøre mig dig underdanig. – Å det var et selvmord. (pp. 263-264)

IRENE: (*hard and cold*) Poet!

RUBEK: Why poet?

IRENE: Because you are soft and spineless and full of excuses for everything you've ever done or thought. You killed my soul – then you go and model yourself as a figure of regret and remorse and penitence ... (*Smiles*) ... and you think you've settled your account.

RUBEK: (*defiantly*) I am an artist, Irene. And I'm not ashamed of those human frailties I may have. Don't you see I was *born* to be an artist. And I'll never be anything other than an artist.

IRENE: (*looks at him with a suppressed malevolent smile, and says gently*) You are a poet, Arnold. (*Smooths his hair*) You great big, middle-aged baby – can't you see that!

RUBEK: (*displeased*) Why do you keep calling me a poet?

IRENE: (*with watchful eyes*) Because there's something exonerating about that word, my friend. Forgiving all sins, and drawing a veil over all human frailty. (*Suddenly changing her tone*) But I was a human being – then! I, too, had a life to live ... And a human destiny to fulfil. All that I put aside ... threw it away in order to serve you. It was suicide. (p. 279)

If we super-impose on this dialogue, as Frode Helland in his fine study of the late plays feels that we are entitled to,[13] the image of Rodin's 'Dikteren' ('Poet') and contrast it with one of his Camille-inspired essays in the female form – of which 'Kilden' 'The Spring' (Danaid) is a fine exemplar – then the situation is beautifully illuminated for us. We don't have to use Irene's highly subjective pejorative adjectives to see that Rodin's study shows a self-absorption of a surely very male kind. Brooding over personal problems gets translated into a criticism of the world, and this in turn, to use Irene's terminology, 'exonerates' the man from faults of his own. Male spirituality which fuses with male ambition, male vanity which fuses with male solipsism and difficulty in giving are all too often inextricably entwined, and Rodin – whose own personality contained all these attributes – has rendered this while still making his stooped masculine figure sympathetic, even worthy of admiration.

By contrast the vulnerability of Danaid/ Camille/ Irene as she lies beside the stream is most definitely linked to the ability to give; unlike the male artist she has made no usurpation of other people's lives. That is why Irene was able to make a greater, a more toll-taking sacrifice than Rubek ever could, and spent years in madness and misery; that is why, for all her hysteria and wild threats and accusations, Camille Claudel lost to Auguste Rodin and the male-hegemonic society that looked after him and applauded his victories, in all senses of that word.

Lack of an over-arching religious faith, a belief in humanity that by no means freed them from destructive conventions about social position, money and the role of the sexes, a belief in themselves and in their own art that didn't protect them from blinding egotism and power-wielding, but withal a fundamental ability to recognize the complexity of life, and the terror inherent in it – these are qualities Rubek and Rodin share. So the question must finally be asked: do they share them with Ibsen too? Is *When We Dead Awaken*, with the internationally acknowledged artist at its centre, a disguised confessional work?

No. The very controversies and debates that his plays continued to provoke to the end of his life, for all the lavish plaudits they also received, remain the great testimony to Ibsen's extraordinary refusal ever to compromise in his art, ever to capitulate to bourgeois and boulevard tastes. He was no kind of Rubek opting for a life of ease and comfort, adulterating a big task of many years, making pot-boilers to please a snobbish public, and then sitting back with champagne and seltzer. He said that he was working hard all the time even when he did not appear to be doing so, and so it surely was. Certainly *When We Dead Awaken* offers us through Rubek apotheosized a picture of what the true artist must be like, but, until those last moments before the high peaks, never through Rubek in his life, and we have to assume that his creations, except for those of his early maturity, when Irene was his helper, were as flawed as his personality.

We can return to the Apollo/Dionysus dialectic which we have seen in operation throughout Ibsen's major plays, and note that his 'dramatic epilogue' ends with the promise of the sun which his characters expect to see but will not. Ibsen's art is sun-honouring, Apollonian in its qualities of rational understanding, moral firmness, common sense and kindness. But it cannot and will not operate without the Dionysian dance – frenzied, painful, ecstatic, despairing – being allowed to run its full course. That is for him the condition of the freedom he at once permits, and celebrates in, his artists.

Conclusion

When Karsten Bernick in *The Pillars of Society* returned from Paris and London, now a sophisticated and charismatic young man, he put all his ample energies into the restoration of his family firm's fortunes, building up from this a locally-based business empire which he ruled ruthlessly. For the sake of success, which indeed came quite spectacularly, he ditched the young woman whose heart he had won, married her sister for her money, used an old friend as a scapegoat for his own misdemeanours, and sent into general currency an untruth calumniating him and of great convenience to himself. This is to say nothing of the sharp business practices he later indulged in, ones which brought to theatregoers' attention questionable or downright dishonest contemporary affairs: the laying-off of men, without adequate union representation, in shipyards and elsewhere because of new labour-saving machinery; the buying-up of land with insider knowledge of the imminent construction of railway-lines; and, worst of all, the scandal of the 'floating coffin' ships bound for America. We become not only aware of Bernick's guilt here (perhaps least convincing in this last instance) but are made privy to his deplorable behaviour in other areas: his contemptuous neglect of his wife which she feels only too keenly, his blindness to his sister's feelings on having become an unpaid social drudge, his harshness to his small son whom he thrashes for insubordination. Yet oddly we do not dislike him; on the contrary, we feel something great and powerful about him, some force that could have been, and still might be, harnassed to good. That good is lodged, so to speak, within the woman whom he once loved and whom he treated so badly, the maverick, fiercely independent feminist Lona Hessel. The play's famous last lines indicate the moral order she is bringing back into his long, deliberately amoral life:

KONSUL BERNICK: Det har jeg også lært i disse dage: det er I kvinder, som er samfundets støtter.

FRØKEN HESSEL: Da har du lært en skrøbelig visdom, svoger. (*lægger hånden vægtigt på hans skulder*) Nej, du; sandhedens og frihedens ånd, – *det* er samfundets støtter. (HU VIII, p. 148)

BERNICK: ... That's something else I've learnt these last few days: it's you women who are the pillars of society.

LONA HESSEL: That's a pretty feeble piece of wisdom you've learnt, Karsten. (*Placing her hand firmly on his shoulder*) No, my friend, the spirit of truth and the spirit of freedom – *these* are the pillars of society. (Vol. V, p. 126)

Nevertheless we cannot help but feel that Karsten Bernick is right in his last affirmation, and that there is something disingenuous in Lona's retort. The male drive towards achievement of mastering ambition, towards realisation of what he feels to be his own potential, a realisation which too often requires not only admiration but subservience from others, puts at risk not only the virtue of honesty, but that of respect for others, the one essential requisite for freedom in any community. Bernick's career and what in himself he has jettisoned to achieve it thus foreshadows Solness' with his 'helpers and servants', and his aspirations to the 'robust' conscience of the Vikings who, after committing plunder and rapine, went on (in his picture of them) to enjoy feasting and connubial pleasures. Just as Bernick has confined Betty to the margins of his attentions, so (if with greater sensitivity to her plight) has Solness Aline. Rubek's ability to regard Irene as an 'episode', from which he can move on, to enjoy wider approbation in the world he wishes to conquer (and does), is also foreshadowed in the first major prose-play of contemporary life Ibsen gave us. And to this we may add the fact we have already noted that, however shallow, however lacking in intellectual qualities we may find her to be, Maja, Rubek's wife, is also a victim of his relegation of the personal to an inferior position in his life.

Thus there seems to be a destructive tension between the drives without which major accomplishments can never take shape, and that emotionally registered recognition of otherness without which all human communication is detrimentally incomplete. We have here to acknowledge that Karsten Bernick is in the eyes of his townsfolk an extremely successful, indeed conscientious Consul who has done unprecedented good things for the community, and that even some knowledge on their part of how much he has compromised the morality with which he started out in life cannot altogether change their high regard and gratitude. And this study has been written to no purpose if it is not clear that Solness and Rubek are richly gifted men too, with substantial works to their credit. Yet – and this brings us back to the discussion of malehood that so vitally informs these plays[1] – the capitulation to their success has vitiated their attainments scarcely less than their private lives. The citizens of the little sea-port may not realise it, but their community is not one where honest dealings and the proclamations of certain basic rights (eg those of the ship-yard workers) can prevail: a bourgeois sense of safety, a kind of proto-consumerist prosperity have blinkered people's awareness of these disagreeable but important truths. Solness' buildings have earned him national and international accolades as well as commissions, but they clearly belong to *one* phase only of Norwegian/European taste and requirements; they will soon be superseded, and he knows it, as do others (the Broviks, the young couple who want the villa out at Løvstrand). Rubek chose not to sustain the artistry he had released in himself in that creation of the young girl who could embody 'Opstandelsens dag', but to go on to work which suited the fashion of the times, but which (we feel) may well pass into obscurity when this has, inevitably, run its course. What happened to the original statue in Rubek's best-known work is a paradigm for the whole situation of these men, these artists – a refusal to recognise woman as needed co-sharer in the human condition, a downgrading of the feminine at the expense of the crudely defined masculine. This is surely borne out by their offences against women being not singular but plural; in *The Pillars of Society* Betty, Martha, Lona, and to a certain extent Dina Dorf also, are victims of Bernick's dedication to success; it is not only Aline whom Solness uses, but numerous young women we do not meet but of whom Kaja Fosli is an outstanding wronged representative. And his relations with Hilde Wangel are charged with unbridled egotism exploitative of her youth. Further, we have just insisted that Rubek should not wholly be pardoned for his behaviour to Maja, and in a vignette he gives us of his early life we gather he promised many a young girl that he would take her to the top of a mountain and show her the world.

There is another aspect of Karsten Bernick's career which should concern us. As Consul he has been responsible for significant improvements to his home-town (a school-house, gas- and water-works) and for its beautification (he has presented a park to the place). But – and this is lamented in general talk both in the final version of the play and in earlier drafts[2] – an unappealing consequence of his consulship is that all artistic activity has declined. Formerly, we hear, the town had a Dancing Club, a Music Society, and a Dramatic Society prepared to stage romantic plays written by one of the townsfolk. These have now been replaced by sewing bees for good causes where books of undenominational piety are sanctimoniously read aloud, and there is much undercover small-town tittle-tattle of a demeaning nature. (This too is something stressed in the earlier drafts.) The expansion of commerce and business in the mid-nineteenth century went hand-in-hand with a utilitarianism that ended up in rank and unrepentant philistinism. The very term, originally a derogatory German appropriation of the biblical name for the Caananites' enemy, brings to mind its employment in the anathemas of Goethe and of Robert Schumann, both in the latter's journalism where the Philistines represent those hostile to the demands of new music and in such compositions as the *Davidsbündlertänze* of 1837-1838, the joyful dances of the League of David (who, in the Bible, defeated the Philistine giant, Goliath).[3] But, especially for British readers, the word is bound up more with Ibsen's older contemporary Matthew Arnold (1822-1888) who in his *Essays in Criticism* (1865-1869) employed it to denote the enemies of the free soul, for those systems preventative of creative relations between the private and the societised individual. We can remember too in *The Pillars of Society* young Olaf's enthusiasm for stories of American adventure and his rapturous welcoming of the circus-troupe who disembark in the town, both compensating him for what he has been deprived of in the society over which his father has so much authority. Indeed the play's treatment of this troupe cannot but remind us of Dickens' similar use of a circus with its clowns and 'Horse-riding' in his most passionately anti-utilitarian novel, *Hard Times* (1854).

Solness and Rubek are neither philistine in themselves nor do they encourage philistinism in others. Both not only possess active imaginations but, to a marked extent, live by them. This was even evidenced in their youth – by the former's love of Viking sagas, by the latter's promises of showing forth the glories of the world from mountain-tops. But both, culpably, have surrendered to the philistines of the greater world, by performing to their demands, tastes and blindnesses, self-betrayals of which they are tormentedly conscious. Solness' predatory involvement with the world of deals, contracts, cash has undoubtedly undermined key qualities in him just as it has catered for other ones, and by the time we meet him he is totally dissatisfied with those homes for people for which he has been responsible. Indeed this dissatisfaction helps to kill him. Rubek has thriven on celebrity even while despising those who have helped him to experience it. He may have gratified some buried integrity in himself by all those animal likenesses in the busts so handsomely commissioned by Establishment persons, but the result has hardly been art of which he can justly be proud.

Philistinism is not a failing of which we can find the other three male artists in our survey guilty. Indeed Osvald, Lyngstrand and Løvborg have all, as it were, been members of Schumann's League of David against the Philistines in their society. They would, we feel sure, have detested life under Bernick's consulship. Osvald has fought for his ideals against the narrowness of Pastor Manders and those forces in his own Norwegian society which upheld him and his like; he has sought liberation in Paris and an alternative credo in its artist circles. Lyngstrand reacted against his father and his narrow commerce-oriented values, we know, and has sustained himself since with ideas of the sculptures he himself will create and of the great classical monuments of Italy and Greece. Ejlert Løvborg, as we have seen, belongs to that section of nineteenth-century society which consciously defined itself against the materialistic, the Philistine: the Bohemian. The inadequacies of both Osvald and Lyngstrand relate to their callowness which in turn is linked to a failure to give women a full place in their lives and visions. Osvald is deceived by the circles he frequents in Paris into an over-evaluation of their liberated life-style that in truth only perpetuates conventional subjugation of woman by man; this is revealed again in his treatment of Regine. Lyngstrand, with sufficient, indeed impressive artistic insight into Ellida, is betrayed by his own half-understood homo-erotic desires into condescending treatment of Bolette and Hilde, behaviour which may well contribute to inability properly to realize his own creative plans.

Ejlert Løvborg is a quite different case, and interestingly he is the only artist of those we have considered who follows Ibsen's own avocation of writer. He is a deliberate flouter of Philistia, and unlike all the others, but especially Solness and Rubek, he has studied his own society to examine its forward-tending currents and has given the future intense consideration. Even if he were to be found wrong in his deductions, it would not, we feel, occasion him the disagreeable surprises that the architect and the world-famous sculptor receive in later life. Nor can Løvborg be accused of undervaluing women. He understands and indeed empathises with Hedda and Thea in ways impossible to the other male artists in this book, and we know – from Ibsen's drafts as well as from the text of the play – that new, more open, more honest relationships between the sexes are an article of faith for him, that they will be key constituents of any desirable society of the future. Yet his stress is on 'companionship', camaraderie. Is not something deeper and more demanding required? Such a stress only gratifies his abundant vanity, that need for approbation and attention of one kind or another which constitutes one of the faces of traditional malehood.

Furthermore – and this seems to me confirmed by his willingness (or half-willingness) to go along with Hedda's Dionysiac fantasies about him – his essential bohemianism has discouraged in him two qualities which (we hope) Karsten Bernick has learned truly to appreciate at the close of *The Pillars of Society*: first, a responsibility that can never traffic in double standards and deceptions, and second, but perhaps more important still, kindness. One is aware when re-reading or seeing again Ibsen's plays that between his people spaces exist, spaces which seem themselves to speak. Are they not speaking of the paramount importance of unsentimental unegotistic love, of the kindness of feeling and deed which each of them could give the others were they not culturally conditioned against doing so? Ibsen does not partake of this conditioning. He himself accords his flawed persons precisely the sort of respect and courtesy that proceeds from the kind of love just adumbrated. He faces up to their faults, he does not flinch from the consequences of them. But he takes these on with a courage of the heart as well as of the intellect, and installs his individuals in works of art towards the meaningful totality of which each makes his or her contribution.

It is an Apollonian achievement, and one in which Christian charity predominates. For all his very real radical sympathies, Ibsen could never tether himself to a political party, and it is small wonder that, for all his detestation of Lammers-like evangelicism and orthodoxies, he never made the break into Nietzschean atheism which Brandes would have liked him of him. Ibsen's art is always concerned with diversity, the contradictions even inside the single human being, and with acknowledgement of this. At the very heart of his oeuvre is his passionate belief, which as an artist he surely realised, in a deeper understanding between the sexes, and he surveyed the world in the hope that such a thing was possible. The Dionysiac vision is too singular, does not allow for the charitable understanding to which his plays are, at bottom, testaments. After all Ejlert Løvborg, analyst of the future and lover of women though he was, never wore those vine-leaves in his hair.

Notes

All Norwegian quotations from Ibsen's works are taken from Henrik Ibsen: *Samlede Verker (Hundreårsutgave)* Vols. I-XXI. Gyldendal norsk forlag, Oslo 1928-1957. Abbreviated HU in text. English translations are taken from *The Oxford Ibsen* (ed. J. W. McFarlane), Oxford University Press, 1960-1977.

Introduction
(pages 11-20)

1. *Oxford Ibsen* Vol. VIII, p. 1.
2. See pp. 218-222.
3. Engelstad, Fredrik: 'The Defeat of Failure and the Failure of Success. Gender Roles and Images of the Male in Henrik Ibsen's Last Plays' in *Proceedings of VII International Ibsen Conference, Grimstad 1993*. Centre for Ibsen Studies 1994.
4. See Collett, Camilla: *The District Governor's Daughters*. Translated from the Norwegian by Kirsten Seaver, pp. 8-9.
5. Nietzsche, Friedrich: *Die Geburt der Tragödie (The Birth of Tragedy)* 1872.
6. Op. cit, pp. 188-217.
7. Coleridge, Samuel Taylor: *Biographia Literaria*. 1817, Everyman's Library Edition (Dent, Dutton) 1967, p. 180.

Ghosts
The Artist as Impressionist: Osvald Alving
(pages 21-46)

Works particularly relevant to this chapter on the arts in France:
Adams, Steven: *The Barbizon School and the Origins of Impressionism*. Phaidon 1997.
House, John: *Monet: Nature into Art*. Yale 1986.
Mathieu, Caroline: *Musée d'Orsay: Guide to the Collections*. Éditions de la Réunion des Musées Nationaux 2004.
Thompson, Belinda: *Impressionism – Origins, Practice, Reception*. Thames and Hudson 2000
Zeldin, Theodore: *France 1848-1945* (two volumes). Oxford University Press 1973

and 1977.

1. See Act Two of *Pillars of Society* (*Oxford Ibsen*, Vol. V, p. 63).
2. See Meyer, Michael: *Henrik Ibsen: The Top of a Cold Mountain 1883-1906*, p. 26. Lindberg was at the time responsible for the first European performance of the play.
3. Quoted in Belinda Thompson: *Impressionism*, p. 163.
4. Appendix III, Commentary on *Ghosts*, *Oxford Ibsen*, Vol. V, p. 467.
5. FrodeHelland and Arnfinn Åslund: 'Dette er ikke en pipe (om Henrik Ibsens *Gengangere*)', *Bøygen 1-96*.
6. See especially Prideaux, Sue: *Edvard Munch: Behind 'The Scream'*, pp. 79-107.
7. Hardy, Thomas: *The Return of the Native*. Folio Society, p. 20.
8. Appendix III, *Oxford Ibsen*, Vol. V, p. 468.
9. *Ibid.*
10. *Ibid.*
11. Nietzsche, Friedrich: *The Birth of Tragedy* and *The Case of Wagner*. Translated with commentary by Walter Kaufmann. Vintage Books 1967.
12. J. P. Jacobsen (1847-1885) translated Darwin's *Origin of Species* into Danish (1871), and his *Descent of Man* in 1874-75. Divided in his loyalties between science and literature, and a proselytizing atheist, he produced some of the finest works of fiction in all Nordic literature, pioneering in their sensibility, philosophy and art, *Mogens* (1872), *Fru Marie Grubbe* (1876) and *Niels Lyhne* (1880). Through this last work he makes an entrance into British culture, since the composer Frederick Delius based his opera *Fennimore and Gerda* (1910) on it. See also in the context of Ibsen and Darwinism the very interesting essay by Asbjørn Aarseth: 'Ibsen and Darwin: a Reading of *The Wild Duck*' in *Modern Drama* (2005).
13. *Oxford Ibsen*, Vol. V, p. 466.
14. The renowned 1911 edition of the *Encyclopaedia Britannica* has been edited to form the LoveToKnow1911: Explanation web-site.
15. Term coined by Richard Dawkins in *The Selfish Gene* (1976).
16. Prideaux, Sue, *op. cit.*, p. 54.
17. *Ibid.*, p. 239.

The Lady From the Sea
The Artist as Hellenist: Hans Lyngstrand
(pages 47-80)

Works particularly relevant to this chapter on sculpture:

Bukdahl, Else Marie: *The Roots of NeoClassicism, Wiedewelt, Thorvaldsen and Danish Sculpture of Today*. Royal Danish Academy of Fine Arts 2004.

Hall, James: *The World as Sculpture: The changing status of sculpture from the Renaissance to the present day*. Chatto & Windus 1999.

Hall, James: *Michelangelo and the Reinvention of the Human Body*. Chatto & Windus 2005.

On the Molde area of Norway:

The Rough Guide to Scandinavia : Denmark, Norway, Sweden and Finland. Ed. Jules Brown, Mick Sinclair *et al* 7th edition. Rough Guides 2006. Visit www.visitmolde.com

1. *Oxford Ibsen*, Vol. VII, Appendix 1, p. 459.
2. Joan Templeton: 'About Jacob Fjelde's Bust of Ibsen' on www.askart.com (for *American Artists' Bluebook*).
3. See Fjelde, Rolf: *Ibsen: The Complete Major Prose Plays.* Farrar Straus Giroux 1978, pp. 588-590.
4. *Oxford Ibsen*, Vol. VII, Appendix 1, p. 448.
5. Vilhelm Foldal is a bent, weary, shabby clerk with a soft felt hat and large horn-rimmed glasses, for whom little in life has gone right. He labours under the delusion that the tragedy he wrote when young was a great literary achievement, has sacrificed years of time and energy to this belief, and has been bolstered up in it by John Gabriel Borkman himself (who all the time knows its real worthlessness). Foldal goes on correcting and improving his 'magnum opus' in the hope that one day it will triumphantly see daylight, thus counterpointing the greater delusions of his old friend and employer; meanwhile his private life grows ever more dismal.
6. Janet Garton in her essay 'The middle plays' in *The Cambridge Companion to Ibsen* points out that strangeness of name characterises the heroine of the previous play *Rosmersholm* (1886), Rebekka West, and the eponymous heroine of the next one, *Hedda Gabler* (1890), to emphasize both their distance from the community and their Otherness.
7. *Oxford Ibsen*, Vol. VII, Appendix 1, p. 450 .
8. *Ibid.*, pp. 449-50.
9. *Ibid.*, p. 450.
10. See introduction by Kirsten Seaver to her translation of Collett, Camilla: *The District Governor's Daughters*, pp. 8-9.
11. *Oxford Ibsen*, Vol. VII, Appendix 1, p. 449.
12. *Ibid.*
13. Ibsen meant a great deal to Thomas Mann. He even taught himself Norwegian in order to read the plays in the original, as James Joyce was later to do. He was only eighteen when he wrote an admiring review of *The Master Builder*. In the very month of his twentieth birthday, June 1895, he played the part of Gregers Werle in a production of *The Wild Duck* in Munich where he was then living. His performance earned him praise. It is tempting to think that Mann retained something of Werle in his probing and uncomfortable concern for truth. See Prater, Donald : *Thomas Mann: a Life*, 1995.
14. See note 2 above.
15. See Meyer, Michael: *Henrik Ibsen: The Farewell to Poetry 1864-1882*, p. 28.
16. *Ibid.*, p. 36.
17. *Oxford Ibsen*, Vol. VII, Appendix 1, p. 450.

18. *Ibid.*, p. 467.
19. Moi, Toril: *Henrik Ibsen and the Birth of Modernism.* Oxford 2006, p. 310.
20. Isherwood, p. 75.
21. John Addington Symonds, Oxford educated and later a fellow of Magdalen College, was an apologist for Hellenism, especially as recovered by the Renaissance. Its attraction for him was bound up with his love of male beauty, and though married, he quietly promoted the need for a more accepting attitude to homosexuality in the society of his times, in pamphlets later taken up by more radical thinkers like Havelock Ellis. His most substantial and influential work was *Renaissance in Italy* (1875-1886).
22. See See Meyer, Michael: *Henrik Ibsen: The Farewell to Poetry 1864-1882*, p. 89.

Hedda Gabler
The Artist as Bohemian: Ejlert Løvborg
(pages 81-124)

Works particularly relevant to this chapter on Scandinavian (Christiania) Bohemianism:
Bjørnstad, Ketil: *Historien om Edvard Munch.* Gyldendal 1993.
Bjørnstad, Ketil: *Jæger*, Gyldendal 2001.
Prideaux, Sue: *Edvard Munch: Behind 'The Scream'.* Yale 2005.
Tanner, Michael: *Nietzsche.* Oxford 1994.

1. Nietzsche, Friedrich: *The Gay Science.* Translated from the German with commentary by Walter Kaufmann. Vintage Books 1974.
2. See Binding, Paul: *Imagined Corners: Exploring the World's First Atlas.* Review 2003.
3. *Oxford Ibsen*, Vol. VII, Appendix II, p. 476.
4. Sprinchorn, Evert: 'Ibsen and the Immoralists'. In *Comparative Literature Studies* (University Park, Pa) 9:1 (1972).
5. Nilsen, Håvard: 'How Ibsen Found His Hedda Gabler'. In *Ibsen Studies* Vol. III No. 1. Taylor & Francis 2003.
6. Spinchorn, Evert, *op. cit.*, p. 71.
7. Quoted in author's own translation in Meyer, Michael: *Henrik Ibsen: The Farewell to Poetry 1864-1882*, p. 162.
8. *Oxford Ibsen*, Vol. VII, Appendix II, p. 483.
9. Archer, William: 'Introduction to *Hedda Gabler* (translated by William Archer and Edmund Gosse)'. Charles Scribner's Sons 1907, pp. 5-6.
10. *Oxford Ibsen*, Vol. VII, Appendix II, p. 481.
11. See Bjørnstad, Ketil: *Historien om Edvard Munch* for a particularly vivid picture of Jæger's impact on his own generation and younger people.
12. *Oxford Ibsen*, Vol. VII, Appendix II, p. 480.
13. See translation of the above by Torbjørn Støverud and Hal Sutcliffe. Arcadia 2001,

p. 34.
14. *Peer Gynt*, HU VI, p. 166.
15. From *Peer Gynt*. Translated by James Kirkup and Christopher Fry with the assistance of James Walter McFarlane and Johan Fillinger. *Oxford Ibsen*, Vol. III, p. 356.
16. *Kejser og Galilæer*, HU VII, p. 175
17. *Emperor and Galilean*. Translated by James Walter McFarlane and Graham Orton. *Oxford Ibsen*, Vol. IV, p. 327.
18. Calasso, Roberto: *The Marriage of Cadmus and Harmony*. Translated from the Italian by Tim Parks. Vintage 1994, p. 44.
19. Nietzsche, Friedrich: *Ecce Homo*. Translated from the German by R. J. Hollingdale. Penguin 1979, p. 134.
20. See Meyer, Michael: *Henrik Ibsen: On Top of a Cold Mountain 1883-1906*, pp. 156-157.

The Master Builder
The Artist as Challenger: Halvard Solness
(pages 125-170)

Works particularly relevant to this chapter on art and architecture:
Duncan, Alastair: *Art Nouveau*. Thames & Hudson 1994.
Frampton, Kenneth: *Modern Architecture: a critical history*. Thames & Hudson 1992.
Hauglid, Roar: *Norwegian Stave Churches*. Dreyers Forlag, Oslo 1970.
Hughes, Robert: *The Shock of the New* (updated edition). Thames & Hudson 1991.
See also: www.kultur-og-idrettsetaten.oslo.kommune.no (on architecture in Oslo).

1. *Oxford Ibsen*, Vol. VIII, p. 1.
2. Sprinchorn, Evert (ed.): *Ibsen: Letters and Speeches*. Translated from the Norwegian by the editor, pp. 302-303.
3. Meyer, Michael: *Henrik Ibsen: The Top of a Cold Mountain 1883-1906*, p. 215.
4. *Ibid.*, p. 213.
5. Auden, W. H. in *The English Auden: Poems, Essays and Dramatic Writings 1927-1939*, ed. Edward Mendelson. Faber 1977, p. 36.
6. *Oxford Ibsen*, Vol. VII, Appendix III, p. 521 (both the original and J. W. McFarlane's translation)..
7. *Henrik Ibsens Samlede Verker 1866-1873, Bind 2*, p. 446.
8. Archer, William; 'Introduction to *The Master Builder*. Translated by William Archer and Edmund Gosse'. Charles Scribner's Sons 1907, pp. 2-3.
9. *Oxford Ibsen*, Vol. VII, Appendix III, p. 522.
10. See Robert Ferguson: *Henrik Ibsen: A New Biography*. Ferguson, also the author of a biography of Hamsun, gives a vivid picture both of Hamsun's lectures themselves and of Ibsen's attendance at them, in the company of Hildur Andersen.

11. See Rem, Tore: *Henry Gibson/Henrik Ibsen: Den provinsielle verdensdikteren.* Cappelen 2006.
12. Tjønneland, Ejvind: 'Allegory, Intertextuality and Death – the problem of symbolism in Ibsen's *The Master Builder*'. In *Proceedings of the VII International Ibsen Conference, Grimstad 1993.* Centre for Ibsen Studies, Oslo.
13. Dietrichson, Jan: 'Ibsen and Lorenz Dietrichson'. *Proceedings of the 10th International Ibsen Conference 2003.* Centre for Ibsen Studies, Oslo.
14. Meyer, Michael: *Henrik Ibsen: The Top of a Cold Mountain 1883-1906*, p. 213.

When We Dead Awaken
The Artist as Man-With-Woman: Arnold Rubek
(pages 171-209)

Works particularly relevant to this chapter on Rodin:
Ayral-Claus, Odile: *Camille Claudel, A Life.* Harry N. Abrams 2002.
Butler, Ruth: *Rodin: The Shape of Genius.* Yale 1993.
Champigneule, Bernard: *Rodin.* Thames & Hudson 1967.
Eisenwerth J. A. Schmoll: *Auguste Rodin and Camille Claudel.* Pegasus Library 1999.
Goldscheider, Ludwig (ed.): *Rodin.* Phaidon 1939/1996.
Prater, Donald: *A Ringing Glass: The life of Rainer Maria Rilke.* Oxford 1986.
Rilke, Rainer Maria: *Selected Letters 1902-1926.* Translated by R. F. C. Hull. Quartet 1988.

1. Nietzsche, Friedrich: *The Birth of Tragedy and The Case of Wagner*, pp. 35-36.
2. Schikaneder, Emanuel: *Libretto for Die Zauberflöte* (The Magic Flute). Translated from the German by Lionel Salter for Archiv recording, 1996.
3. *Oxford Ibsen*, Vol. VIII, pp. 299ff.
4. Joyce, James (ed. Kevin Barry): *Occasional, Critical and Political Writings.* Oxford 2000, p. 47.
5. Quoted in Hillman, James (ed. Thomas Moore): *A Blue Fire.* Routledge 1989, p. 115.
6. *Lille Eyolf*, HU XII, p. 215.
7. *Oxford Ibsen*, Vol. VIII, p. 54.
8. Nietzsche, Friedrich: *The Birth of Tragedy* and *The Case of Wagner*, p. 183.
9. Goldscheider, Ludwig (ed.): *Rodin*, p. 416.
10. Champigneulle: *Rodin*, p. 144.
11. Clark, Kenneth: *Civilisation.* BBC/John Murray 1969, p. 319.
12. *Op. cit.*, pp. 258-260.
13. Helland, Frode: *Melankoliens spill. En studie i Henrik Ibsens siste dramaer*, pp. 394-395. Helland sees another work of art, to be found in Orvieto, to be of seminal importance to Ibsen's last play – a most interesting thesis which falls outside the scope of this study.

Conclusion
(pages 211-217)

1. See again Fredrik Engelstad: 'The Defeat of Failure and the Failure of Success. Gender Roles and Images of the Male in Henrik Ibsen's Last Plays'. In *Proceedings of VII International Ibsen Conference, Grimstad 1993*. Centre for Ibsen Studies 1994.
2. *Oxford Ibsen*, Vol. V, pp. 133-135.
3. See Taylor, Ronald: *Robert Schumann: His Life and Work*, especially pp. 152-154.

Bibliography

Primary sources:

Ibsen, Henrik: *Samlede Verker (Hundreårsutgave)* Vols. I-XXI. Gyldendal norsk forlag, Oslo 1928-1957.
McFarlane, J. W. (ed.): *The Oxford Ibsen*. Oxford University Press, 1960-1977.

Secondary literature:

Aarseth, Asbjørn: 'Ibsen and Darwin: a Reading of *The Wild Duck*'. In *Modern Drama* Vol. 48, No. 1. University of Toronto Press 2005.
——: *Ibsens samtidsskuespill. En studie i glasskapets dramaturgi.* Universitetsforlaget 1999.
——: 'Greenhouse, Zoo, Aquarium'. In *Ibsen Studies* Vol. IV, No. 1. Taylor & Francis 2004.
Adams, Steven: *The Barbizon School and the Origins of Impressionism*. Phaidon 1997.
Alison, Jane & Brown, Carol: *Border Crossings*. Barbican Art Gallery 1992.
Andersen, Merete Morken: *Ibsen håndboken*. Gyldendal 1995.
Auden, W. H., in: *The English Auden: Poems, Essays and Dramatic Writings 1927-1939*, ed. Edward Mendelson. Faber 1977.
Ayral-Claus, Odile: *Camille Claudel, A Life*. Harry N. Abrams 2002.
Bjørnstad, Ketil: *Historien om Edvard Munch*. Gyldendal 1993.
——: *Jæger*. Gyldendal 2001.
Brandes, Georg: *Hovedstrømninger i det 19de Aarhundredes Litteratur*. Gyldendal 1872.
Bukdahl, Else Marie: *The Roots of NeoClassicism. Wiedewelt, Thorvaldsen and Danish Sculpture of Today*. Royal Danish Academy of Fine Arts 2004.
Butler, Ruth: *Rodin: The Shape of Genius*. Yale 1993.
Calasso, Roberto: *The Marriage of Cadmus and Harmony*. Translated from the Italian by Tim Parks. Vintage 1994.
Champigneulle, Bernard: *Rodin*. Thames & Hudson 1967.
Clark, Kenneth: *Civilisation*. BBC/John Murray 1969.
Coleridge, Samuel Taylor: *Biographia Literaria 1817*. Everyman's Library Edition (Dent, Dutton) 1967.
Collett, Camilla: *The District Governor's Daughters*. Translated from the Norwegian by Kirsten Seaver. Norvik Press 1991.
Dawkins, Richard: *The Selfish Gene*. Oxford 1976.

de Figueiredo, Ivo: *Henrik Ibsen, Mennesket*. Aschehoug 2006 (first volume, up to the period of *Brand* and *Peer Gynt*).

Dietrichson, Jan: 'Ibsen and Lorenz Dietrichson'. In *Proceedings of the 10th International Ibsen Conference 2003*. Centre for Ibsen Studies, Oslo.

Duncan, Alastair: *Art Nouveau*. Thames & Hudson 1994.

Eide, Tom: *Ibsens dialogkunst. Ettik og Eksistens i 'Når vi døde vågner'*. Universitetsforlaget 2001.

Engelstad, Fredrik: 'The Defeat of Failure and the Failure of Success. Gender Roles and Images of the Male in Henrik Ibsen's Last Plays'. In *Proceedings of the VII International Ibsen Conference, Grimstad 1993*. Centre for Ibsen Studies 1994.

Eisenwerth J. A. Schmoll: *Auguste Rodin and Camille Claudel*. Pegasus Library 1999.

Ewbank, Inga-Stina: 'The last plays'. In *The Cambridge Companion to Ibsen*, ed. J. W. McFarlane. Cambridge 1994.

Ferguson, Robert: *Henrik Ibsen: A New Biography*. Richard Cohen Books 1996.

—— (ed): *Said About Ibsen*. Translated from the Norwegian by Robert Ferguson. Gyldendal 2006.

Frampton, Kenneth: *Modern Architecture: a critical history*. Thames & Hudson 1992.

Garton, Janet: 'The middle plays'. In *The Cambridge Companion to Ibsen*, ed. J. W. McFarlane. Cambridge 1994.

Gross, Kenneth: *Dream of the Moving Statue*. Cornell University Press 1992.

Goldscheider, Ludwig (ed.): *Rodin*. Phaidon 1939/1996.

Gullestad, Siri : 'Fear of Falling; Some Unconscious Factors in Ibsen's Play, *The Master Builder*'. In *Scandinavian Psychoanalytical Review* 1994.

Haakonsen, Daniel: *Henrik Ibsen: mennesket og kunstneren*. Aschehoug (new edn) 2003.

Habermas, Jurgen: *The Philosophical Discourse of Modernity*. Translated from the German by Frederick Lawrence. MIT Press 1987.

Hall, James: *The World as Sculpture: The changing status of sculpture from the Renaissance to the present day*. Chatto & Windus 1999.

——: *Michelangelo and the Reinvention of the Human Body*. Chatto & Windus 2005.

Hauglid, Roar: *Norwegian Stave Churches*. Dreyers Forlag, Oslo 1970.

Helland, Frode: *Melankoliens spill. En studie i Henrik Ibsens siste dramaer*. Universitetsforlaget 2000.

——: 'Petrified Time: Ibsen's response to modernity with special emphasis on *Little Eyolf* . In *Ibsen Studies* Vol. III, No. 2. Taylor & Francis 2003.

Helland, Frode & Åslund, Arnfinn: 'Dette er ikke en pipe (om Henrik Ibsens *Gengangere*)'. In *Bøygen 1* 1996.

Hemmer, Bjørn: *Ibsen: Kunstnerens vei*. Vigmostad & Bjørke 2003.

Hillman, James (ed. Thomas Moore): *A Blue Fire*. Routledge 1989.

House, John: *Monet: Nature into Art*. Yale 1986.

Hughes, Robert: *The Shock of the New*. Thames & Hudson 1991 (updated edn).

Ibsen, Bergliot: *The Three Ibsens: Memories of Henrik Ibsen, Suzannah Ibsen and Sigurd Ibsen*. Translated from the Norwegian by Gerik Schjelderup. Hutchinson 1951.

Isherwood, Christopher: *Lost Years: A Memoir 1945-1951* (ed. Katherine Bucknell). HarperCollins 2000.

Johansen, Jørgen Dines: 'Mimetic and diegetic space in Ibsen's later plays'. In *Acta Ibseniana No. 1: Ibsen and the Arts. Painting – Sculpture – Architecture* (ed. Astrid Sæther). Unipub, Oslo 2002.

——: 'Art is (Not) a Woman's Body'. In *Proceedings of VII International Ibsen Conference, Grimstad 1993*. Centre for Ibsen Studies 1994.

Joyce, James (ed. Kevin Barry): *Occasional, Critical and Political Writings*. Oxford 2000.

Kent, Neil: *The Soul of the North: A Social, Architectural and Cultural History of the Nordic Countries, 1700-1940*. Reaktion 2000.

Kittang, Atle: *Ibsens Heroisme fra 'Brand' til 'Når vi døde vågner'*. Gyldendal 2002.

Lampert, Catherine & Le Normand-Romain, Antoinette: *Rodin*. Royal Academy of Arts, London 2006.

McFarlane, James Walter: *Ibsen and Meaning: Studies, Essays and Prefaces 1953-1987*. Norvik 1989.

—— (ed.): *The Cambridge Companion to Ibsen*. Cambridge 1994.

Madsen, Peter: 'The Destruction of Rome'. In *Acta Ibseniana No. I: Ibsen and the Arts. Painting – Sculpture – Architecture* (ed. Astrid Sæther). Unipub, Oslo 2002.

Mathieu, Caroline: *Musée d'Orsay: Guide to the Collections*. Éditions de la Réunion des Musées Nationaux 2004.

Meyer, Michael: *Henrik Ibsen: The Making of a Dramatist 1828-1804*. Rupert Hart-Davis 1967.

——: Henrik Ibsen: *The Farewell to Poetry 1864-1882*. Rupert Hart-Davis 1971

——: Henrik Ibsen: *The Top of a Cold Mountain 1883-1906*. Rupert Hart-Davis 1971.

Moi, Toril: *Henrik Ibsen and the Birth of Modernism*. Oxford 2006.

Monrad , Kasper & Siden, Karin (eds): *Nordiskt Skeleskrifte / The Light of the North*. Nationalmuseum Stockholm 1995.

Nietzsche, Friedrich: *The Birth of Tragedy* and *The Case of Wagner*. Translated from the German, with commentary by Walter Kaufmann. Vintage 1967.

——: *Ecce Homo*. Translated from the German by R. J. Hollingdale. Penguin 1979.

——: *The Gay Science*. Translated from the German with commentary by Walter Kaufmann. Vintage 1974.

Nilsen, Håvard: 'How Ibsen Found His Hedda Gabler'. In *Ibsen Studies* Vol. III, No. 1. Taylor & Francis 2003.

Northam, John: *Ibsen: A Critical Study*. Cambridge 1973.

Prater, Donald: *A Ringing Glass: The life of Rainer Maria Rilke*. Oxford 1986.

—— : *Thomas Mann: a Life*. Oxford University Press 1995.

Prideaux, Sue: *Edvard Munch: Behind 'The Scream'*. Yale 2005.

Rem, Tore: *Henry Gibson/Henrik Ibsen: Den provinsielle verdensdikteren*. Cappelen 2006.

Rilke, Rainer Maria: *Selected Letters 1902-1926*. Translated by R. F. C. Hull. Quartet 1988.

Schikaneder, Emanuel: *Libretto for Die Zauberflöte* (The Magic Flute). Translated from the German by Lionel Salter for Archiv recording, 1996.

Sehmsdorf, Henning K.: '*Bygmester Solness*: Two Legends about St Olaf'. In *EDDA: Nordisk Tidskrift for Litteraturforskning* 1967.

Sprinchorn, Evert: 'Ibsen and the Immoralists'. In *Comparative Literature Studies* University Park, Pa. 9:1 1972.

——: 'Syphilis in Ibsen's *Ghosts*'. In *Ibsen Studies* Vol. IV, No. 2. Taylor & Francis 2004.

—— (ed.): *Ibsen: Letters and Speeches*. Hill & Wang 1946.

Symonds, John Addington: *Renaissance in Italy*. Smith, Elder & Co. 1875-86.

Sæther, Astrid (ed.): *Acta Ibseniana No. 1. Ibsen and the Arts. Painting – Sculpture – Architecture*. Unipub, Oslo 2002.

—— (editor and contributor): *Acta Ibseniana No. 2. Ibsen, Tragedy and the Tragic*. Unipub, Oslo 2003.

Tanner, Michael: *Nietzsche*. Oxford 1994 .

Taylor, Ronald: *Robert Schumann: His Life and Work*. Granada 1982.

Templeton, Joan: *Ibsen's Women*. Cambridge 2001.

Thompson, Belinda: *Impressionism – Origins, Practice, Reception*. Thames & Hudson 2000.

Tjønneland, Ejvind: 'Allegory, Intertextuality and Death – the problem of symbolism in Ibsen's *The Master Builder*'. In *Proceedings of the VII International Ibsen Conference, Grimstad 1993*. Centre for Ibsen Studies, Oslo.

Wells, Marie: 'Ghosts and White Horses: Ibsen's *Gengangere* and *Rosmersholm*'. In *Scandinavica* Vol. 37, No. 2. Norvik 1988.

——: 'Ibsen, God and the Devil'. In *Contemporary Approaches to Ibsen 1994*. Universitetsforlaget 1994.

Wærp, Lisbeth Pettersen: 'Ibsen's Poetics, "The Tragic Muse", *Brand* (1866) and *When We Dead Awaken*, a dramatic epilogue (1899)'. In *Ibsen Studies* Vol. III, No. 2. Taylor & Francis 2003.

—— (ed.): *Livet på likstrå: Henrik Ibsens 'Når vi døde vågner'*. Cappelen 1999.

Young, Robert: *Time's Disinherited Children: Childhood, Regression, and Sacrifice in the Plays of Henrik Ibsen*. Norvik 1989.

Zeldin, Theodore: *France 1848-1945*. Vols 1-2. Oxford University Press 1973 and 1977.

Østerud, Erik: 'In Pandora's Jar. Ibsen's *Master Builder* in between Antiquity and Modernity'. In *Acta Ibseniana No. I: Ibsen and the Arts, Painting – Sculpture – Architecture* (ed. Astrid Sæther). Unipub, Oslo 2002.

——: '*Når vi døde vågner* på mytologisk bakgrund'. In *Ibsen Årbok 1963-1964*. Universitetsforlaget 1964.

——: 'Viewing the Nude: Body and Existence in Space and Time: a study of Henrik Ibsen's *When We Dead Awaken*'. In *Ibsen Studies* Vol. V, No. 1, 2005.

MICHAEL ROBINSON (ED.)

Turning the Century
Centennial Essays on Ibsen

Since 1962 the British journal *Scandinavica* has published a wealth of articles on Nordic literature and culture. To commemorate the centenary of the death of the Norwegian playwright Henrik Ibsen (1828-1906), a selection of the finest articles printed in *Scandinavica* on the subject of Ibsen's work is published in this volume.

The selection has been made to reflect the breadth and variety of scholarship into Ibsen's plays during the past four decades. The articles cover a wide range of general topics, from his reception in England and an analysis of early perfomances of the plays in London to studies of his language and style, as well as individual essays on specific plays. These include *Love's Comedy*, *Ghosts*, *An Enemy of the People*, *Rosmersholm*, *The Lady from the Sea*, *The Master Builder*, and *When We Dead Awaken*. Contributors include James MacFarlane, James Northam, Kristian Smidt, Brian Johnson, Egil Törnqvist and Erik Østerud.

ISBN 10: 1 870041 64 X
ISBN 13: 978 1 870041 64 5
UK £14.95
(paperback, 224 pages)

ROBIN YOUNG

Time's Disinherited Children
Childhood, Regression and Sacrifice in the Plays of Henrik Ibsen

More than most dramatists, Ibsen was concerned to imply – through what his characters do or say on stage – a sense of the past. How he achieved this, draft by draft, and how the past lives of his characters determine their present actions are taken as the focal points of this major study of Ibsen's work. The true 'disinherited children' in the plays are adults who, unable to outgrow their own childhood, allow it to distort or even destroy the lives of those around them. How Ibsen explores this theme, from the early poetry and Viking dramas to the last plays, is related throughout to the work of his predecessors and contemporaries, and to cultural and social developments in the Norway of his day.

More than a conventional thematic study, *Time's Disinherited Children* offers a fresh and thought-provoking reassessment of Ibsen's achievement as poet and dramatist.

ISBN 10: 1 870041 06 2
ISBN 13: 978 1 870041 06 5
UK £9.95
(paperback, 244 pages)

For further information, or to request a catalogue, please contact:
Norvik Press, University of East Anglia (LLT), Norwich NR4 7TJ, England
or visit our website at <u>www.norvikpress.com</u>